Charity
Checklists

2nd edition

Cecile Gillard

icsa

The Governance
Institute

First edition published 2014
Second edition published 2019

Published by
ICSA Publishing Limited
Saffron House, 6–10 Kirby Street
London EC1N 8TS

Typeset by Patricia Briggs
Printed in Great Britain by Lightning Source, Milton Keynes, Buckinghamshire

British Cataloguing in Publication Data
A catalogue record for this book is available from the British Library.

ISBN 978-1-86072-761-0

Table of Contents

About the author

Cecile is a specialist in charity and company law, charity and company secretarial administration and the governance and regulation of charities. Her work supports charities, social enterprises (including CICs) and civil society organisations, as well as their professional advisers.

Cecile advises on legal and regulatory issues, governance, corporate legal administration and constitutional matters for charities, social enterprises and civil society organisations. She also leads trustee training, board development and board assessment activities. Clients range from faith-based groups, arts, heritage and cultural organisations, sports and recreational bodies to charities that address health, deprivation and social welfare issues.

A regular contributor to journals and publications, such as ICSA's Governance and Compliance Magazine, and a speaker at professional training events, Cecile's other published titles include: *How to Run a Charity* and *Charity Law and Governance: A Practical Guide* (both ICSA Publishing).

Cecile periodically serves on working parties for organisations including ICSA and the Charity Law Association, helping to produce best practice guides and comment on proposed charity and company law reform. Cecile is a member of the Charity Law Association and a Professional Subscriber of ICSA.

In her 'spare' time, Cecile is a trustee of a grant making charity that supports the education and development of children and young people and a voluntary director of a CIC that seeks to empower young people to realise their potential. She enjoys birdwatching and loves showing members of the public the magnificent peregrine falcons that breed in the Avon Gorge. She also enjoys classical music and is a lifelong Bristol City fan.

Preface

The ICSA *Charity Checklists* provides a handy, quick-reference guide to the more common legal and administrative procedures charities may have to deal with. The checklists are a guide to point out important matters to consider and outline steps that may need to be taken. Each topic provides some general commentary on the particular matter, a checklist of items to be considered and, where appropriate, an outline of procedural steps that may need to be taken, some information on filing requirements at Companies House and/or the charity regulator(s), as well as general notes and references for sources of additional information.

This is not a legal reference book, so there is no detailed explanation of relevant law and regulations. Where further information is needed on legal rules and requirements, readers are pointed towards a range of other publications available from ICSA: The Governance Institute.

Charities take a variety of different legal forms. This book concentrates on some of the most common or important, which are as follows:

▶ Charitable incorporated organisation (CIO) – this is a corporate body *only* available for use by a charity in England and Wales. A CIO has its own distinct legal identity and independent legal capacity. It provides limited liability protection to its members and its trustees. (There are equivalent legal forms specific to Scotland and Northern Ireland; however, some of the legal rules and detailed regulations that apply to them differ from those applicable to CIOs in England and Wales.)

▶ Company limited by guarantee (CLG) – this is a private limited company, registered under the CA 2006. It has both members and trustees. A company has its own distinct legal identity and independent legal capacity. It provides limited liability protection to its members and its trustees.

▶ Members' association – a members' association is unincorporated. It has both members and trustees. It does not have its own legal identity or legal capacity. It does not provide limited liability protection to its members and its trustees.

▶ Trust – a trust is unincorporated, it only has trustees (there are no members). There is no limited liability protection. Under the law of England and Wales a trust does not have its own legal identity or independent legal capacity. (The position is different under the law of Scotland, where trusts are regarded as having legal identity.)

It should be noted that the specific legal form of an individual charity will have a significant impact on many legal and administrative procedures.

Further, the specific provisions of the individual charity's constitution will be of considerable importance in relation to some procedures.

Many fundamental principles of charity law are of general application to all charities across the UK. However, there is also a specific and distinct body of statutory charity law for each of the jurisdictions (England and Wales, Scotland, Northern Ireland) with a charity regulator for each (Charity Commission, The Office of the Scottish Charity Regulator and the Charity Commission for Northern Ireland).

The charity regulatory system in England and Wales requires charities to register unless they are small non-CIO charities, or exempt or excepted from registration.

▶ Small non-CIO charities with annual income under £5,000 are not required to register.

▶ Exempt charities are not required to register. They have a principal regulator (other than the Charity Commission) – for example, the Department for Education is the principal regulator for academy schools. Exempt charities are subject to the general principles of charity law, but some provisions of the Charities Act 2011 do not apply to them. The relevant principal regulator has an obligation to promote compliance with charity law by the trustees of exempt charities. Where intervention by the Charity Commission is necessary, the relevant principal regulator can ask the Commission to exercise its powers.

▶ Excepted charities are not required to register if their annual income is below £100,000. There are various groups of excepted charities, such as some churches, chapels and other Christian denominations, scout and guide groups and some armed forces charities. Excepted charities are directly regulated by the Charity Commission and the Commission may use its powers in relation to these charities.

Larger income formerly excepted charities have generally become subject to the registration obligation and are now on the register of charities, as a result of changes to charity regulatory obligations in recent years. The regulations that retain the remaining exceptions are due to remain in place until March 2021.

Registered charities in England and Wales are the main focus of this book. Some material has been included in relation to charity regulation in the other jurisdictions, particularly in the context of UK-wide charities (which are often described by the charity regulators as 'cross-border' charities) and the charity regulatory regime in Scotland. At the time of writing, the regulatory requirements of charity law in Northern Ireland for non-Northern Ireland constituted charities have not yet been brought into force.

CIOs are subject to English charity law in general, to CIO-specific statutory provisions in the Charities Act 2011 and to several sets of detailed CIO-specific regulations. CIOs must be registered with the Charity Commission, regardless of their income level.

Company law applies throughout the UK. The main statutory provisions are set out in the Companies Act 2006. However, those provisions are supplemented by numerous statutory instruments, which include considerable regulatory requirements. These supplementary regulations have significant impact on many legal and administrative procedures.

For companies incorporated prior to 1 October 2009, some of the previous company law rules and procedures remain applicable (because of supplementary company law regulations). For example, if the company's articles require the appointment of a secretary or the holding of an AGM, that requirement is still effective and binding.

As a general rule of thumb, the previous legal status quo is often preserved for these 'old' companies unless and until they alter their articles or their members pass resolutions on particular matters to 'opt-in' to the full modern company law regime. However, that is not inevitably the case. Some rules in the 2006 Act are mandatory, regardless of the company's previous arrangements or the provisions in its articles.

Considerable care must therefore be taken when dealing with procedures in an 'old' company that may not have modernised its constitution or removed these carried forward restrictions.

This book will particularly assist charity secretaries, clerks to trustee boards and others, such as senior charity managers, who have responsibilities in relation to key regulatory and accountability compliance matters, legal record-keeping and the practical procedures associated with the legal administration of their charities. It will also serve as a quick reference work for charity trustees and officers, as well as professional advisers including solicitors, chartered secretaries, accountants, auditors and independent examiners.

Charity law and regulation are intended to ensure public accountability and the safeguarding of charitable funds and assets. The underlying point and purpose of the correct legal administration of a charity is, though, far more than mere legal and regulatory compliance. Rather, it is about building a firm foundation for good governance, enabling the charity to be effective in achieving its charitable purposes, delivering lasting positive social impact and making a real difference for good. If this book contributes to that, both its author and its publisher will be delighted.

Cecile Gillard
August 2018

Acronyms and abbreviations

AGM	annual general meeting
CA 2006	Companies Act 2006
CIC	community interest company
CIO	charitable incorporated organisation
ChA 2011	Charities Act 2011
CLG	company limited by guarantee
HMRC	Her Majesty's Revenue & Customs
old company	company incorporated prior to 1 October 2009 that has not updated its articles and modernised its legal administrative arrangements to bring it completely within the full CA 2006 regime
OSCR	Office of the Scottish Charity Regulator
RSB	Recognised Supervisory Body
SAIL	Single Alternative Inspection Location
SCIO	Scottish charitable incorporated organisation
SORP	Statement of Recommended Practice – Accounting by Charities
TUPE	Regulations Transfer of Undertakings (Protection of Employment) Regulations
VAT	value added tax

Agreement for short notice of general meeting (company)

Introduction

General meetings of the members of a company are subject to a range of rules and procedural requirements. The most important of these arise from the provisions of CA 2006 and associated regulations, although there is some limited scope for divergence within the individual company's articles.

The statutory notice period for general meetings may usually be shortened, provided the consent of relevant members is obtained.

The members in question must together represent not less than 90% of the total voting rights at that meeting of all the members (CLG). (This can be altered by the individual company's articles to a higher percentage, not exceeding 95%.)

Checklist

▶ Can consent to short notice be requested or does the particular situation require a full period of notice?

▶ It is not permissible to propose a resolution to remove a director or to remove an auditor on short notice.

**ss. 168 and 510
Companies Act 2006**

▶ Is it practical to seek the consent, considering the total number of members and the practicalities and costs of contacting them to seek consent?

Procedure

▶ Draft the consent to short notice.

▶ Consider applicable provisions of the company's articles in relation to communications with members.

▶ If electronic communications are being used, consider the relevant provisions of the CA 2006.

**Schedules 4 and 5
Companies Act 2006**

▶ Circulate the draft consent to the members (either with the notice of the general meeting or cross referring to the notice, if the notice has already been circulated to the members).

▶ Ensure the deadline for replies is stated and adequate guidance is given to the members about completion, signature and return.

▶ It is advisable to ask consenting members to print their names against their signatures (many signatures are illegible).

▶ Monitor responses and ensure a sufficient percentage of members give consent to enable the meeting to be held on the proposed shorter notice period.

Filing requirements

▶ Consent to short notice of a general meeting does not need to be filed at Companies House.

▶ The signed consent should be kept in the company's own records of the meeting.

Notes

▶ Although consent could be provided verbally, a written record must be made of the consent and of the members who provided it. It is clearly more appropriate to obtain a signed written consent.

▶ In other types of membership charity, there may be the possibility of members agreeing a shorter period of notice for a members' meeting than the standard notice period applicable for that meeting in the particular charity. If so, the relevant procedures are likely to be set out in the particular charity's constitution.

Annual accounts and annual trustees' report

Introduction

A charity holds funds and assets in order to pursue its charitable purposes for the public benefit. So the wider public, as well as donors, funders and charity regulator(s), have an interest in the correct custody and application of those funds. Timely filing of annual accounts and the annual trustees' report is also a key driver of public trust and confidence. Those are key reasons why charity regulators are so insistent that annual accounts and trustees' reports must be properly prepared, in compliance with the law, and filed within relevant time limits.

Annual accounts and trustees' reports are an integral part of a charity's public accountability.

Oversight of public accounting and reporting compliance by charities is a key function of charity regulators.

Checklist

▶ Most charities must prepare an annual trustees' report to accompany their annual accounts.

▶ Most charities have a statutory obligation to have either an audit or an independent examination of their annual accounts. (Sometimes this is an obligation imposed by the charity's own constitution.)

▶ Annual accounts are a matter of public record and the public have the right to access these documents. The method of access may be via the charity regulators' websites or via Companies House or by a request to the charity for a copy of the most recent accounts.

▶ Every copy of the accounts issued should be accompanied by the relevant trustees' report.

▶ Every copy of the accounts issued by a CLG must also state the names of the signatories to the trustees' report and the balance sheet. **s. 433 Companies Act 2006**

▶ The main legal and reporting requirements and standards are as follows:

England and Wales

Unincorporated charities	Charities Act 2011 Charities (Accounts and Reports) Regulations 2008 SI 2008/629 Charities SORP
CLGs	As above and Companies Act 2006
CIOs	The Charitable Incorporated Organisations (General) Regulations 2012 SI 2012/3013 Charities SORP

Scotland

Unincorporated charities	Charities and Trustee Investment (Scotland) Act 2005
	Charities Accounts (Scotland) Regulations 2006 SSI
	   2006/218
	Charities Accounts (Scotland) Amendment Regulations
	   SSI 2010/287 CA 2006
	Charities SORP

CLGs	As above and Companies Act 2006

SCIOs	Charities and Trustee Investment (Scotland) Act 2005
	Charities Accounts (Scotland) Regulations 2006
	   SSI 2006/218
	Charities Accounts (Scotland) Amendment Regulations
	   SSI 2010/287 CA 2006
	Charities SORP
	The Scottish Charitable Incorporated Organisations
	   Regulations 2011 SSI 2011/44

Table of accounting thresholds (England and Wales)

Annual gross income	Type of accounts	Type of scrutiny
Below £25,000	Receipts and payments option (*not*: companies)	None (unless audit required)
Above £25,000 but below £250,000**	Receipts and payments option (*not*: companies)	Independent examination option unless audit required for any reason
Above £250,000 but below the current Charities Act audit threshold of £500,000	Accruals	Independent examination option unless accounts value of gross assets more than £3.26m** or audit required for any other reason
Above £500,000	Accruals	Charities Act audit – unless Companies Act audit is required

The Charities Act accounts scrutiny requirement is for a statutory audit (unless, in the case of a charitable company, a Companies Act audit is required for any reason) if the year's gross income for any charity exceeds £500,000, or if it exceeds £250,000** and the balance sheet value of the charity's gross assets exceeds £3.26m, with an option for independent examination below that level and above £25,000 gross income.

Above £250,000 gross income, only an appropriately professionally qualified examiner is eligible to carry out an independent examination of the charity.

** The 'accounts threshold' of £250,000 gross income and all the other Charities Act accounting thresholds are amendable by statutory instrument.

Those charities with an annual gross income of up to £10,000, i.e. those within the 'light touch' regulatory regime, need not submit a copy of their annual report and accounts to the Charity Commission unless they are specifically asked for them – as is also the case for all excepted charities and for all registered charities with up to £25,000 gross income.

Scotland

▶ Scotland has its own accounting legislation to underpin the Charities SORP and to regulate the accounts and reports of charitable companies, as well as to regulate accounts prepared on the alternative basis of receipts and payments for small non-company charities. Chapter 6 of the Charities and Trustee Investment (Scotland) Act 2005 requires all charities to maintain 'proper' accounting records and to prepare from them and file with the OSCR within nine months an annual 'statement of account', including a trustees' report, in accordance with Regulations made under s. 44(4) of the 2005 Act, and to retain all this information for at least six years from the end of the financial year to which it relates.

▶ The main differences from the SORP's English 2008 Regulations are that its related Scottish Regulations (SSI 2006/218, as amended by SSI 2010/287) require:

▷ full compliance with the SORP's 'methods and principles' for all accruals-based accounts (charitable companies included) as well as for the trustees' report accompanying them;

▷ accounts on the alternative receipts and payments basis permitted by reg 9 to be drawn up as specified in Part 1 of Sch 3 thereto, with certain additional information as set out in Part 2 of Sch 3 unless provided in the accompanying trustees' report, for which Sch 2 specifies the minimum information to be disclosed;

▷ a statutory audit of all accruals accounts where the balance sheet value of the charity's gross assets exceeds £3.26m (£2.8m for financial years starting before 1 April 2011); and

▷ an independent examination in all cases where a statutory audit is not required.

▶ The Scottish Regulations permit (but do not require) the combining of annual accounts into a single set, covered by a single trustees report, for all 'connected charities' (meaning those with common or related charitable purposes or which are under common trusteeship or are administered in common). In that circumstance, the statutory audit or independent examination requirement is determined by reference to the charity with the highest gross income (not the aggregate for all of them).

▶ There is no statutory or non-statutory concession for the OSCR to be able to dispense with a parent charity's own SoFA if it files group consolidated accounts with the OSCR. This is because, unlike the English Regulations, the SORP's Scottish Regulations overlay the Companies Act's accounting provisions and specifically require consolidated accounts in addition to the parent charity's own accounts.

▶ Instead of English charity law's requirement of a list of assets and liabilities where receipts and payments accounting is adopted, Part 1 of Sch 3 to reg 9 of the Scottish Regulations requires a year-end 'statement of balances'.

▶ For the trustees' report, accompanying accounts prepared under reg 9, Sch 2 specifies similar information to that required by the SORP where the charity is below the statutory audit threshold, but also requires an analysis of donated facilities and services, if any, that the charity received during the financial year. (These non-cash transactions will not be reported in the receipts and payments account.)

Procedure

▶ Prepare accounts and trustees' report in accordance with relevant legal requirements and applicable reporting standards.

▶ Arrange approval of accounts and approval of the annual trustees' report, also arrange authorisation of signatories for the accounts and for the trustees' report. (Note members' approval of the accounts may be required in some unincorporated membership charities; see checklist 'Annual accounts – approval'.)

▶ Ensure audit or independent examination of the accounts is completed as required by law or by the constitution.

▶ Arrange distribution of copies to members (if applicable).

▶ Ensure filing deadlines are met (note that filing with more than one regulator may be necessary and filing deadlines are *not* the same for all regulators).

Filing requirements

▶ See checklist: 'Annual accounts – approval'.

Notes

▶ The Charity Commission makes all filed accounts and reports available online on its website. So does Companies House.

▶ The OSCR does not yet make all charity accounts available online. However, for charities that are companies it does provide a live link to the Companies House website, where a search can locate the company and copies of its filed accounts can be accessed.

More information

▶ Charities SORP: www.charitysorp.org.

Annual accounts – approval

Introduction

A charity's annual accounts need formal approval.

In a charitable trust, without members, that approval will be given by the trustees.

In an unincorporated members' association, it is common for the charity's constitution to require approval by the members (usually at the AGM).

In a CLG, the annual accounts must be approved by the trustees before they are audited/independently examined and copies sent to the members. The accounts may also be presented to the members at the AGM, if the articles require this or the trustees consider it appropriate (it is not a statutory requirement to do so).

In a CIO or a SCIO, the accounts must be approved by the trustees.

In other types of membership charity, the constitution and/or law or regulation may require approval by the members.

Checklist

▶ Consider who is required to approve the accounts (trustees or members).

▶ Distinguish requirements for formal approval from requirements to circulate copies to members and/or present the accounts to the members at the AGM.

▶ The CA 2006 requires approval of the accounts and authorisation of the signatory to the balance sheet (who signs on behalf of the board) and also approval of the directors' report (i.e. the annual trustees' report) and authorisation of the signatory to the report (who signs on behalf of the board).

ss. 414(1) and 419(1)
Companies Act 2006

▶ The balance sheet must be signed by at least one trustee on behalf of the board; the name(s) of the signing trustee must be stated together with the date of approval.

ss. 414(2) and
433 (1) and (2)
Companies Act 2006

▷ If audited, the audit report must be signed by the auditors and the date of approval shown. If the auditors are a firm, the audit report must be signed by the senior statutory auditor, who must sign in their own name on behalf of the firm and their name must be stated.

**ss. 503–505
Companies Act 2006**

[The name of the senior statutory auditor may be omitted if there are risks to personal safety (conditions apply).]

▷ If the accounts have been independently examined, the independent examiner must sign the independent examiner's report, stating the examiner's name and relevant qualifications.

Procedure

▷ CLG/CIO/trust – convene a board meeting to approve the accounts and authorise the signatory (it is both usual and sensible also to approve the trustees' report and the signatory to that report at the same meeting)

▷ Other types of charity – if the formal approval of the accounts by the members is required, make appropriate arrangements for that.

▷ Ensure the correct full charity name is stated.

▷ Ensure the registered charity number is included and is correct. If the charity is a cross-border charity, include its Scottish Charity number as well.

▷ CLG – ensure the registered company number is included and is correct (it must appear at least on the first page).

▷ Arrange completion of audit or independent examination procedures. Note that the auditors/independent examiner will need a signed copy of the final approved accounts in order to complete the audit or examination and issue a signed copy of their report to the trustees.

▷ Circulate copies of the accounts and accompanying annual trustees' report to members and others entitled to receive copies.

▷ Arrange presentation to the members at the AGM (if appropriate or required).

**s. 423 Companies
Act 2006**

▷ CLG – after the accounts have been approved by the trustees, full copies of the final accounts must be circulated to all members, any debenture holders (there are unlikely to be any in a charitable company) and to anyone else entitled to receive notice of general meetings. The copies must be sent out before the end of the period allowed for filing accounts at Companies House.

▷ Arrange filing at Companies House (CLGs).

▷ Arrange filing with charity regulator(s).

Filing requirements

▷ Signed copies of the accounts must be filed at Companies House within nine months of the year-end. Where electronic filing is used, relevant security and verification procedures must be followed.

▷ Copies must also be filed with the appropriate charity regulator(s) (unless exemptions apply). The time limit for filing with the Charity Commission is 10 months (from the financial year-end); for filing with the OSCR the time limit is nine months.

Notes

▷ Although the signatory for the balance sheet must be one of the trustees, the board can authorise the CLG's secretary to sign the trustees' report. It is more sensible to authorise a trustee to sign both items.

▷ The trustees must provide a copy of the most recent annual accounts to anyone who makes a written request. A two-month time limit applies.   **s. 172 Charities Act 2011**

▷ The Charity Commission makes copies of filed accounts available to the public on the Commission's website. The OSCR does not do this for charities on the Scottish Charity Register.

▷ Companies House makes copies of filed company accounts available to the public on its website.

▷ Ensure copies provided to Companies House and charity regulator(s) comply with relevant document filing regulations and standards. (Documents must be suitable for digital scanning and digital imaging.)

▷ Also ensure the copies filed include all required names and that signatories state their capacities (e.g. senior statutory auditor), as well as original signatures (or electronic equivalents).

Annual general meeting

Introduction

Annual general meetings are meetings of the *members* of a charity.

A charity may be directly obliged to hold an annual general meeting by its constitution or indirectly obliged to do so (e.g. if there is a requirement in the constitution for full or partial retirement of the trustee board at an annual general meeting).

The Companies Act 2006 does not impose a statutory requirement for CLGs to hold annual general meetings. However if the articles of a particular CLG require an AGM the company must hold such meetings unless and until it alters its articles.

Non-membership charities, such as unincorporated charitable trusts, will not need to hold an annual general meeting in the strict sense, as they have no members. However some may have a pattern of trustees' meetings that involves a particular annual meeting of the trustees to deal with specific matters (e.g. to determine grant allocations for the following year).

Checklist

▶ Check whether the charity is a membership charity (if not AGMs are not relevant).

▶ Consider whether there is any obligation to hold an AGM (typically this will be a constitutional requirement).

▶ A CIO using the Charity Commission 'Association' model constitution is obliged to hold AGMs (the 'Foundation' model does not include this provision).

▶ Consider whether there is a need to re-appoint the auditors or independent examiner.

s. 487
Companies Act 2006

▶ Note that in a CLG or trading subsidiary, an auditor is deemed to continue in office.

▶ Annual re-appointment is not required unless:

   1. the auditor was appointed by the trustees (rather than the members);

2. the articles require re-appointment;
3. the members exercise their right to prevent deemed re-appointment;
4. the members resolve that the auditor should not be re-appointed; or
5. the trustees have resolved that no auditor should be appointed for the financial year in question (usually this is because the company is entitled to audit exemption).

▷ Check whether the constitution specifies the normal or ordinary business of the meeting. Normal or ordinary business at an AGM is usually:

1. Presentation of annual accounts and trustees' report (in an unincorporated charity the constitution may require formal approval by the members; in a CLG the accounts will already have been approved by the trustees, prior to the AGM).
2. Appointment of new trustee.
3. Re-appointment of trustees who are retiring and are both willing and eligible to stand for re-appointment to a further term.

▷ If the auditor is to be re-appointed, the meeting may also need to consider authorisation of the auditor's remuneration (or grant authority for the trustees to determine the remuneration).

▷ Check the constitution carefully with regard to retirement of directors. Retirement may be required in relation to fixed periods of office or because of a retirement by rotation system.

▷ Note that retirement and re-appointment of a new trustee, appointed since the previous AGM, may also be required by the constitution.

▷ Consider whether any other business needs to be put to the meeting.

▷ Most other business will be considered to be special business. Full details need to be set out on the notice. (The constitution may also specify certain matters that are to be considered special business and provide additional procedural requirements for those matters.)

**s. 283
Companies Act 2006**

▷ If a special resolution is to be proposed to the members of a CLG at the AGM, the full text of the resolution and a statement that it is being proposed as a special resolution must be included on the notice.

Procedure

▷ Convene a trustees' meeting to give formal approval to the AGM arrangements and to approve the proposed business of the AGM, the formal notice of the meeting and authorise despatch of the notice.

▷ Prepare the notice and despatch to members and others entitled to receive notice of the meeting.

▷ Calculate notice period taking into account any statutory minimum notice periods (e.g. Companies Act minimum periods for a CLG) or any minimum periods specified in the charity's constitution. Also take into account any deemed delivery date rules in the constitution.

▶ Ensure the contents of the notice comply with the constitution and any applicable statutory rules (particularly Companies Act 2006 rules for a CLG).

▶ Ensure correct despatch/communications methods are used and all necessary formalities attaching to those methods are observed.

▶ In a CLG, if the notice is to be sent by electronic communication (posted on a website or sent by email) the Companies Act 2006 rules and procedures for electronic communications between CLGs and their members apply.
See Schedule 4 and 5 Companies Act 2006

▶ Note that other types of charity wishing to use electronic communications to send the notice to their members, including CIOs, should check their constitutions to ensure they do have power to send meeting notices by electronic communication.

▶ Include correct statements about members' rights to appoint proxies, especially in a CLG. State the deadline for return of proxy forms (in a CLG this must not be longer than 48 hours prior to the start of the meeting).
s. 324 Companies Act 2006

▶ Enclose with the notice all other relevant documents (e.g. copies of the accounts and trustees' annual report, proxy form).

▶ If the meeting is being convened on short notice, obtain the required prior consent of members. (It is unlikely that an AGM will be held on short notice.)

▶ In a CLG non-member trustees and the auditors must be provided with a copy of the notice. This may be a constitutional requirement in other types of charity.
s. 502(2) Companies Act 2006

▶ Validate proxy forms received and any documents relating to the appointment and authority of representatives of corporate members.

▶ Prepare sign-in sheet for use at the reception desk.

▶ Make practical arrangements for the conduct of voting (e.g. ballot papers for contested trustee elections).

▶ Consider whether independent scrutineers should be arranged to count votes taken at the meeting.

▶ Before the meeting commences, check credentials of those attending to ensure only those entitled to speak and vote do so (usually this is members or their proxies).

▶ Check a quorum is present before the formal business begins. The charity's constitution normally specifies the quorum for members' meetings.

▶ Ensure voting is conducted correctly, in accordance with the charity's constitution and applicable statutory provisions (e.g. Companies Act 2006 for a CLG).

▶ Comply with the charity's constitution and any applicable statutory rules regarding voting methods (show of hands or poll) and with the voting rights of different membership classes.

▶ Be aware of required voting majorities. For a CLG, the Companies Act specifies a simple majority for ordinary resolutions and a 75% majority *of votes cast* for special resolutions. For other types of charity, the constitution may specify required voting majorities for particular resolutions.

Filing requirements

▶ There may be a filing or notification requirement with regard to Companies House or charity regulators, depending on what resolutions were passed and what business was dealt with at the meeting (for example if there were new trustees appointed).

▶ In a CLG, copies of any special resolutions passed must be filed at Companies House within 15 days of the date of the meeting. Certain ordinary resolutions also have to be filed.

**ss. 29 and 30
Companies Act 2006**

Notes

▶ Many charities combine their AGM with a members' social event or an event that is open to wider stakeholders, such as local councillors and representatives of major funders or partner organisations. Where this is the case, ensure there is a clear distinction between the formal AGM and the other events. Also ensure that only members of the charity or their duly appointed proxies are allowed to vote at the AGM.

▶ Make sure the practical arrangements for the venue are suitable and appropriate, including disability access and participation assistance for people with disability needs such as sight loss or hearing impairment.

▶ In order to take advantage of the deemed re-appointment of the auditor in a company, it is necessary for the original appointment of that auditor to have been made by the members (rather than the trustees). If the original appointment was made by the trustees, one subsequent re-appointment by the members is required in order for the deemed re-appointment rules to apply.

**ss. 314–317
Companies Act 2006**

▶ Unless there is a constitutional requirement to do so, it is not necessary to read out the notice of meeting or the auditor's report or independent examiner's report at the meeting.

▶ It is wise to have some spare copies of the meeting papers available at the meeting, especially the annual accounts and reports.

More information

▶ See checklists: 'General meetings – notice periods and short notice' and 'General meetings – conduct and voting'.

Annual returns

Introduction

Charities are required to file charity annual returns to the charity regulators.

CLGs must also file a company confirmation statement at Companies House.

Charity annual returns provide an annual snapshot of key information, including the name, registered or principal office of the charity and a full list of its trustees.

The principal responsibility for ensuring these requirements are met lies with the trustees although they may delegate the actual process to the charity secretary or clerk to the trustees, a senior manager within the charity or to the charity's professional advisers (particularly the charity's accountants or its solicitors).

Failure to file returns within the applicable time limits is a breach of charity and/or company regulatory requirements. Both the trustees and the charity are subject to potential penalties for such non-compliance. The Charity Commission may also regard non-compliance as evidence of potential misconduct or mismanagement of the charity by the trustees.

Checklist

Charity annual return – England and Wales

▶ A CIO must file a charity annual return regardless of annual income level.

▶ Non-CIO charities with annual income over £10,000 must file a charity annual return.

▶ Non-CIO charities with lower income levels must update the details held about them by the Charity Commission (for example the named contact's details may have changed).

▶ If the charity's annual income is over £25,000 a copy of its annual accounts and trustees' report must be attached when the annual return is submitted.

▶ The return provides key information such as the name of the charity and how to contact it, details of its charitable purposes, activities and geographic area of operation, as well as financial data.

▶ For smaller charities, this financial information must be provided:

▷ Start and end dates for the financial period covered by the return (for example 01/04/2018 to 31/03/2019).

▷ Total income and total spending for that period.

▷ Total spending outside England and Wales (if applicable).

▶ A charity with income above £500,000 is required to provide additional financial information in the return.

▶ A charity with income above £25,000 must submit a copy of its annual accounts and trustees' report, with the audit report or independent examiner's report, with its charity annual return.

▶ As part of the charity annual return, the trustees of all charities must declare that there are no serious incidents or other matters they should have reported to the Charity Commission but have not yet reported.

Charity annual return – Scotland

All charities must submit a charity annual return to the OSCR.

Those with gross annual income over £25,000 must also submit a Supplementary Monitoring Return, to provide further information (particularly additional financial information).

A signed copy of the charity's annual accounts and trustees' report must also be filed with the return.

Company annual return

▶ The return (form AR01 or electronic equivalent) sets out the company's full legal name, its registered company number and its registered office address. It also contains details of the directors, company secretary (if there is a secretary), the type of company (e.g. CLG) and its principal business activities.

▶ Where certain statutory registers are kept at a location other than the registered office, details of that alternative location must be provided.

▶ Companies *limited by shares*, such as trading subsidiaries of charities, also have to list their shareholders and any changes that have occurred during the year and provide these details of their share capital:

1. Aggregate amount of share capital issued, paid up and unpaid on each share class.
2. Total number of shares issued and their nominal value.

Procedure – charity annual return (England and Wales)

▶ The charity annual return must be submitted online via the Charity Commission website.

▶ The charity's registered number and online password are both required in order to use this Charity Commission online service.

▶ Check or complete all relevant details on the return.

▶ Ensure the trustees are aware of and content with the return contents.

▶ Submit the return (via the relevant regulator's website).

Filing requirements

▶ Non-CIO charities with annual income *under* £10,000 are not required to file a charity annual return with the Charity Commission.

▶ For charities on the Scottish Charity Register, there are no filing exemptions – all types of charity must file a charity annual return with the OSCR regardless of their financial size.

▶ All companies must file a confirmation statement with Companies House each year, regardless of their financial size or activity level (even dormant companies must do so).

▶ *Filing deadlines* are as follows:

▷ **Charity annual return (England and Wales)** within 10 months of the charity's financial year-end.

▷ **Charity annual return (Scotland)** within nine months of the charity's financial year-end.

▷ **Company confirmation statement** at least once a year and within 14 days of the end of the 'review period'. For new companies the review period starts on the date of incorporation and ends 12 months later. For existing companies, the review period starts on the day after the last confirmation statement was made and ends 12 months later. If the statement is filed early, a fresh 12 month review period begins from that filing date.

Filing fees:

▶ There is a statutory filing fee for a company confirmation statement (£13 if it is filed online, £40 if it is filed in paper format).

▶ There are no filing fees for charity annual returns.

Notes

▶ The Charity Commission no longer accepts paper charity annual returns; charities *must* use the online filing facility on the Charity Commission website: www.charitycommission.gov.uk.

▶ If a charity fails to file its return with the Charity Commission, that charity's public details will be marked to show documents 'overdue'. After a further six months the Commission considers removing the charity's details from the register and taking further action in relation to the default.

▶ The OSCR actively monitors both submission dates and contents of annual documents and takes steps to ensure any defaults are corrected.

▶ The Charity Commission expects charities to update changes in the details held about them by the regulator as they occur, rather than waiting for the charity annual return due date to make such notifications. Although not a strict legal requirement this is good practice which charities would be well advised to follow.

▶ There is no financial late filing penalty imposed on companies that file their confirmation statements late. However, such failure does expose the directors to potential criminal sanctions (a fine). In practice the mere threat of such action by Companies House is usually sufficient to ensure the default is quickly corrected.

▶ Criminal proceedings that may be taken against directors as a result of non-filing of confirmation statements is a separate matter from, and can be in addition to, any late filing penalty imposed against the company for filing its accounts late.

▶ Although the criminal penalty for failure to file a company confirmation statement does also apply to any secretary in office, in practice it is likely to be the directors who will be pursued for non-compliance.

▶ If the company continues to fail to file its annual documents, the Registrar of Companies may also take steps to strike the company off the register of companies.

Annual trustees' report

Introduction

Trustees must prepare an annual trustees' report.

The report accompanies the annual accounts and provides a wider commentary on the charity's strategic objectives and its performance during the year reported on. The report can, and should, 'add value' to the financial data provided by the accounts.

The trustee board as a whole is responsible for the contents of the report and for ensuring those contents include all the relevant material required by law and applicable accounting and reporting standards (in particular the Charities SORP).

The accounting and reporting standards for charities recognise that numbers are not, of themselves, enough to show the overall picture of a charity's activities and its end of year position. Further, the figures alone cannot tell the story of the public benefit that has been provided and the good the charity is doing – whereas an imaginative trustees' report certainly can.

Checklist

▶ Ensure the report complies with all applicable legislation and with SORP (as it applies to the type and size of charity).

▶ Consider whether the charity is subject to an alternative SORP, for example the sector-specific SORPs relevant to academy schools, colleges of further or higher education, Church of England Parochial Church Councils, mutual societies, industrial and provident societies, registered social landlords.

Public benefit

The report must include:

1. A report of the activities undertaken by the charity to further its charitable purposes for the public benefit.
2. A statement by the trustees as to whether they have complied with their duty to 'have regard' to the Charity Commission's guidance on public benefit.

See s. 17(5)
Charities Act 2011

Other contents

▶ **Reference and administrative material**, including the charity's full legal name and any operating name(s) it uses and the charity registration number. Cross-border charities must also provide their Scottish charity number.

▶ The address of the principal office must be stated.

▶ For a CLG, the address of its registered office must be stated.

▶ The names of all trustees must be stated; this should include all who served for any part of the year being reported on. If trustees have joined the board after that year but before the approval of the report, their names should also be given.

▶ The name of the Chief Executive Officer and the names of any staff to whom the trustees have delegated day-to-day management must be given (i.e. senior management staff).

▶ Names and addresses of all relevant professional advisers must be stated (e.g. solicitors, bankers, auditors or reporting accountants/ independent examiners, investment advisers).

▶ **Structure, governance and management** – this section must set out the legal form of the charity (trust, unincorporated members' association, CLG, CIO etc.), specify the nature of the governing document and indicate the method(s) for appointment of trustees.

▶ There should be details of how new trustees are inducted, plus information about the general training and development of trustees.

▶ The organisational structure must be described (e.g. committees and their roles, in the context of the governance role of the trustee board) and the decision-making processes should be explained.

▶ If the charity is part of a wider network, information should be given about that.

▶ Details of relationships with related parties must be given (SORP defines 'related parties').

▶ There must be a statement about risk management, including the review processes by which risks are identified and the systems and procedures adopted by the board to manage those risks.

▶ **Objectives and activities** – this section should make clear the aims and objectives set by the charity, the strategies and activities undertaken to achieve those and set matters in the context of the longer term strategies and objectives that have been set.

▶ The information must include a summary of the *charitable purposes* (as set out in the governing document), an explanation of the charity's aims, including what changes or differences it seeks to make by its activities, an explanation of the main objectives for the year being reported on and the strategies for achieving the stated objectives, as well as details of significant activities that contribute to obtaining those objectives.

▷ If the charity makes grants as a major activity, the grant-making policy must be stated.

▷ If there are material social investment programmes and/or material use of volunteers, information must be provided about those areas.

▷ **Achievements and performance** – this section must provide information about the achievements of the charity (and any subsidiaries) during the year being reported on. In particular, it should review the charitable activities, explaining performance against objectives, give details of material fundraising activities, including performance achieved against objectives set and commenting on material expenditure as well as projected future income.

▷ Details of material investments and their performance against the investment objectives should be given.

▷ Any factors outside the charity's control that are relevant to the achievement of its objectives should be commented upon. Those might include relationships with employees, service users, other beneficiaries and funders and the charity's position in the wider community.

▷ **Financial review** – a review of the charity's financial position is required (and that of any subsidiaries). The principal financial management policies adopted during the year should be stated.

▷ The policy on financial reserves, the level of reserves held and why they are held must be indicated. If material sums have been designed for particular purposes the amounts and reasons must be given, together with intended timing of future expenditure. If there is a deficit or surplus on the target reserves sum this must be indicted, together with the steps being taken to address the difference between the target and actual figures.

▷ Principal funding sources must be indicated.

▷ Information about how expenditure during the year has supported the charity's key objectives must be included.

▷ If there are material investments, the investment policy and its objectives, including any social, environmental or ethical considerations, should be indicated.

▷ **Plans for future periods** – the charity's plans for future periods need to be explained, including key aims and objectives and details of activities planned to support these.

▷ **Funds held as custodian trustee** – if the charity holds any funds in the capacity of custodian trustee details must be given.

Procedure

▶ Prepare the report in accordance with legislative requirements and applicable reporting standards.

▶ Arrange approval by the trustee board.

▶ Ensure the trustees authorise the relevant signatory.

▶ Minute the approval of the report and the authorisation of the signatory.

▶ Arrange filing of the report, with the annual accounts, with all relevant regulators.

Filing requirements

▶ The trustees' annual report, with the accounts, must be filed with charity regulators.

▶ A CLG must include the report (drawn up to comply with relevant company law requirements for a charitable company) with the accounts it files at Companies House.

▶ For charities in England and Wales that are exempt or excepted from charity registration with the Charity Commission, the trustees' report will need to be submitted with the annual accounts to their alternative principal regulator, for example the Higher Education Funding Council for England (higher education institution charities) or Department for Education (academy schools) or Prudential Regulation Authority (charitable industrial and provident societies).

▶ All charities in Scotland are registered on the Scottish Charity Register, so submission of the trustees' annual report with the accounts must be made to the OSCR.

Notes

▶ There is no required order for the material that must be dealt with in the trustees' annual report. So the statement of the charity's charitable purposes and the most important information, such as the impact of its activities and the public benefit the charity has delivered, can be addressed before all the required (but rather dull) legal and administrative information.

More information

▶ The main Charity SORP and a range of sector specific other SORPS and accounting and reporting standards are available online from the ICAEW library: www.icaew.com/en/library/subject-gateways/accounting/accounting-by-industry.

Articles – alteration (CLGs)

Introduction

The articles of association are a company's constitution.

A CLG incorporated on or after 1 October 2009 only has articles, which include the external aspects of the company's constitution (for example the limited liability guarantee clause) and the internal aspects (for example how new members are admitted to membership and how trustees are appointed).

Older companies had a two part constitution when they were originally incorporated – a memorandum of association which dealt with the external aspects, and articles which dealt with the internal aspects. Both are now treated as being the articles of the company in accordance with the provisions of s. 28 Companies Act 2006. An older company that has not already altered and updated its memorandum and articles to combine the two documents into one comprehensive set of articles may decide to do so.

Alterations to articles require approval by special resolution of the company's members.

Any alteration of a CLG's objects (its charitable purposes) always requires the prior consent of the relevant charity regulator(s) – Charity Commission, the OSCR, the Charity Commission for Northern Ireland.

Certain other alterations are 'regulated alterations' that cannot be made without the prior consent of the Charity Commission.

Any attempt to make a change to relevant provisions, without the required consent, is ineffective.

Checklist

▶ Are any regulatory consents required?

▶ If so, what is the process and projected timescale for obtaining those consents?

▶ Consider the potential implications if permission is in fact refused. Note that the regulators sometimes negotiate a compromise wording with an applicant.

▶ Note that cross-border charities may have to obtain consent from more than one charity regulator.

▶ Does the CLG have classes of members? If so, class consents to any variation of the rights of membership classes will also be needed.

▶ Ensure the proposed changes comply with current charity and company law.

▶ Ensure the proposed changes 'fit' with the rest of the articles.

▶ Consider the best approach to the amendments – alteration of some parts of the present articles, with any required consequential changes to other clauses or adoption of a full set of new articles.

▶ If a full set of new articles is to be adopted, consider which clauses must be carried over from the old to the new because of legal, regulatory or practical reasons.

▶ Ensure terminology is consistent between any retained/carried forward clauses and new clauses.

Procedure

▶ Obtain any required prior regulatory consents (e.g. consent from the Charity Commission or the OSCR to any proposed change to the charitable purposes [objects]).

▶ Convene a trustees' meeting to approve the convening of a general meeting of the members to consider a special resolution to effect the proposed changes (or to authorise circulation of a members' written resolution).

▶ The trustees should either authorise the draft meeting notice or authorise the company secretary to prepare and issue the notice.

▶ Ensure sufficient notice period is given (including delivery date or deemed delivery date). The Companies Act specifies a 14-day minimum notice period (excluding delivery date and date of meeting) unless the articles of the company require a longer period.

▶ Despatch notice by appropriate methods.

▶ If the meeting is to be held on short notice, circulate written consent to short notice to the members for signature.

▶ Arrange class meetings or the circulation of written class consents if the proposed changes to the articles involve a direct or an indirect variation of the rights of one or more classes of members.

▶ Hold the general meeting, ensuring a quorum is present and voting is correctly conducted. A special resolution requires a 75% majority of votes cast.

▶ If the resolution has been circulated as a proposed written resolution, it requires consent by the eligible members who represent 75% of the voting rights and the required signatures must be obtained within 28 days of the circulation date.

Filing requirements

▶ A copy of the relevant special resolution and the amended articles must be filed at Companies House within 15 days.

▶ If any of the changes required prior regulatory consent, a copy of the consent must also be included.

▶ If the objects have been altered, form CC04 (Statement of company's objects) is also required.

▶ If the changes involved alteration of the rights of any class of members, relevant class consents and form SH12 (Notice of particulars of variation of class rights) must also be filed.

Notes

▶ The model articles for a guarantee company, prescribed by Companies Act regulations, are not suitable for use as the articles of a charitable company without modification.

▶ Likewise, the model share company articles are not suitable for use as the articles of a charity's trading subsidiary without some alterations and additions to the provisions of the model.

Date changes take effect

s. 31(2)(c)
Companies Act 2006

▶ Any alteration to the objects does not take effect until the Registrar of Companies registers the relevant documents on the register of companies.

▶ Other changes take effect on the passing of the relevant special resolution.

▶ However, note that if the change is a regulated alteration, for which prior Charity Commission consent is required, the change will not be effective if that consent has not been obtained.

More information

▶ See checklists: 'General meetings' and 'General meetings – conduct and voting'.

Audit, auditors and audit exemption

Introduction

A charity may have to appoint auditors and have its annual accounts audited because:

▷ it has a statutory obligation to have its annual accounts audited; or

▷ it has a constitutional obligation to do so.

The trustees of a charity that is not obliged to have its accounts audited may decide to appoint auditors and have an audit carried out for reasons of additional transparency and re-assurance or because a key partner organisation, such as a major funder, wishes to receive audited accounts from the charity.

The legal and regulatory requirements regarding audit differ to some extent between the different legal forms that charities take and between the various jurisdictions of the UK.

Checklist

Auditors – England and Wales

▶ Charities subject to a statutory audit requirement must appoint a registered auditor, or some other person authorised by statute or to whom the Charity Commission has granted dispensation to carry out statutory audits of charity accounts.

Auditors – Scotland

▶ Under the Scottish charity accounting regulations, if the term 'audit' is used in a charity's constitution or governing document, the charity must have its accounts audited by either:

▷ a registered auditor;

▷ the Auditor General for Scotland; or

▷ an auditor appointed by the Accounts Commission for Scotland (responsible principally for public bodies).

Audit

▷ An audit provides reasonable assurance that accounts are free from material misstatement (whether caused by error, fraud or other irregularity).

Auditor's report

▷ The auditor's report is addressed to the trustees. It is a matter of public record and is attached to the publicly filed copy of the charity's annual accounts.

Registered auditors

▷ The UK regulatory system for auditors requires registered auditors to be registered with a Recognised Supervisory Body. The main RSBs are the principal professional bodies for the accounting profession in the UK.

Audit exemption – England and Wales

Table of external scrutiny requirements and exemption thresholds – charities in England and Wales

Statutory audit or other scrutiny report	Charitable companies	Other charities
None	Gross income ceiling £25,000	Gross income ceiling £25,000*
Report by an independent examiner**	Gross income ceiling £500,000	Gross income ceiling £500,000
Full statutory audit report: Charities Act 2011	Gross income over £500,000 (£250,000 if book value of gross assets over £3.26m) or else no 'company audit exemption' claim	Gross income of charity or group over £500,000 (£250,000 if book value of gross assets over £3.26m)
Full statutory audit report: Companies Act 2006	Thresholds: turnover £6.5m; gross assets £3.26m; 50 staff (or 'audit exemption' not claimed)	Not applicable

* For Church of England Parochial Church Councils, independent scrutiny is required under church accounting regulations.
** The independent examiner must be suitably qualified, in accordance with relevant regulations, if the charity's gross income exceeded £250,000.

Scotland

▶ Different thresholds and exemption provisions apply to unincorporated charities under charity law in Scotland. There will be a statutory audit requirement if:

▷ the gross income for the year is £500,000 or more; or

▷ gross assets at the financial year-end exceed £2,800,000 and the charity has prepared accrued accounts.

▶ Charitable companies are subject to the same thresholds as are applicable to charitable companies in England and Wales because company law has UK-wide application.

Northern Ireland

▶ Northern Ireland specific accounting and reporting requirements apply to charities on the Northern Ireland Register of Charities. CCNI guidance is available on the CCNI website and see the Charities (Accounts and Reports) Regulations (Northern Ireland) 2015.

Procedure

Auditors and auditing – standards

▶ Registered auditors are required to comply with relevant professional and ethical standards. Audits must be carried out in accordance with international auditing standards.

Filing requirements

▶ The auditor's report needs to be attached to the annual accounts when those accounts are filed with relevant regulators.

More information

▶ Guidance for auditors on relevant auditing standards and ethical and professional standards is available from the Financial Reporting Council and relevant professional bodies, such as the Institute of Chartered Accountants in England and Wales, the Institute of Chartered Accountants for Scotland, Chartered Accountants Ireland (which is the professional body for the chartered accounting profession in Northern Ireland as well as Ireland) and the Association of Chartered Certified Accountants.

Auditors – appointment

Introduction

A charity may have to appoint auditors because:

▷ it has a statutory obligation to have its annual accounts audited; or

▷ it has a constitutional obligation to do so.

The trustees of a charity that is not obliged to have its accounts audited may decide to appoint auditors and have an audit carried out for reasons of additional transparency and re-assurance or because a key partner organisation, such as a major funder, wishes to receive audited accounts from the charity.

The legal and regulatory requirements regarding compulsory audit differ to some extent between the different legal forms that charities take and between the various jurisdictions of the UK.

Checklist

▶ Is there a legal or regulatory obligation to appoint auditors?

▶ Is there a constitutional requirement to appoint auditors and arrange an audit of the charity's annual accounts?

▶ Has a funder or other relevant party requested audited annual accounts?

▶ Have the trustees taken a decision that audit would be appropriate, even though there is no obligation for the charity to have its accounts audited?

▶ If the answer to any of the above is affirmative, the charity should ensure it appoints auditors.

▶ If auditors are *not* required, consider whether an independent examiner should be appointed to carry out an independent examination of the accounts.

Procedure

Unincorporated charity

▶ The procedure will largely depend on the charity's constitution. In a non-membership charity (for example an unincorporated charitable trust) it is likely that the trustees will appoint the auditor. In a membership charity the appointment may need to be made by the member (e.g. at the AGM).

CIO

▶ The trustees are responsible for ensuring the CIO meets relevant statutory requirements with regard to the preparation of annual accounts and the audit or independent examination of those accounts. The trustees will appoint the auditors (if audit is required) unless the particular CIO's constitution requires appointment by the members.

CLG

▶ Companies must appoint auditors unless they are dormant or audit exempt.

**ss. 477, 479A, 480
Companies Act 2006**

▶ Where auditors do not need to be appointed the directors should specifically resolve not to appoint them, on the grounds that audited accounts are not likely to be required for the financial year in question.

▶ Where auditors are required, the directors may resolve to appoint them in any of the following circumstances:

a) as the company's first auditors;
b) to fill a casual vacancy (e.g. a vacancy arising from the resignation of the previous auditors); or
c) to appoint auditors following a previous period when the company was exempt from audit so it did not have auditors in office.

▶ An auditor is deemed re-appointed each year *unless*:

**s. 487
Companies Act 2006**

a) the auditor was appointed by the directors;
b) the articles require re-appointment (e.g. at the AGM);
c) the members exercise their right to prevent deemed re-appointment (see s. 488 CA 2006);
d) the members have resolved that the current auditor shall not be re-appointed; or
e) the directors have resolved that no auditor should be appointed for the financial year in question.

▶ Note that because of (a) there must be one re-appointment by the members before the 'deemed to continue in office' provisions can apply.

Qualifications and independence

▷ A charity's auditor must be suitably qualified and independent (for example not an officer, trustee or employee of the charity).

▷ Auditors are registered with a Recognised Supervisory Body in accordance with the UK's requirement for the regulation of the audit profession.

▷ A registered auditor may be an individual, a partnership or a corporate body, such as a limited liability partnership or a company.

▷ For CIOs and unincorporated charities, relevant charity law provisions apply in these matters.

▷ For a CLG, the auditor must be qualified in accordance with company law provisions.

Filing requirements

▷ A statutory audit report submitted with the annual accounts to charity regulators or to Companies House must comply with relevant requirements with regard to wording, format and document quality standards.

Notes

▷ The accounting and audit obligations for CIOs flow from the Charities Act 2011.

▷ Full charity law based statutory audit of a CIO's accounts is required if the income is over £500,000 (£250,000 if the book value of the assets exceeds £3.26 million) or the CIO is part of a group of organisations. If the income is lower, an independent examination is permitted in place of an audit.

▷ The accounting and audit obligations for CLGs flow from the Companies Act 2006 as modified by the Charities Act 2011 and relevant regulations.

▷ The members of a CLG who represent at least 10% of the total number of members may require an audit of its accounts for any year (i.e. regardless of the company otherwise being exempt from Companies Act audit requirements).

s. 476
Companies Act 2006

Scotland

▷ For *unincorporated* charities and SCIOs on the Scottish charity register, there is a statutory audit requirement if:

▷ the gross income for the year is £500,000 or more; or

▷ the gross assets at the financial year-end exceed £2.8 million and the charity has prepared accrued accounts.

▷ CLGs are subject to the same thresholds as apply to companies in England and Wales because company law has UK-wide application.

Northern Ireland

▶ Non-company charities are subject to the audit requirements of the Charities (Accounts and Reports) Regulations (Northern Ireland) 2015.

▶ CLGs are subject to the same independent scrutiny and exemption thresholds as apply to companies in England and Wales because company law has UK-wide application.

More information

▶ See checklists: 'Audit, auditors and audit exemption' and 'Auditors – procedures for changes of auditors'.

Auditors – procedures for changes of auditors

Introduction

A change of auditors of a CLG triggers requirements to notify Companies House.

A change of auditors (in any type of charity) does not of itself trigger a notification requirement with regard to the relevant charity regulator(s). However, depending on the circumstances that led to the change, a 'whistleblowing' requirement may arise for the outgoing auditors.

Checklist

▶ Auditors leaving office should consider whether a 'whistleblowing' duty arises.

▶ The charity should consider what procedures are required with regard to the departure of the outgoing auditors and, if applicable, the appointment of new auditors.

Procedure

Company – statement by auditor leaving office

▶ An auditor who ceases to hold office as auditor of a company must provide a statement setting out any circumstances relevant to that cessation of office that should be brought to the attention of members or creditors of the company or stating that there are no such circumstances.

s. 519
Companies Act 2006

▶ If the statement does set out circumstances that ought to be brought to the attention of members or creditors, the company must, within 14 days of deposit of that statement with the company:

s. 520
Companies Act 2006

   a) send a copy of the statement to all those who are entitled to receive copies of the statutory accounts of the company; or
   b) apply to the court for relief from that requirement.

▶ If an application to court is made, the auditor must be notified of that by the company within 21 days of the date of deposit of the statement.

Company – early cessation of office

▶ If an auditor ceases to hold office as auditor of a company before the end of his or her term of office, both the auditor and the company are obliged to notify the appropriate audit authority.

ss. 522–525 Companies Act 2006

Company – special procedures for appointing a different auditor

▶ Special procedures apply if a company proposes to appoint a different auditor in place of an auditor whose term of office has expired or is to expire. These apply when the change is taking place from one financial year to the next.

ss. 514 and 515 Companies Act 2006

▶ The underlying intention of these requirements is to ensure the outgoing auditor has the opportunity to make representations that will be seen by the members of the company.

▶ The requirements apply if:

   a)   no period for appointing auditors has ended since the outgoing auditor ceased to hold office; or
   b)   such a period has ended and an auditor should have been appointed but was not.

▶ The 'period for appointing auditors' is the period of 28 days beginning with:

   a)   the end of the time allowed for sending out copies of the company's annual accounts for the previous financial year to the members; or
   b)   if earlier, the day on which the copies of the company's annual accounts for the previous year are sent out.

s. 485 Companies Act 2006

▶ If the resolution is proposed as a written resolution, the company must send a copy of the proposed resolution to the person proposed to be appointed and to the outgoing auditor.

▶ If the resolution is to be proposed at a general meeting, e.g. the AGM, special notice of the proposed resolution is required. That is, notice of the propose resolution must be given to the company at least 28 days before the meeting at which the resolution is to be proposed. On receipt of that notice, the company must send a copy of it to the person proposed to be appointed and to the outgoing auditor. The auditor has the right to attend the meeting under general auditor's rights (s. 502 CA 2006).

▶ In either case (meeting or written resolution) the outgoing auditor is entitled, within 14 days of receiving notice from the company of the proposed resolution, to require the company to circulate written representations to the members. If such representations are made, the company must circulate them unless it applies to court for permission not to do so on the grounds that the auditor is using the statutory provisions to secure needless publicity for defamatory matter.

Filing requirements

▷ In the absence of notification from the company to the auditor that it has applied to court as above, the auditor must send a copy of the statement to Companies House within seven days of the expiry of the 21-day period allowed for making the application to the court.

Notes

▷ A charity in a legal form other than a CLG may have to follow particular procedures on a change of its auditors because of provisions in its own constitution.

▷ Note that there will normally be a professional adviser/client contractual relationship between the auditors and the charity. Consideration should be given to the correct steps to end that relationship and to deal with any outstanding issues (e.g. unpaid fees due to the outgoing auditor).

▷ Removal of an auditor of a company is subject to special rules and procedures – see checklist: 'Auditors – removal'.

More information

▷ The joint guidance from the charity regulators 'Reporting matters of material significance: guidance for auditors and examiners' (issued jointly by all three UK charity regulators – available on the Charity Commission website).

▷ Charity Commission guidance on trustees reporting serious incidents: www.gov.uk/government/organisations/charity-commission.

Auditors – removal

Introduction

Removal of auditors should be distinguished carefully from other reasons for the cessation of office of an auditor (including voluntary resignation or reaching the end of a term of office and not seeking re-appointment).

Forcible removal of auditors from office is serious matter (and a rare event). It is likely to signify there are major problems in relation to the charity.

Where a forcible removal is being considered the charity should seek appropriate professional advice.

Checklist

▶ Obtain appropriate professional advice before proceeding with an attempted forcible removal.

Procedure

▶ In a CLG, forcible removal of auditors is subject to Companies Act requirements (see further below).

▶ In other types of charity, the constitution may give the trustees power to remove the auditors or it may provide for any proposed removal to be considered by the charity's members.

Company – removal of auditor

ss. 510–513
Companies Act 2006

▶ An auditor can be removed from office by ordinary resolution of the members of the company. This must be passed at a general meeting (a written resolution cannot be used).

▶ Special notice of the proposed resolution is required. That is, notice of the proposed resolution must be given to the company at least 28 days before the meeting at which the resolution is to be proposed. On receipt of that notice, the company must send a copy of it to the auditor who is proposed to be removed.

▶ The auditor has the right to require written representations to be circulated to the members of the company.

▶ The auditor can attend and be heard at the meeting.

s. 502
Companies Act 2006

▶ An auditor who has been removed from office has the right to attend and be heard at any general meeting at which it is proposed to fill the vacancy created by that removal.

s. 513
Companies Act 2006

Filing requirements

▶ Where a resolution to remove an auditor is passed, the company must give notice of that to the Registrar of Companies within 14 days (it is an offence to fail to do so) [Form AA03].

s. 512
Companies Act 2006

Notes

▶ Note that there will normally be a professional adviser/client contractual relationship between the auditors and the charity. Consideration should be given to the correct steps to end that relationship and to deal with any outstanding issues (e.g. unpaid fees due to the outgoing auditor).

▶ Removal of a company auditor in accordance with the Companies Act procedures does not deprive the auditor from any entitlement he or she may have to damages in respect of that termination (or in respect of the termination of any other office that terminates as his or her office as auditor is terminated).

More information

▶ The joint guidance from the charity regulators 'Reporting matters of material significance: guidance for auditors and examiners' (issued jointly by all three UK charity regulators – available on the Charity Commission website).

▶ Charity Commission guidance on trustees reporting serious incidents: www.gov.uk/government/organisations/charity-commission.

Auditors – resignation

Introduction

Auditors may choose to resign from office voluntarily. This should be distinguished carefully from other reasons for the cessation of office of an auditor (including reaching the end of a term of office and not seeking re-appointment).

Checklist

▶ Is the change of auditors due to a voluntary resignation or is it because of some other reason? (If it is for another reason, additional procedures may be required.)

▶ Ensure the audit arrangements for the current year are properly completed.

▶ Auditors leaving office should consider whether a 'whistleblowing' duty arises.

Procedure

▶ Obtain signed letter of resignation from the outgoing auditors.

▶ The charity should consider what further procedures are required with regard to the departure of the resigning auditors and, if applicable, the appointment of new auditors.

Company – statement by auditor leaving office

s. 519
Companies Act 2006

▶ An auditor who ceases to hold office as auditor of a company must provide a statement setting out any circumstances relevant to that cessation of office that should be brought to the attention of members or creditors of the company or stating that there are no such circumstances. For further details see checklist: 'Auditors – procedures for changes of auditors'.

Filing requirements

▶ When there is a change of auditor, if the outgoing auditor of a company exercises his or her right to provide written representations to be circulated to the members of the company, the outgoing auditor must file a copy of the representations at Companies House.

Notes

▶ If an auditor of a company ceases to hold office before the end of his or her term of office, both the company and the auditor are obliged to notify the appropriate audit authority.

ss. 522–525
Companies Act 2006

▶ If the outgoing auditor provides a written statement of circumstances that ought to be brought to the attention of members or creditors, a copy of that must be sent by the company to all those who are entitled to receive copies of the company's statutory accounts.

s. 520
Companies Act 2006

Bank account

Introduction

The trustees have ultimate responsibility for the charity's banking arrangements.

The trustees should ensure that there are adequate procedures regarding the charity's bank accounts and transactions on those accounts, as part of the charity's overall financial controls and risk management. As the Charity Commission points out:

> 'Financial controls are important for charities of all sizes. Even small charities with relatively simple structures and low-risk activities need to protect their assets and get the most out of their resources… It is important that all those working in the charity whether trustees, staff or volunteers take the issue of internal financial controls seriously.'

> [CC8 Internal Financial Controls for Charities]

Banks have their own standard forms of bank mandates which they will require completed when a new bank account is being opened for a charity. There will also be standard forms to make changes to the banking arrangements (e.g. alter the signatories).

All board decisions relating to bank accounts and banking arrangements for the charity should be carefully recorded in minutes of the relevant trustees' meeting.

Checklist

▶ Income should be banked as quickly as possible.

▶ There are particular risks with regard to the processing and banking of cash donations. The trustees should ensure procedures are robust and that their effectiveness is reviewed regularly.

▶ There should be no undue delay in processing incoming funds and recording all receipts of funds.

▶ Agree, document and apply clear limits on financial authority levels for all personnel (paid or volunteer).

▶ Keep cheque books/paying in books and passwords for online banking secure.

▶ Never permit the pre-signature of blank cheques.

▶ Review bank mandates, authorised signatories and authority levels regularly.

▶ Keep proper records of all accounts held by the charity and review and update these periodically as accounts/banking service suppliers change.

▶ Review the appropriateness of banking service suppliers periodically – consider value for money, service quality and, if appropriate, ethical issues.

Procedure

New bank account

▶ Convene a trustees' meeting to consider the terms of the bank mandate for the proposed account and, if thought fit, to approve those.

▶ Authorise relevant signatories.

▶ Document these decisions in the minutes of the meeting.

▶ Provide the bank with the completed mandate (retaining a copy with the minutes of the relevant trustees' meeting) and certified copies of the relevant board resolutions (or copies of the board meeting minutes, being careful to retain the original minutes).

▶ Also provide all required anti-money laundering evidence, verifications of the signatories and their signatures and evidence of the charity and its basic legal details (including list of trustees, charity registration details, company registration details and copy certificate of incorporation [CLGs] and a copy of the charity's constitution).

▶ Ensure all appropriate security arrangements are put in place (see further below).

▶ Ensure suitable practical arrangements are agreed with the bank and put in place (including frequency of statements, the medium by which the charity prefers to receive those statements [if the bank offers a choice, e.g. electronic communication/online or by post], to which address and person statements should be sent etc.).

General

▶ Check and follow the requirements of the charity's constitution with regard to banking arrangements and the authorisation of transactions on the charity's bank accounts.

▶ Ensure there are adequate verification and authorisation procedures for both cheque payments and electronic transactions on the charity's bank accounts.

▷ Dual authority (i.e. two signatories/authorising parties) should normally be required for all transactions on the bank account, regardless of the transaction mechanism.

Electronic banking

▷ The same level of financial controls should be applied to electronic banking as to other forms of banking arrangements. In particular, dual authority requirements should be applied.

BACS, direct debits, standing orders

▷ Apply the usual principles for financial security, including dual authority.

▷ Ensure suitable practical arrangements are in place for the use of any of these payment methods on the charity's bank accounts.

▷ Only specifically authorised individuals should be empowered to set up arrangements to make payments by direct debit, standing order or BACS. Such authority should be limited to a small number of people, with a list of authorised individuals being approved and recorded for this purpose.

▷ The documents setting up the payments should be retained as part of the charity's accounting records.

▷ The payments should be monitored so that the charity can ensure that the arrangement is cancelled when the charity stops using relevant goods or services.

Debit and credit cards

▷ Agree a clear policy for the use of payment cards (debit and/or credit cards), if the charity is to make use of such cards as a payment mechanism on any of its bank accounts. This should include the criteria for their issue, spending limits and security arrangements. Consider the need to place restrictions on when and how card payments may be used.

▷ Communicate the policy and required procedures for the use of payment cards clearly, in writing, to all trustees and staff using such cards.

▷ Ensure relevant payment cards are cancelled and destroyed, if the individual ceases to work for the charity or if the authorisation of the particular card's use is withdrawn.

▷ Ensure copies of credit or debit card statements are sent directly to the charity's finance team and not the individual card holder. The statements should be properly analysed and checked.

▷ Arrange periodic review of card use to ensure it is in line with agreed policies and procedures.

Filing requirements

▶ The Charity Commission expects a charity to notify the details of its principal bank account(s). The data is kept on a private part of the Commission's records and is not accessible to the public.

▶ The bank(s) used by the charity (but not details of the specific bank accounts) need to be stated in the trustees' annual report. That report is open to public access.

More information

▶ CC8 Internal Financial Controls for Charities (Charity Commission).

▶ CC26 Charities and Risk Management (Charity Commission).

▶ See also the Charity Commission guidance 'Protecting charities from harm' and several pieces on charities working internationally – available on the Commission's website.

▶ Charity Fraud: A Guide for the Trustees and Managers of Charities – this guide is produced jointly by regulatory bodies, investigative agencies and charity sector support bodies including the Charity Commission, National Fraud Authority, NCVO, Charity Finance Group. www.cfg.org.uk.

Business names

Introduction

A business name (sometimes called a trading name) is a name or title
by which a company is known and operates which is different to its
registered corporate name.

Charities often prefer to call a business or trading name an 'operating name'.

It is the registered corporate name (i.e. the company's name as set
out in its certificate of incorporation and recorded on the register of
companies at Companies House) that is the company's formal legal name.
That formal legal name must appear on a wide range of documents and
communications.

Checklist

▶ Carry out basic checks to seek to establish if the proposed business
name to be adopted, or a closely similar name, is already registered
for another organisation (e.g. an online company name check of the
records at Companies House).

▶ Remember that third party legal rights in a name can arise in other
ways than formal company name registration.

▶ Consider whether any trade mark searches might be advisable, to
reduce the risk of infringing a third party's trademark rights.

▶ A name, or part of it, may be subject to all or any of the legal rights
mentioned below, in favour of third parties. Care must be taken to
consider such matters prior to adopting use of a business name and
appropriate checks and searches should be arranged.

▷ Common law rights acquired through usage (there may be a risk
of a 'passing off' action by a third party against the charity).

▷ Domain name rights.

▷ Trade or service mark registrations (in the UK or overseas).

▷ Other legal registrations (in the UK or overseas).

▷ Copyright/other intellectual property rights.

▶ If a charity operates internationally it should check whether there are any local legal, regulatory, registration or disclosure requirements for an organisation that uses a business name. It should also be careful to check what the local legal position is regarding third party rights over names and the potential risks to the charity if it should infringe such rights.

▶ Be careful about the meaning of words and phrases in other languages, cultural issues and the risks of causing unintended offence.

Procedure

▶ Where a company chooses to use a business name, the company becomes subject to the requirements of Part 41 of the Companies Act 2006. In summary, these are:

▷ that any name implying connection with government or a public authority requires approval;

▷ the use of prescribed sensitive words or expressions requires approval;

▷ some proposed names or phrases require the consent of a government department or relevant body;

▷ where approval has been given in accordance with the above requirements it may subsequently be withdrawn;

▷ names that indicate an inappropriate company type or an inappropriate other legal form cannot be used;

▷ a name giving a misleading indication of the organisation's activities cannot be used.

Disclosure requirements

▶ The full legal name of an organisation that uses a business name must be given on a wide range of documents and in a wide range of communications.

▶ Company regulations require that any company using a business name must include its company name on relevant material and items and make it clear that the business name is being used by that company. These requirements also apply to the company's premises.

Sensitive words

▶ It may be necessary to obtain various consents or permission before using certain 'sensitive' words in a business name (for example, the consent of the Charity Commission is required before the word 'charity' can be used).

Filing requirements

▶ There is no register of business names in the UK.

▶ Check the position in other territories where the charity operates, as there may be local registration or notification requirements.

Notes

▶ The use of 'charity' and 'charitable' are restricted by English charity law.

▶ In Scotland, there are charity law restrictions on the use of those terms and also the term 'Scottish charity'.

▶ Company regulations and the Companies Act 2006 contain a wide range of restrictions with regard to company names, as well as the use of 'sensitive' words in company and business names.

▶ In addition, the use of some words deemed to be offensive is banned by regulations.

▶ There is a system for adjudication of name disputes involving companies, through the Company Names Adjudicator. The Adjudicator is based at the Intellectual Property Office. The IPO publishes helpful guidance on its website: www.ipo.gov.uk.

More information

▶ The Companies and Business Names (Miscellaneous Provisions) Regulations 2009.   **SI 2009/1085**

Chair of trustees – appointment

Introduction

Every board needs a chair to oversee the functioning of the board and chair board meetings. The charity's constitution usually sets out some broad responsibilities and powers for the chair with regard to the conduct of board meetings.

It is good practice for the board to approve a written role description for the chair and to review and update this from time to time. The role description should be consistent with the relevant provisions of the charity's constitution.

The chair of the board of trustees will normally be appointed from among the serving trustees. Many charity constitutions only permit a serving trustee to be appointed as chair.

Some charity constitutions provide that as a person is appointed to the chair role they automatically become a charity trustee of that charity.

Some constitutions provide a deliberate succession path, for instance requiring a person to serve for a period as a vice-chair before they can be considered for appointment as chair of the board.

Checklist

▶ Consider legal criteria for eligibility to serve as a charity trustee (as the chair will be a trustee).

▶ In a CLG, consider legal criteria for eligibility to serve as a company director (e.g. minimum age 16).

▶ Check eligibility criteria in the constitution (e.g. current membership of the charity may be required).

▶ Consider pre-appointment checks and due diligence that are required or desirable.

▶ Take into account the 'fit and proper persons' requirements under Finance Act 2010 and HMRC's guidance on meeting those requirements.

▶ Consider safeguarding issues and any checks or verifications needed in relation to those.

▶ Verify the candidate's identity and home address details.

▶ Check appointment method specified in the constitution (appointment by decision of the members at the AGM may be required or the board may be empowered to appoint its own chair).

▶ Consider whether the candidate must first be admitted to membership and/or appointed as a trustee before they can be appointed as chair of the board.

▶ Review the chair role description and update as appropriate.

▶ Ensure the candidate has a copy of the role description and a copy of the constitution (including all amendments to date).

▶ Consider whether the candidate, if appointed, may need any support or training as they take up their new role.

Procedure

▶ Carry out pre-appointment checks and verifications (if appropriate or required).

▶ Obtain all appropriate contact details for the candidate, if not already held.

▶ Follow appropriate procedures to make the appointment, in accordance with the constitution.

▶ Ensure the appointment decision is recorded in the minutes of the relevant meeting.

▶ Notify charity regulator(s) if the appointment involves appointment of a new trustee and notification of that is a requirement. It is good practice to notify trustee changes to the charity regulator(s) even if there is no strict legal requirement to do so.

▶ Notify any other relevant regulators (e.g. Companies House).

▶ Make necessary register entries if the appointment involves appointment of a new trustee:

▷ Register of directors (CLG).

▷ Register of trustees (CIO).

▶ Consider and action practical matters in consequence of the appointment (e.g. changes to website, literature, documents, alteration of bank account signatories).

▶ Make a note of the date of commencement of office and any applicable term of office and its end date.

Filing requirements

▶ CIO – there is an obligation to notify the Charity Commission of changes among the CIO's trustees, so if the appointment of the new chair involves appointment of a new trustee ensure this obligation is met.

▶ CLG – appointment of a new director must be notified to Companies House within 15 days (form AP01). Notification of the appointment of a *serving director* as chair is not required.

Chair of trustees – cessation of office

Introduction

It is healthy for the principal offices within a charity to change hands periodically, including the office of chair. A charity's constitution may ensure this happens in relation to the chair by providing limited periods of office and/or limits on the number of terms that may be served by an individual or an overall limit on the number of years' service permitted in a particular office or permitted for a trustee generally.

A chair may cease to hold office because of any of these reasons:

▷ Voluntary resignation as chair (check the constitution carefully to see if a former chair may remain on the board as a trustee and, if so, what the limits are on his or her remaining period of office as a trustee; also consider issues of good governance – it is not always helpful for the new chair to have a predecessor at his or her shoulder!)

▷ Cessation of office as a trustee (only a trustee should serve as chair of the board).

▷ Completion of a term of office (without any re-appointment to a new term).

▷ Bankruptcy (this automatically disqualifies the individual from charity trusteeship).

▷ Other disqualification by law (as a charity trustee or as a company director, as the latter also disqualifies the individual from charity trusteeship).

▷ Death.

Procedure

Resignation

▶ It is best practice to obtain a written resignation letter.

▶ Ensure the resignation is recorded in the minutes of the relevant meeting. The minute should make it clear if the trustee remains a trustee after the resignation as chair.

- Notify charity regulator(s) if required or desirable (particularly if the resignation involves cessation of office as a trustee).

- Notify any other relevant regulators (e.g. Companies House form TM01 cessation of office of an individual director).

- Make necessary register entries if the resignation involves cessation of office as a trustee:

  - Register of directors (CLG).

  - Register of trustees (CIO).

- Consider and action practical matters in consequence of the resignation (e.g. changes to website, literature, documents, alteration of bank account signatories).

- Address appointment of a new chair.

- Consider any interim arrangements necessary to chair board meetings held in the meantime (note the constitution may include provisions about the chairing of meetings in the absence of a chair of the board).

Other cessations of office

- Most of the above steps will also apply.

Filing requirements

- CIO – there is an obligation to notify the Charity Commission of changes amongst the CIO's trustees, so if the appointment of the new chair involves appointment of a new trustee ensure this obligation is met.

- CLG – appointment of a new director must be notified to Companies House within 15 days (form AP01). Notification of the appointment of a *serving director* as chair is not required.

Notes

- It is wise to carry out at least some succession planning, ready for future changes of chair. This should include periodic review of the skills needed for the office in the charity's situation and periodic review of the chair's role description.

- Where a charity's constitution specifies limited terms of office for a chair the succession planning process can be timetabled accordingly.

- Arrange any consequential actions relating to the change of chair (e.g. alterations to website, stationery and documents, alteration of bank account signatories).

Chair of trustees – role and responsibilities

Introduction

Every board needs a chair to oversee the functioning of the board and chair board meetings. The charity's constitution usually sets out some broad responsibilities and powers for the chair with regard to the conduct of board meetings.

It is good practice for the board to approve a written role description for the chair and to review and update this from time to time. The role description should be consistent with the relevant provisions of the charity's constitution.

Checklist

Role

▶ The chair's overall role is to lead the charity's board of trustees, ensuring that it fulfils its responsibilities for the governance of the charity.

Responsibilities – general

▶ The chair's principal responsibilities are:

▷ Leadership of the board of trustees (as the governing body of the charity) in its role of setting the direction and strategy of the charity.

▷ Ensuring that the board of trustees acts in furtherance of the charity's charitable purposes for the public benefit.

▷ Ensuring that the board of trustees deploys the charity's resources to further the charity's charitable purposes for the public benefit and in accordance with legal requirements.

▷ Planning the annual cycle of board meetings and committee meetings.

▷ Setting the agenda for meetings of the board of trustees.

▷ Monitoring that decisions taken at meetings are implemented.

Chairing of board meetings

▶ The chair must ensure that board meetings are conducted in an orderly fashion in accordance with the charity's constitution. The chair should seek to ensure that all trustees have the opportunity to participate in the discussions at meetings, so all voices and points of view are heard and the board can read a balanced and well thought through conclusion.

Chairing of general meetings of the members

▶ In a membership charity typically the chair of the board will also have responsibility for chairing general meetings of the members (e.g. the AGM).

▶ Some charity constitutions provide for the holder of some other role to chair the AGM (e.g. the honorary president of the charity).

Procedure

▶ Chairing of meetings should be carried out in accordance with applicable provisions of the charity's constitution.

Filing requirements

▶ The chair should be identified in the trustees' annual report.

▶ There is no specific filing or notification obligation in relation to the charity regulators (or Companies House for a CLG) when a chair is appointed or ceases to hold office. However, there may be if the change involves:

▷ appointment of a *new* trustee; or

▷ cessation of office of a trustee.

Charity regulators

Introduction

England and Wales

The general scheme of regulation for charities in England and Wales is public registration (unless an exemption or exception applies), regulatory oversight by the Charity Commission and public accounting and reporting, on an annual basis.

The intended removal of most of the exemptions and exceptions from charity registration has made slow progress, so a very significant number of charities are still not on the Charity Commission's register of charities.

The charity regulatory regime flows principally from the Charities Act 2011, supplemented by various regulations. However, some statutory provisions of charity law are still in older legislation.

Scotland

▶ The general scheme of regulation for charities in Scotland is comprehensive registration on the Scottish Charity Register, regulatory oversight by the OSCR and public accounting and reporting, on an annual basis. There are no exemptions from registration.

▶ The charity regulatory regime flows principally from the Charities and Trustee Investment (Scotland) Act 2005, supplemented by various regulations.

▶ As well as organisations constituted under the law of Scotland that are charities, any organisation constituted under the law of any other territory, that meets the charity test and has relevant connections/activities in Scotland, must also register (e.g. a charity constituted under the law of England and Wales). This requirement applies if the organisation:

1. is managed or controlled wholly or mainly in Scotland;
2. occupies land or premises in Scotland; or
3. carries out activities in any office, shop or similar premises in Scotland.

▶ The OSCR has issued guidance explaining how it interprets and applies these conditions. The guidance indicates the circumstances in which organisations constituted in other territories should apply for registration: www.oscr.org.uk.

Checklist

Role of the charity regulators

▶ The prime role of the UK's three charity regulators is to ensure charitable funds and assets are protected and correctly applied, to maintain public registers of charities required to be registered and to ensure that charities comply with their public accountability obligations. (They do not have the resources to police overall compliance with the whole gambit of charity law.)

▶ The regulators cannot and do not generally direct or manage charities or intervene in the governance of charities by their trustee boards. Nor will they involve themselves in member disputes or issues of good governance.

▶ However, if in a particular situation there is a substantial and immediate risk to charitable funds or assets, the regulators do have intervention and protective powers available to them.

▶ In addition, the regulators do have a role where trustees have fallen significantly short of the standards required of them by the law. For example the Charity Commission can and, depending on the particular circumstances, may exercise some of its regulatory powers where it considers there is evidence of misconduct or management by charity trustees.

Charity Commission – legal basis

▶ The legal basis for the Charity Commission is set out in the Charities Act 2011.

▶ The Charities (Protection and Social Investment) Act 2016 has extended the range of powers available to the Charity Commission.

▶ The Commission is a corporate body, with statutory objectives, functions and duties.

▶ The Commission is independent of government and outside the direction or control of ministers. It is accountable to Parliament through the Home Secretary and is ultimately answerable to the courts.

Charity Commission – statutory objectives

▶ The Charity Commission's statutory objectives are:

1. To increase public trust and confidence in charities.
2. To promote awareness and understanding of the public benefit requirement (i.e. the obligation for charities to provide public benefit).

3. To promote compliance by charity trustees with their legal obligations in exercising control and management of the administration of their charities.
4. To promote the effective use of charitable resources.
5. To enhance the accountability of charities to donors, beneficiaries and the general public.

Charity Commission – statutory functions

▶ The Charity Commission's statutory functions are:

a) To determine whether or not institutions are charities.
b) To encourage and facilitate the better administration of charities.
c) To identify and investigate the apparent misconduct or mismanagement in the administration of charities, and take remedial or protective action in connection with misconduct or mismanagement.
d) To determine whether public collection certificates should be issued and remain in force.
e) To obtain, evaluate and disseminate information in connection with the performance of the Commission's functions of the meeting of its objectives.
f) To give information or advice, or make proposals, to ministers, on matters relating to the Commission's functions or objectives.

▶ It is because of items (a) that the Charity Commission is responsible for keeping the public register of charities in England and Wales and also deals with new charity registrations. This is also the function under which the Charity Commission issues guidance on the public benefit requirements and monitors whether or not existing charities deliver suitable public benefit.

Charity Commission – general duties

▶ The Charity Commission's general duties (specified in the Charities Act 2011) are:

1. To act in a way compatible with its objectives and most appropriate to meeting them.
2. To act in a way compatible with the encouragement of charitable giving and voluntary participation in charity work.
3. To have regard to the need to use its resources in the most efficient, effective and economic way.
4. To have regard to the principles of best regulatory practice (including the principles under which regulatory activities should be proportionate, accountable, consistent, transparent and targeted only at cases in which action is needed).
5. To have regard to the desirability of facilitating innovation by or on behalf of charities.
6. To have regard to such generally accepted principles of good corporate governance as it is reasonable to regard as applicable to the Commission.

Charity Commission – intervention powers

▶ The Charity Commission has a range of powers of intervention. These divide into temporary protective powers and remedial powers:

1. The temporary protective powers enable charity assets deemed to be at risk to be protected quickly. Charity trustees or employees can be suspended pending potential removal, additional trustees or a receiver and manager to be appointed and transactions or property transfers can be made subject to Charity Commission prior approval.
2. The remedial powers include removal of trustees or employees or the making of a scheme for the charity's administration. These may be used during an inquiry.

▶ In both cases the Charity Commission can only act if it believes there has been misconduct or mismanagement in the charity's administration and its property needs protection.

Charity Commission – additional powers

▶ The Charity Commission has a number of additional powers, including:

▷ Subject to certain conditions being met, it can grant relief from liability for breach of trust or breach of duties to trustees, by an order. The power (which will only rarely be exercised) is available if the Commission considers the trustees acted honestly and reasonably and ought fairly to be excused from the breach.

▷ The Commission has power to waive the disqualification of any former trustee after a five-year period.

▷ The Commission can issue formal warnings when it considers that there has been a breach of trust or duty or other misconduct or mismanagement in a charity. Such warnings can be issued to the charity or to the trustees. Prior notice that the regulator is considering issuing a warning is given and the charity/trustees may make representations with the specified timescale. If the Commission does decide to proceed with a warning it may also choose to publish the warning on its website.

▷ The Commission has power to give formal advice to charities (it does not frequently do so).

▷ The Commission has power to determine the membership of a membership charity, in cases of doubt. This can be done when a formal inquiry has been opened or at the request of the charity itself.

▷ The Commission has power to direct the transfer of funds in a charity bank account that has been dormant for five or more years to another suitable charity.

▷ The Commission can enter premises and seize documents or information, under the authority of a warrant. This can be used when a formal inquiry has been opened.

▷ The Commission has power to disqualify trustees, at its discretion (without the need to seek a court order) in the exercise of one of the Commission's new powers under the 2016 Act. The order is made on the grounds that the person is considered unfit to be a trustee. Particular conditions must be met to enable the Commission to consider use of the power.

The OSCR – legal basis and functions

▶ The OSCR is established under the Charities and Trustee Investment (Scotland) Act 2005. Its functions are to:

▷ Determine whether bodies are charities.

▷ Keep a public register of charities (the Scottish Charity Register).

▷ Encourage, facilitate and monitor compliance by charities with the provisions of the Act.

▷ Identify and investigate apparent misconduct in the administration of charities and to take remedial or protective action in relation to such misconduct.

▷ Give information or advice, or make proposals, to Scottish ministers on matters relating to the OSCR's functions.

The OSCR – powers

▶ The OSCR has broadly similar powers to those of the Charity Commission, including intervention and investigatory powers intended to safeguard charitable funds and assets.

Charity Commission for Northern Ireland

▶ The Charity Commission for Northern Ireland (CCNI) is the independent regulator of charities in Northern Ireland, responsible for charity registration in Northern Ireland.

▶ The legal basis for and the powers of CCNI flow from the Charities Act (Northern Ireland) 2008 and supplementary regulations made under that Act.

▶ CCNI is a non-Departmental Public Body supported by the Department for Social Development in Northern Ireland.

Filing requirements

Annual reporting

▶ All the UK's charity law regimes require annual reporting to the relevant charity regulator. In essence, this is the filing of a charity annual return and the filing of annual accounts and an annual trustees' report (though there are some exemptions for the smallest charities in England and Wales, as well as 'lighter touch' reporting obligations for small to medium sized charities in England and Wales and in Scotland).

Event reporting

▷ Certain events trigger a public reporting requirement or an obligation to notify the relevant charity regulator. These range from relatively routine matters of public record, where the public details of a charity change (e.g. changes amongst the trustee board or a change to the public contact details for the charity) through to serious incident reporting obligations, where particular incidents such as suspected fraud or theft must be notified to the regulator on a confidential basis for potential investigation.

Notes

Alternative principal regulators

▷ There are a number of alternative principal regulators for certain groups of exempt charities in England and Wales.

▷ Exempt charities include most universities and colleges of further or higher education (their principal regulator is the Higher Education Funding Council for England or the Higher Education Funding Council for Wales), various national museums and galleries (their principal regulator is the Department for Culture, Media and Sport), the Royal Botanic Gardens, Kew (its principal regulator is the Department for the Environment, Food and Rural Affairs), academy schools, free schools and the governing bodies of foundation, voluntary aided, voluntary controlled and foundation special schools, sixth form college corporations (in England their principal regulator is the Department for Education, in Wales for most of these educational bodies the principal regulator is the Welsh Government).

▷ Alternative principal regulators are charged with promoting compliance with charity law obligations by exempt charities and their trustees. In practice it is difficult for principal regulators to be effective in discharging this responsibility, as they do not have comparable powers to the Charity Commission.

Charity status – key consequences

Introduction

Being a charity in law has some key consequences for the organisation, for its funds and assets and for the people involved in the organisation – any members (if it has a membership structure) and, particularly, for its charity trustees.

Checklist

▶ The organisation is inherently outward focused.

▶ The organisation must pursue its own charitable purposes (as set out in its constitution) and do so for the public benefit. Note that charity law in Scotland requires a charity to *provide* public benefit (or intend to do so, in the case of a new organisation) as one of the two requirements of the charity test (the other requirement being that the purposes of the organisation are charitable under the law of Scotland).

▶ The funds and assets must be protected and used correctly, towards the charitable purposes of the organisation and in accordance with charity law restrictions and requirements.

▶ No significant private or commercial benefits must arise from the organisation's activities (any such benefits must be only those that are necessary and incidental to the pursuit of the charitable purposes).

▶ The organisation is regulated by charity law and overseen by relevant charity regulator(s).

▶ The organisation is publicly accountable and must provide detailed annual accounts and an annual trustees' report (unless it has exemptions from reporting obligations – e.g. the smallest English registered charities have such exemptions).

▶ The members have no commercial interests, they do not 'own' the charity in the way that members of a commercial company do.

▶ The trustees are stewards and custodians, with legal duties.

▶ In a CIO or SCIO the *members* also have some legal duties.

CIOs – accounting and reporting

Introduction

CIOs are subject to statutory accounting and reporting obligations.

This is part of the 'quid pro quo' for the benefits a CIO enjoys by being a corporate body and a charity.

Checklist

Accounting standards

▶ CIOs must prepare their annual accounts in accordance with charity accounting standards, in particular the Charities SORP.

Basis of accounts

▶ If the CIO's income is £250,000 or less it may opt to prepare its accounts on a receipts and payments basis. If the income is higher, accruals accounts must be prepared.

Trustees' responsibilities

▶ The trustees have collective responsibility for ensuring that the CIO prepares annual accounts in accordance with applicable legal requirements and reporting standards.

▶ They are also responsible for preparing an annual trustees' report that complies with relevant legal requirements and reporting standards.

Trustee approval

▶ The trustees must formally approve both the annual accounts and the trustees' annual report.

Independent scrutiny

▶ The annual accounts of a CIO are subject to independent scrutiny requirements under charity law.

▶ Full statutory audit is required if the income is over £500,000 (£250,000 where the book value of the assets exceeds £3.26 million) or the CIO is part of a group of organisations.

▶ If the income is lower, but above £25,000, an independent examination is permitted instead of an audit. The examiner must be qualified in accordance with relevant regulations.

▶ In all cases, these are gross income thresholds, so income from all sources must be taken into account.

Filing requirements

▶ A CIO must complete a charity annual return to the Charity Commission (this is filed online via the Charity Commission website).

▶ A CIO must file annual accounts and a trustees' report with the Charity Commission. The accounts must comply with charity reporting standards, especially the Charities SORP.

▶ The accounts and trustees' annual report must be filed with the Charity Commission within 10 months of the financial year-end.

▶ Filing must be carried out electronically, via the Charity Commission website.

▶ There are *no* filing exemptions for the accounts and trustees' reports of smaller CIOs (unlike the exemptions that apply to other small charities).

Charity Commission specification, under regulation 54(1)(e), Charitable Incorporated Organisations (General) Regulations 2012, SI 3012 of 2012

More information

▶ See checklist: 'CIOs – general'.

CIOs – alteration of constitutions

Introduction

A CIO must have a constitution that meets the requirements of the Charities Act 2011 and relevant CIO specific regulations.

The constitution may only be altered as permitted by the relevant legal provisions and in accordance with relevant procedural requirements of the CIO's own constitution.

Checklist

▶ Initial considerations:

▷ Does the proposed alteration require prior Charity Commission consent?

▷ What procedural requirements in the particular CIO's constitution will need to be considered and observed? (Particularly with regard to members' meetings and members' decisions.)

Alterations that require prior Charity Commission consent

▶ The following alterations require *prior* Charity Commission consent:

▷ A change to the charitable purposes of the CIO.

▷ A change that would authorise benefits to trustees or connected persons.

▷ An alteration to the winding up clause (i.e. the dissolution provisions).

Date the change becomes effective

▶ Any change to the constitution of a CIO does not take effect until it is registered with the Charity Commission. (This is the case whether or not the alteration required prior Charity Commission consent.)

▶ This is an important difference from the position for other types of charity, where alterations normally take immediate effect as the members approve the changes (except for changes to the charitable purposes [objects] of a CLG which take effect when registered by Companies House).

Procedure

▶ An alteration to a CIO's constitution may only be made with the approval of the CIO's members.

▶ The trustees will therefore authorise the convening of a general meeting of the members (or the circulation of a written resolution).

▶ The requirements of the CIO's constitution with regard to the convening and conduct of general meetings of the members must be observed (including notice period, contents of the notice, delivery methods, the use of proxies, quorum rules, chairing of the meeting and voting rights and practical arrangements).

▶ A 75% majority of votes cast is required if the relevant resolution is proposed at a general meeting of the CIO's members.

▶ If the decision is to be taken in writing, *unanimity* is required.

Filing requirements

▶ A copy of the members' resolution approving the changes, together with a copy of the amended constitution, must be sent to the Charity Commission within 15 working days from the date of the resolution.

▶ If the alteration required the Commission's prior consent, a copy of that consent should also be included.

More information

▶ See checklist: 'CIOs – general'.

CIOs – constitutions general

Introduction

A CIO must have a constitution that meets the requirements of the Charities Act 2011 and relevant CIO specific regulations.

Checklist

▶ A CIO's constitution must either be in the form specified by regulations made by the Charity Commission or 'as near to that form as the circumstances admit'.

▶ The constitution must be in English unless the CIO's principal office is in Wales, in which case the constitution may be in English or in Welsh.

Matters that must be included

▶ These matters must be included in a CIO's constitution:

▷ Name of the CIO.

▷ Its charitable purposes.

▷ Whether its principal office is in England or Wales (it is not necessary to set out the full address).

▷ Whether or not its members are liable to contribute to its assets if it is wound up and, if they are, up to what amount.

▷ Membership eligibility and provisions for the admission of members and cessation of membership (the statutory minimum number of members is one, the constitution could set this at a higher level).

▷ Provisions for the appointment and cessation of office of the trustees (and any eligibility criteria for appointment).

▷ The minimum number of trustees, if that is to be more than one (as is both likely and advisable, the Charity Commission regards three as good practice).

▷ Provisions regarding the taking of trustees' decisions by resolutions in writing, or by electronic means outside board meetings, if the trustees are to have these powers.

▷ The names of the first trustees (for a new CIO).

▷ Procedural rules including rules for meetings (of members and of trustees).

▷ Proxy rights for members, if they are to have such rights (the rights are not automatic as they would be in a charitable company).

▷ Postal voting rights for members, if they are to have such rights.

▷ Provisions for automatic use of electronic communications or a website to formally communicate with its members, if the CIO intends to do that.

▷ Provisions for use of the seal, if the CIO is to have a seal (the CIO may but does not have to have a seal).

▷ Directions about the application of the CIO's property on its dissolution for similar charitable purposes.

Charity Commission models

▶ The Charity Commission has made regulations providing two model constitutions (see The Charities Act 2011 (Charitable Incorporated Organisations) (Constitutions) Regulations 2012). These regulations were, made by order of the Charity Commission pursuant to its powers under section 206(5) of the Charities Act 2011.

▶ The two models are as follows:

▷ A 'foundation' model in which the only voting members of the CIO are the trustees.

▷ An 'association' model for a CIO that has a wider membership, beyond the trustees.

▶ There are important differences between the two, for example the 'association' model includes an obligation to hold an annual general meeting at least once every 15 months.

▶ Use of these models is not a legal obligation and the Commission is taking a flexible approach to CIOs that want to use a custom drafted constitution (provided that document contains the features that are specifically required for a CIO by the Charities Act and the CIO regulations).

Procedure

▶ When a new CIO is registered with the Charity Commission a suitable constitution must be provided with the relevant documents for the registration application (which is made online via the Charity Commission website). The Commission checks that this complies with the requirements of relevant legal provisions regarding the contents of a CIO's constitution (see checklist above). The constitution takes effect on registration.

▷ Subsequent changes can be made to a CIO's constitution, provided the required approval is given by the CIO's members. Note that changes do not take effect until they are registered with the Charity Commission.

Filing requirements

▷ A CIO's constitution must be filed with the Charity Commission.

▷ Changes to the constitution must be filed with the Charity Commission. The changes do not take effect until this has been done.

Notes

▷ CIO constitutions are not made generally available on the register of charities by the Charity Commission. However, if a member of the public requests a copy of a particular CIO's constitution the Commission will provide a copy to the enquirer.

▷ If making a trustee's name known publicly could place the trustee at risk of personal violence or intimidation, the Charity Commission will be prepared to redact the name from any copy of the constitution it sends out in response to a request from a member of the public. Note that it is important to discuss any perceived risk with the Commission when setting up a new CIO (the names of the first trustees do have to be listed in the constitution provided to the Commission with the CIO registration application).

More information

▷ See checklists: 'CIOs – general' and 'CIOs – alteration of constitutions'.

CIOs – conversion of CLGs to CIOs

Introduction

Many charities take the legal form of a CLG.

There are specific legal provisions permitting the conversion of a charitable CLG to the charitable incorporated organisation (CIO) legal form.

Whether the CIO legal form would be appropriate for an existing CLG and what, if any, particular issues might be involved in the conversion requires careful consideration. Each charity should consider its own needs and circumstances, with appropriate specialist professional advice, before following a conversion process.

Checklist

▶ Check whether the company is an exempt charity; if it is it cannot convert to a CIO.

▶ Ensure all required filing with the Charity Commission and Companies House is up-to-date – the conversion process cannot be followed unless this is the case.

▶ Consider whether there are any sensitive words in the name that may require consents or a non-objection letter to enable the resulting CIO to use the desired name.

▶ Consider whether the charity needs to make any regulated alterations at the same time it makes the required changes for conversion (for example changes to its charitable purposes or the application of final funds on dissolution of the charity). If it does a prior step the procedure to obtain prior Charity Commission consent and then make those changes must be followed.

▶ Check there are no outstanding legal proceedings against the CLG; if there are the conversion process cannot proceed.

▶ Check the CLG is not subject to a dissolution process or in liquidation or administrative receivership; if it is the conversion process cannot proceed.

Procedure

- ▶ Prepare a suitable CIO form of constitution.

- ▶ Trustees convene a general meeting of the members of the CLG to consider special resolutions to authorise the conversion, adopt a suitable CIO form of constitution and make any other required or appropriate changes (or authorise the circulation of written resolutions).

- ▶ Ensure the notice of meeting and draft resolutions comply with all relevant company law requirements.

- ▶ Check that the meeting is quorate.

- ▶ Ensure the required 75% majority of votes cast is achieved to pass each special resolution. Note that if written resolutions are used in place of a meeting, each one must be passed unanimously by all the members of the CLG.

- ▶ Ensure minutes of the meeting are prepared, authenticated and kept in accordance with the usual requirements.

- ▶ Prepare trustees' declaration of eligibility to serve as charity trustees (available on the Charity Commission website) and ensure all trustees sign the declaration.

- ▶ Apply for conversion online via the Charity Commission website.

Filing requirements

- ▶ Submit the required application for conversion and accompanying documents to the Charity Commission online via the Commission's website.

Notes

- ▶ The legal provisions enable the existing CLG to become a CIO, without the need for a transfer of funds, other assets and activities to a new successor charity.

- ▶ The same charity number will remain attached to the charity as a CIO.

- ▶ Because the charity remains but in a different legal form, it should be able to retain its current bank account and arrangements with service providers, suppliers and other third parties. Depending on the circumstances, third parties may ask for some form of 'due diligence' process or evidence or they may require their own administrative process to be followed to take account of the change to CIO.

- ▶ Although, broadly, all funds and assets remain the property of the CIO, the position can be more complex with regard to potential legacies that have not yet taken legal effect (i.e. the person who has made the bequest in their will is still alive).

▶ The usual restrictions on charity names apply to CIOs, for example the name of the altered charity cannot be the same as that of any other charity.

More information

▶ See the Charitable Incorporated Organisations (Conversion) Regulations 2017 and the relevant guidance on the Charity Commission website.

CIOs – general

Introduction

A CIO is a corporate body registered only with the Charity Commission (not Companies House) under the Charities Act 2011 and the CIO specific regulations.

The CIO legal form can only be used by a charity established under the law of England and Wales (there are equivalent legal forms that may be established under the law of Scotland and of Northern Ireland).

The CIO legal form is specific to registered charities in England and Wales, so it *cannot* be used by:

▷ a charity that is exempt or excepted from charity registration requirements;

▷ a charity constituted under the law of any other territory (including the other territories within the United Kingdom); or

▷ a non-charity.

Checklist

Distinctive features of CIOs

▶ Key distinctive features of CIOs include:

▷ The members have a statutory duty (see checklist: 'CIOs – members').

▷ There are no exemptions from registration with the Charity Commission (*all* CIOs must be registered with the charity regulator, regardless of income level).

▷ There are *no* exemptions from filing a CIO's trustees' annual report and accounts with the Charity Commission (*all* CIOs must file these, regardless of income level).

(Other legal types of charity do *not* have to file their report and accounts if their annual income is under £25,000).

Registration and regulation

▶ A CIO is created by registration with the Charity Commission. It comes into being as that registration occurs (the equivalent of the date of incorporation of a company).

▶ There are CIO specific regulatory requirements.

▶ There are lighter touch regulatory requirements for the detailed contents and format of the accounts of a smaller CIO (see checklist: 'CIOs – accounting and reporting').

Part 11, Charities
Act 2011 and
The Charitable
Incorporated
Organisations
(General) Regulations
2012, SI 3012 of 2012

Statutory power

▶ A CIO has statutory power to do anything that is calculated to further its charitable purposes.

Principal office

▶ A CIO must have a principal office in England and Wales (this is the equivalent of a company's registered office).

Assets

▶ There is a statutory obligation for the CIO to use and apply its assets in furtherance of its charitable purposes and in accordance with its constitution.

Members

▶ A CIO must have at least one member, usually there is more than one.

Trustees

▶ A CIO must have trustees. They have both the general responsibilities and duties of charity trustees and also CIO specific duties.

Constitution

▶ A CIO's constitution must either be in the form specified by regulations made by the Charity Commission or 'as near to that form as the circumstances admit'. Certain areas must be dealt with in the constitution (see further details in the checklist: 'CIOs – constitutions general').

▶ The constitution must be in English unless the CIO's principal office is in Wales, in which case the constitution may be in English or in Welsh.

▶ Alterations to the constitution do not take effect until they are registered with the Charity Commission. Note that some alterations require prior Charity Commission consent.

Public accountability

▶ A CIO's annual accounts and trustees' annual report are available to the public via the Charity Commission website.

- In addition to annual reporting obligations, CIOs are subject to a range of public accountability obligations and requirements:

  ▷ Obligations to disclose the CIO's name at its premises, in the same items and communications in which a company would be required to disclose its name and also in conveyances (defined in the relevant statutory provisions as any instruments that create, transfer, vary or extinguish an interest in land).

  ▷ Obligations to disclose various details and information on documents and in communications (including emails and websites, as well as hard copy documents).

  ▷ The requirement to include 'Charitable Incorporated Organisation' or 'CIO' at the end of the organisation's name (or Welsh equivalents).

See the Charitable Incorporated Organisations (General) Regulations 2012, SI 3012 of 2012

Mergers/amalgamations

- There are specific statutory provisions and related procedures for the amalgamation of two or more CIOs.

Transfer of undertaking

- There are specific statutory provisions and related procedures for the transfer of a CIO's undertaking to another CIO.

Conversions

- There are specific statutory provisions and related procedures for the conversion of certain other legal types of charity into CIOs.

- The Charities Act 2011 and supplementary regulations provide for the conversion of community interest companies and CLGs into CIOs.

Procedure

- Some procedures are subject to statutory provisions, which are in many circumstances mandatory (e.g. the procedure to alter a CIO's constitution).

- Other procedures will be subject to the provisions of the particular CIO's constitution.

Regulatory consents

- A CIO must obtain prior Charity Commission consent before it can take certain actions or make certain changes (for example a proposed alteration to its charitable purposes).

Filing requirements

- CIOs have a range of filing obligations in these areas:

  ▷ Annual accounting and reporting.

▷ Event/transaction notifications to the Charity Commission (some of these obligations are CIO specific rather than simply general charity obligations).

▶ Note that the Charity Commission does *not* hold any public register of charges created by CIOs. (Security relating to land would usually be registered against the title to the relevant land at the Land Registry.)

Notes

Scotland

▶ Charity law in Scotland makes provision for the registration and regulation of Scottish Charitable Incorporated Organisations (SCIOs). Key differences between these provisions and those applicable to CIOs include:

▷ There are different statutory duties for SCIO trustees and SCIO members.

▷ There are different rules about the areas that a SCIO's constitution must address (for example there must be provisions about conflicts of interest).

▷ There is a statutory obligation to hold an AGM at least once in every 15 months.

▶ The OSCR has not produced model SCIO constitutions.

▶ There are also statutory provisions for the conversion of existing charities to SCIOs.

Chapter 7, Charities and Trustee Investment (Scotland) Act 2005, The Scottish Charitable Incorporated Organisations Regulations 2011, SSI 44 of 2011, The Scottish Charitable Organisations (Removal from the Register and Dissolution) Regulations 2011, SSI 237 of 2011

Northern Ireland

▶ A version of the CIO legal form is to be introduced in Northern Ireland under the new charity law and regulatory regime being implemented there. Specific regulations will be required, to supplement the provisions in the Charities Act (Northern Ireland) 2008. (At the date of preparation of this book there was no projected timetable for this.)

More information

▶ See: The Charitable Incorporated Organisations (General) Regulations 2012, SI 3012 of 2012.

▶ The Charitable Incorporated Organisations (Insolvency and Dissolution) Regulations 2012, SI 3013 of 2012.

▶ See checklists: 'CIOs – accounting and reporting', 'CIOs – alteration of constitutions', 'CIOs – constitutions general', 'CIOs – conversion of CLGs to CIOs', 'CIOs – general', 'CIOs – members', 'CIOs – registers and records' and 'CIOs – trustees'.

CIOs – members

Introduction

A CIO must have members as well as trustees. Subject to the provisions of the particular CIO's constitution, the members may be the same people as the trustees or different people.

Generally the role of the members is passive. It is the *trustees* of the CIO who are responsible for the governance and the strategic management of the CIO.

Checklist

Number of members

▶ There must be at least one member, in practice there will usually be more than one (and the particular CIO's constitution may well require a minimum number higher than one).

Decisions that must be taken by the members

▶ Certain decisions must be taken by the members, in particular:

▷ alterations to the CIO's constitution;

▷ approval of amalgamation with another CIO;

▷ authorisation for the transfer of the CIO's undertaking to another CIO; and

▷ a decision to dissolve the CIO.

Members' rights

▶ The rights of a CIO's members are partly statutory (flowing from the Charities Act 2011 and the CIO regulations) and partly dependant on the individual CIO's constitution.

Members' statutory duty

▶ A CIO's members are subject to a statutory duty to exercise their membership powers in such a way that they decide, in good faith, will be most likely to further the CIO's charitable purposes.

Membership provisions in the constitution

▶ Certain matters regarding members and membership must be dealt with by a CIO's constitution (see checklist: 'CIOs – constitutions general').

Register of members

▶ A CIO must keep a register of members, recording particular information about its members and their class of membership (for further details see checklist: 'CIOs – registers and records').

▶ This register is open to inspection by members, auditors or the CIO's independent examiner and a range of regulatory and investigatory bodies. It is not open to public access.

s. 220 Charities Act 2011

Members' liability

▶ CIO members are not usually exposed to personal liability to any significant degree. The CIO is a corporate body so it has prime responsibility for its own debts and other liabilities and it is the CIO's own assets that are at risk.

▶ The members of a particular CIO may, or may not, have liability to make a fixed level contribution to the CIO's assets in the event of a winding up. The CIO's constitution will specify this and, if there is a liability, it will state the relevant fixed sum. The sum is likely to be nominal (typically £1).

▶ Breach of the members' statutory duty could potentially give rise to personal liability in accordance with the usual breach of duty legal principles.

Procedure

▶ Members' decisions must be taken in accordance with the CIO's constitution.

▶ Some decisions are also subject to additional statutory requirements, which can include prior Charity Commission consent and/or formal notification to the Charity Commission.

Filing requirements

▶ Certain members' decisions will require formal notification to the Charity Commission (for example a decision to alter the constitution, which does not take effect until it has been registered with the Commission).

Notes

▶ The CIO regulations are:

▶ The Charitable Incorporated Organisations (General) Regulations 2012, SI 2012/3012.

▶ The Charitable Incorporated Organisations (Insolvency and Dissolution) Regulations 2012, SI 2012/3013.

▶ The Charities Act 2011 (Charitable Incorporated Organisations) (Constitutions) Regulations 2012. These regulations were, made by order of the Charity Commission pursuant to its powers under section 206(5) of the Charities Act 2011.

More information

▶ See checklist: 'CIOs – general'.

CIOs – registers and records

Introduction

CIOs must keep a register of trustees and a register of members.

CIOs must keep accounting records.

Various other records will need to be kept (for example in relation to tax and VAT matters, employees, compulsory insurances such as employers' liability insurance and third party insurance in respect of vehicles). The detailed requirements applicable to a particular CIO will in part depend on the nature of its assets and activities.

Checklist

Register of trustees

▶ The register of trustees must record:

> ▷ name of each trustee;

> ▷ service address for each trustee (this may be the trustee's home address however the trustee may choose to use some other alternative address, for example the address of the CIO's principal office);

> ▷ date of appointment of each trustee;

> ▷ date of cessation of office, for any former trustee;

> ▷ if the CIO is a foundation CIO (i.e. only the trustees are members) and it has more than one class of members, the register must indicate the membership class to which each trustee belongs;

> ▷ for a corporate trustee:

>> a) its registered or principal office as its service address; and

>> b) the relevant company registration information (including registered company number and the territory in which it is registered). For corporate bodies registered outside the EEA additional details are required (including the law by which it is governed).

S.26 and Schedule 1, Part 2 The Charitable Incorporated Organisations (General) Regulations 2012

S.26 and Schedule 1, Part 1 The Charitable Incorporated Organisations (General) Regulations 2012

Register of members

▶ The register of members must record:

▷ name of each member;

▷ service address for each member (this may be the member's home address however the member may choose to use some other alternative address);

▷ date of admission to membership of each member;

▷ date of cessation of membership, for any former member;

▷ if there is more than one class of members the register must state the membership class to which the member belongs; and

▷ if the CIO only has one member the register must include a statement to that effect with the date the CIO became single member.

Inspection rights – register of trustees

▶ The public may access the register of trustees to inspect the information it contains.

▶ Various regulatory and investigatory bodies may access this register.

▶ Auditors or independent examiners may access this register.

Inspection rights – register of members

▶ A member or a trustee of a CIO may inspect the register of members, or request a copy of all or part of the register, where:

▷ the request is made for the purpose of carrying out the requester's duties as a member or trustee; or

▷ the requester wants to inspect or see a copy of their entry on the register.

▶ Various regulatory and investigatory bodies may access this register.

▶ Auditors or independent examiners may access this register.

▶ This register is not open to general public access.

▶ If the CIO is being wound up and all or any of the members are liable to contribute to its assets, then a person can ask to see, or be provided with a copy of, all or part of the register in order to recover a member's contribution. The trustees may ask for reasonable payment to recover the costs of meeting such a request.

Other records

▶ A CIO must keep records of:

▷ appointments of officers made by the CIO's trustees;

▷ proceedings at general meetings of the members of the CIO;

▷ meetings of the charity trustees and meetings of committees of the trustees – those records must include:

➤ the names of the trustees at the meetings;
➤ the decisions made at the meetings; and
➤ where appropriate, the reasons for the decisions.

▶ These records must be kept for a minimum period of six years from the date of the meeting, resolution or appointment.

Procedure

▶ Records, including registers, may be kept in electronic form provided they can be reproduced in hard copy form.

Filing requirements

▶ It is not necessary to file copies of the registers with the Charity Commission. However, changes amongst the trustees must be notified to the Commission.

Notes

▶ A service address must be a real address, where documents can be delivered.

▶ A CIO is legally required to have both members and trustees. Subject to the terms of its own constitution, a CIO may choose to have a membership that is wider than its trustee board (an 'association' CIO) or it may structure itself so that its members and trustees are the same people (a 'foundation' CIO).

▶ Entries relating to a former member can be removed from the register of members 10 years from the date of cessation of membership.

▶ If the CIO has more than 50 members, the register of members must be kept in such a form as to constitute an index.

More information

▶ See the Charitable Incorporated Organisations (General (Regulations) 2012 SI 3012/2012.

CIOs – trustees

Introduction

A CIO must have trustees, as well as members. Subject to the provisions of the particular CIO's constitution, the members may be the same people as the trustees or different people.

The trustees are the governing body, with collective responsibility for the governance and strategic leadership of the CIO.

Checklist

Number of trustees

▶ Usually a CIO will have at least three trustees.

▶ The particular CIO's constitution may specify a minimum and/or maximum number of trustees.

Minimum age

▶ The minimum age for a CIO trustee is 16.

CIO specific trustees' duties

▶ In addition to the usual duties of charity trustees, a trustee of a CIO has the following CIO-specific duties:

   s. 221, Charities Act 2011

▷ A duty to exercise the trustee's powers and perform the trustee's functions in a way the trustee decides, in good faith, will be most likely to further the CIO's charitable purposes.

▷ In the performance of the trustee's functions, a duty to exercise such care as is reasonable in the circumstances, having regard in particular to:

➤ any special knowledge or experience the trustee has, or purports to have; and

➤ if the trustee acts in the course of a business or profession, any special knowledge or experience it is reasonable to expect of a person acting in the course of that kind of business or profession.

Disclosure of interests

▶ CIO trustees have a specific statutory obligation to disclose any material interest they have in any arrangement or transaction that a CIO proposes to enter into.

See s. 222(1),
Charities Act 2011

▶ If they fail to do so they may not benefit personally from the arrangement or transaction.

▶ Note that this statutory provision does not of itself give authority for a CIO's trustees to receive personal benefits. Rather the usual legal and governance principles apply – that personal benefits are only permitted if, and to the extent that, there is specific authority [in the constitution or, less likely, some other source].

Conflicts of interest

▶ CIO trustees are subject to the usual legal rules and principles that apply to charity trustees regarding conflicts of interest.

▶ The trustees must obey the provisions of the particular CIO's constitution with regard to conflicts (the constitution should, but does not have to, include suitable provisions).

Trustee provisions in the constitution

▶ Certain matters regarding the trustees, how they are appointed and how they cease to hold office, together with aspects of how they take decisions and discharge their responsibilities must be set out in the CIO's constitution (see checklist: 'CIOs – constitutions general').

▶ Public listing of trustees.

▶ The names of a CIO's trustees are publicly listed on the Charity Commission website.

▶ A new CIO, applying to the Charity Commission for registration, must list the names of its first trustees in its constitution. (This requirement can give rise to confusion later, when trustees have changed.)

▶ If public identification of a trustee would put that person at risk of violence or intimidation it is possible to seek the Charity Commission's agreement to withhold the name from the public record. However, this cannot normally be done retrospectively.

Register of trustees

▶ CIOs must keep a register of trustees, recording particular information about its trustees (for further details see checklist: 'CIOs – registers and records').

▶ This register is open to general public access, as well as to inspection by members, auditors or the CIO's independent examiner and a range of regulatory and investigatory bodies.

Public accountability and disclosure obligations

▶ The trustees have principal responsibility for ensuring the CIO meets its public accountability obligations, including its annual accounting and reporting obligations.

▶ The annual accounts and trustees' report are publicly accessible on the Charity Commission website. In addition, a CIO must provide copies to a member of the public who requests them.

▶ They must also ensure the CIO meets its public disclosure obligations (for example disclosure of its name at its premises and various disclosures in documents and communications, including emails, and on its website).

▶ Non-compliance with the disclosure obligations can have serious consequences. Criminal penalties can be imposed on the trustees and anyone else who was at fault. In addition, a court can potentially reject legal proceedings brought against third parties by the CIO, in relation to the non-compliant item.

Trustees' liability

▶ The trustees are generally protected from personal liability as the CIO is a corporate body that effectively provides limited liability protection. The CIO therefore has prime responsibility for its own debts and other liabilities and it is the CIO's own assets that are at risk.

▶ This protection may not be available if the trustees are in breach of their duties (particularly if that involves a breach of trust) or if the CIO becomes insolvent.

Procedure

Trustees' meetings and decisions

▶ The procedures for trustees' meetings and decision making by trustees are largely subject to the provisions of the individual CIO's constitution.

Filing requirements

Notifying trustee changes to the Charity Commission

▶ CIOs are obliged to notify the Charity Commission of changes amongst their trustees (the notification should be contemporaneous with the event, not left until the next annual reporting cycle). As well as new appointments and cessations of office, any changes to the trustees' details must also be notified (for example a change of address).

Annual accounting and reporting

▶ A CIO must complete a charity annual return to the Charity Commission (this is filed online via the Charity Commission website).

▶ A CIO must file annual accounts and a trustees' report with the Charity Commission. The accounts must comply with charity reporting standards, especially the SORP standards.

▶ There are *no* filing exemptions for the accounts and trustees' reports of smaller CIOs (unlike the exemptions that apply to other small charities).

More information

▶ See checklists: 'CIOs – accounting and reporting' and 'CIOs – general'.

Community benefit societies

Introduction

Community benefit societies are corporate bodies formed and registered under the Co-operative and Community Benefit Societies Act 2014. Only some of them are charitable.

Checklist

▶ Charitable registered societies are exempt charities, so they are not required to register with the Charity Commission.

▶ A significant proportion of the charitable registered societies that exist are involved in the social housing sector, often as registered providers of housing, subject to principal regulatory oversight by the Homes and Communities Agency.

▶ Registered societies are registered on the Mutuals Register held by the Financial Conduct Authority.

▶ The Mutuals Register holds records of around 10,000 organisations, including registered societies (both charitable and non-charitable). It is open to public access online via the FCA website.

▶ Registered societies must pay a periodic fee to the FCA calculated on a sale that relates to their total assets.

▶ The principal legislation for registered societies is the Co-operative and Community Benefit Societies Act 2014.

Procedure

▶ Most procedures are subject to statutory requirements set out in the Co-operative and Community Benefit Societies Act 2014.

Filing requirements

▶ Registered societies have annual accounting and reporting obligations. An annual return and the annual accounts must be filed with the FCA; they are accessible to the public.

▶ There will be a filing or notification requirement in consequence of
the key decisions and changes, including:

▷ change of name;

▷ change to the registered society's rules;

▷ transfer of engagement;

▷ dissolution; and

▷ conversion to or from a registered society.

▶ Fees apply to some of these filing and notification obligations.

Notes

▶ Charitable registered societies will be 'community benefit societies',
one of the two types of registered society (the other is co-operatives).
Note that registered societies established as co-operatives cannot be
charities.

▶ Some conversions are permitted (for example, subject to certain
conditions being met and required procedures being followed, a
registered society can convert to a company and vice versa)

More information

▶ For access to the Mutual Register see:

▷ Financial Conduct Authority: www.fca.org.

▶ For further information on the regulation of registered providers
of social housing see:

▷ National Housing Federation: www.housing.org.uk.

▷ Homes and Communities Agency:
www.homesandcommunities.co.uk.

Companies House – electronic filing

Introduction

Companies are required to file a range of documents and data with Companies House:

▷ Annual reporting documents (annual accounts; company annual return).

▷ Event notifications (a wide range of events and changes trigger a filing requirement).

At least 75% of the material filed at Companies House by companies is sent by electronic communication (this figure is increasing year on year).

Checklist

▶ There are two key mechanisms for electronic filing – WebFiling and software filing.

WebFiling

▶ Companies House WebFiling service is available free of charge to all via the Companies House website.

Software filing

▶ Companies House software filing option enables the electronic transfer and acknowledgement of data between presenters and Companies House via XML.

▶ Such software filing is of greatest benefit to those who file documents on a daily or weekly basis. It is therefore less likely to be used by charities themselves.

▶ Software filing requires purchase of commercial software or the development of suitable software in-house by the relevant organisation that wants to present electronic data to Companies House in this way.

▶ Note that the electronic filing capabilities of commercial software vary considerably. Some are limited to routine notifications while others also allow electronic submission of accounts. A smaller number of software suppliers provide packages that can be used for e filing in relation to more complex or unusual transactions and a wider range of types of corporate body, beyond private limited companies.

Document quality

▶ Documents filed electronically with Companies House must comply with the specifications set out for electronic filing by the Registrar of Companies in the Registrar's Rules.

▶ The formats for software filing are contained in the rules published on Companies House website.

▶ The website also provides all the formats that are needed for electronic filing.

Statutory fees

▶ There are significantly lower statutory fees applicable if electronic, rather than paper-based, filing is used to submit a document to Companies House.

E-reminders

▶ Presenters who have registered to use Companies House WebFiling can also sign up for free e-reminders on relevant companies. This is a convenient way to ensure you do not overlook filing deadlines on annual items such as accounts and company annual returns.

Procedure

WebFiling – user registration

▶ A user registers via the Companies House website. They must provide an email address. Companies House will then transmit a unique user passcode to them at that address.

WebFiling – company authentication

▶ To gain access to WebFiling for a particular company you must first be a registered user of WebFiling (see above).

▶ For a company that may wish to file data via WebFiling you need to obtain an authentication code. Companies House posts the code to the company's registered office address.

Software filing

▶ Relevant commercial software packages provide an electronic filing process via the user's computer and secure links to Companies House.

▶ For organisations wishing to develop their own bespoke software, with an electronic filing functionality, a Technical Interface Specification is available from Companies House to assist the software developers.

Notes

▶ Under the Companies Act 2006 the Registrar of Companies is given authority to make rules governing certain areas in relation to the filing of documents at Companies House. They are regarded as being secondary legislation, made under section 1117 of the Act, and include the form, manner of delivery and method of authentication for documents, whether delivered in electronic format or as a paper document.

More information

▶ See 'Registrar's Rules' available on the Companies House website: www.gov.uk/guidance/registrars-rules.

Companies House

Introduction

Companies House is the official public registry of companies in the UK. It also keeps data for certain other corporate entities including limited liability partnerships.

Companies House is an Executive Agency of the Department for Business, Innovation and Skills.

The United Kingdom's company registration system dates back to 1844, when the first public registration system for companies was introduced.

The principal law governing modern company registration matters is set out in the Companies Act 2006 and associated regulations.

Checklist

▶ The main functions of Companies House are to:

▷ incorporate and dissolve companies;

▷ examine and store company information delivered under the Companies Act 2006 and related legislation; and

▷ make this information available to the public.

Procedure

▶ Companies House publishes a range of guidance on its website including general guidance intended to assist companies in complying with their public filing and reporting requirements and statements about major policy changes or changes to Companies House practices.

▶ The level of electronic communications between companies and Companies House is extremely high, with very few items now being filed in paper form. Significant differentials have been introduced, so that the statutory fee attaching to the paper equivalent item is significantly higher than the fee attaching to that item if it is filed by electronic means (e.g. the statutory incorporation fee and the confirmation statement fee).

Filing requirements

▶ Company filing obligations arise from legislation, mainly the Companies Act 2006 and associated regulations. Where a company is being wound up, particular additional filing obligations arise under the insolvency legislation (whether the winding up is a solvent or an insolvent winding up).

Proper delivery

▶ To comply with a filing obligation a company must meet the requirements of 'proper delivery'. A properly delivered document is one that meets all the requirements of the Registrar's Rules and the legislation under which it is delivered.

▶ In particular a document is properly delivered when:

▷ it contains all the information required by the legislation;

▷ it meets the legislative and Registrar's Rules requirements as to form (it is in the right format for that item in paper or in electronic form) and it can be scanned or copied;

▷ it has been authenticated and includes the company name and number (where required);

▷ it has met any applicable requirements for delivery (e.g. if it has been sent electronically it is a type of document and in a format that the Registrar of Companies can accept electronically);

▷ it complies with any language requirements and/or is accompanied by a certified translation if the document is not in English;

▷ it uses only permitted characters in names and addresses (i.e. characters, letters, symbols);

See Registrar of Companies and Applications for Strike Off Regulations 2009

▷ it meets the Registrar's requirements for certification or verification of a document as an accurate or correct copy or translation; and

▷ it is accompanied by the correct filing fee (if applicable).

Registrar's Rules

▶ The Registrar of Companies has authority to make rules governing certain areas in relation to the filing of documents at Companies House. These rules address matters such as the form, manner of delivery and method of authentication for documents provided to Companies House, whether they are delivered by a company in electronic format or as paper documents.

s. 1117 CA 2006

Notes

▶ There is an individual Registrar of Companies for England and Wales, for Scotland and for Northern Ireland. However Companies House operates a combined UK register of companies, so information on a company registered in any of the UK's three jurisdictions can be found on that register.

More information

▶ Companies House publishes its annual accounts and report on its website. As well as financial data about the registry's operations this provides a wide range of performance data.

▷ www.gov.uk/government/organisations/companies-house.

Conflicts of interest

Introduction

Charity trustees are in a fiduciary role which gives them a core obligation of undivided loyalty to the charity they serve. In meeting that obligation, a charity trustee has a fundamental duty to act in what he honestly believes to be the best interests of the charity's charitable purposes.

In consequence of these key principles, there are further legal principles that seek to prevent conflicts of interest arising:

> ▷ A trustee must not allow himself or herself to be in a position where his or her duty of undivided loyalty to the charity conflicts with another interest (the 'no conflict' rule).

> ▷ A trustee must not make a profit from his or her trust (the 'no profit' rule).

> ▷ One aspect of the 'no conflict' rule is the 'self-dealing rule' (a transaction between a charity and the trustee, even if for full consideration, is liable to be set aside).

> ▷ Trustees are expected to act 'with clean hands' and to be honest and transparent at all times.

These are strict rules, which apply even where a trustee acts honestly and in good faith and even where it cannot be shown the interests of the charity have been damaged.

Checklist

▶ Consider the fundamental legal principles regarding conflicts of interest in charities.

▶ Provide guidance and training for trustees and senior staff. All trustees should be aware of the Charity Commission's guidance on conflicts of interest (available on the Commission's website).

▶ Adopt a conflicts of interest policy with appropriate procedures (including annual updates of trustees' interests and requiring declarations of any interests at the opening of board meetings). The policy should be periodically reviewed and updated.

▶ Ensure trustee recruitment procedures include declarations of interests by potential trustees.

▶ Check the provisions of the constitution regarding conflicts of interest (be careful to ensure the constitution is not at odds with any relevant statutory provisions or other applicable legal principles).

▶ Follow relevant procedures set out in the constitution (noting the caveat above).

▶ If the charity is a CIO, consider the relevant CIO statutory provisions (including the CIO specific trustee duties).

▶ If the charity is a CLG, consider the relevant Companies Act provisions (including directors' general statutory duties, as modified for charities; the duty and obligation for directors to disclose interests in proposed or existing transactions and arrangements).

▶ Be aware that legal rules on conflicts generally extend to indirect as well as direct interests.

▶ Consider connected persons (individuals or organisations) when addressing issues of personal interests and potential conflicts of interest.

▶ Recognise that relevant interests that might conflict may include situations where a trustee has legal duties of loyalty (e.g. as an employee or director or trustee or officer of another organisation) or personal loyalty commitments, as well as situations where there is a financial or other material interest.

▶ Be particularly careful about potential transactions with or payments or benefits to trustees and individuals or organisations connected with trustees and check the current Charity Commission guidance on these areas, as well as the relevant restrictions and requirements in the charity's constitution.

▶ Note that restrictions on trustee benefits and payments extend to arrangements involving a charity's trading subsidiary.

▶ Be aware of the risks to the charity's reputation and good standing (there may be such risks involved even though a particular situation is not strictly unlawful).

▶ Document carefully all disclosures of interests and all decisions taken about potential conflicts of interest.

▶ Ensure all required public disclosures are made (e.g. related party transaction reporting or trustee related transactions/payments disclosures required in the annual accounts).

Procedure

▶ Procedures will vary according to the circumstances and the legal type of charity, as well as the provisions of its constitution and the application of particular statutory provisions.

Filing requirements

▶ There are likely to be public disclosures obligations where transactions involve benefits or payments to trustees or related parties.

Notes

▶ The legal rules and principles in relation to conflicts are fundamental tenets of charity law.

▶ Exceptions in particular charities, in particular situations, although possible, require explicit legal authority. Exceptions are rare and always narrow. If a charity and its trustees seek to rely on one they must be extremely careful it does indeed apply and that they are acting within its strict legal boundaries.

▶ These are complex and high risk areas of law and governance. Extreme care should be taken and trustees should consider taking professional advice on particular situations and circumstances.

Constitutions – other types of charity

Introduction

A charity's constitution is its governing document, sometimes called the governing instrument. The initial constitution is generally the charity's founding document.

It is important to recognise that over time alterations may have been made to the original constitution. When dealing with the charity's legal administration and internal management and when considering any action by or on behalf of the charity or any transaction involving the charity, it is essential to consider the constitution and to ensure you are viewing the current version, including all amendments made that remain in effect.

Some types of restructuring can result in the substitution of an entirely new and different constitution (for example if an unincorporated charity transfers its funds and assets to a successor incorporated charity, such as a CLG, or converts itself into a CIO).

Checklist

Form and contents

▶ The form and contents of a charity's constitution depend on:

▷ the legal form of the charity (unincorporated members' association, trust etc.);

▷ any specific legal or regulatory rules that apply because of the nature of the charitable purposes and the activities of the specific organisation (e.g. if it is a registered social landlord); and

▷ the choices made by the organisation's members when the constitution was adopted (in membership charities) or the decisions of the founders and original trustees (in a trust).

Name of the constitution

▶ The name of the constitution varies depending on the legal form of the particular charity:

Type of charity	Name of constitution
Trust	Trust deed or trust document
Charitable company	Articles of association
Members' association	Constitution or rules
CIO or SCIO	Constitution
Registered society	Rules

Notes:
1. A charitable trust may have been created under the terms of a will.
2. Companies incorporated prior to 1 October 2009 had a two-part constitution (memorandum and articles of association). The Companies Act 2006 provides that the memorandum of an old company is now to be treated as part of its articles.
3. Articles of association are often simply described as 'articles'.

Constitution – trustees' duties

▶ The trustees must ensure they govern and manage the charity in accordance with its constitution.

▶ In particular they must ensure that:

▷ the charity does not go beyond its charitable purposes or its powers;

▷ the board acts within its powers;

▷ any limitations on the charity's powers or the trustees' powers are observed; and

▷ other restrictions in the constitution are properly observed (e.g. restrictions on how the charity's funds and assets may be used, limitations on its activities and how or where those can take place, restrictions and prohibitions on benefits and payments to, or transactions with, members or trustees of the charity.

▶ When using any powers that flow from the constitution, the trustees must be satisfied that the proposed course of action is a proper use of those powers and is in the best interests of the charity's charitable purposes.

Impact and effect

▶ Generally constitution is king and the provisions of the constitution must be strictly observed (for example if the constitution requires the appointment of an auditor and the audit of the charity's annual accounts).

▶ The constitution generally remains effective unless and until it is altered or the charity changes into another legal form (in which case the constitution of the successor charity will then apply).

▶ However, there are areas in which the law will override any inconsistent or contradictory provision in a charity's constitution, for example:

▷ statutory accounting and reporting obligations;

▷ deadlines for the filing of annual accounts and the trustees' annual report and for the filing of the charity annual return; and

▷ statutory obligations relating to regulatory consents (for example the obligation to obtain prior consent from the relevant charity regulator(s) before altering the charity's charitable purposes).

Unincorporated members' association

▶ Unincorporated members' associations are heavily dependent on their individual constitutions (largely because there is no overall statute that governs and regulates such associations).

▶ The constitution will set out the charitable purposes. It is also likely to deal with some or all of these areas:

▷ Minimum and any maximum number of trustees.

▷ Appointment of trustees and cessation of office.

▷ Officers, including how they are appointed and perhaps some aspects of their role and functions.

▷ Trustees' powers.

▷ Procedures for meetings and decisions of trustees.

▷ Admission and cessation of membership.

▷ Members' rights and responsibilities/obligations.

▷ Procedures for meetings and decisions of members.

▷ Administrative provisions for the internal management of the association.

▷ Provisions for the holding, management and application of the association's funds and assets to further its charitable purposes.

▷ Alteration of the constitution.

▷ Dissolution of the organisation and the transfer of its assets to similar charitable purposes.

Trust

▶ Charitable trusts can be established by will, in which case the terms of the charitable trust set out in the will are the constitution. They take effect on the death of the testator.

▶ A trust established during the founder's lifetime will be established under a trust deed (or a declaration of trust). That document, which takes effect on execution, is the trust's constitution.

▶ Trust law provides some of the governance framework for charitable trusts in England and Wales and there are also some relevant specific statutory provisions, in particular the Trustee Act 2000. That Act provides a range of statutory powers for the trustees, as well as various obligations and duties, in particular with regard to investment powers, the management of investments and land transactions.

▶ However, the powers of trustees and the requirements and procedures for the governance and management of the trust are to a large extent dependent on the terms of the trust deed. That deed will set out the charitable purposes. It is also likely to deal with:

▷ minimum and any maximum number of trustees;

▷ appointment of trustees and cessation of office;

▷ trustees' powers;

▷ procedures for meetings and decisions of trustees;

▷ administrative provisions for the management of the trust and its property;

▷ alteration of the trust deed; and

▷ dissolution of the trust and the transfer of its assets to similar charitable purposes.

Orders and schemes

▶ It is now rare to have to seek a Charity Commission order or scheme to make changes to the constitution of an unincorporated charity, largely because of the Charities Act powers and procedures described above. However, if the charity has land that is subject to trusts or there are other forms of legal restrictions on the charity's assets (such as endowment provisions or other special trusts) the Charities Act powers will not be available. It may then be necessary to seek a formal order or scheme, agreed with the Charity Commission. In such situations legal advice should be taken.

Registered society

▶ A registered society is a particular type of corporate body, registered under the Co-operative and Community Benefit Societies Act 2014. Charitable registered societies in England and Wales are exempt from registration with the Charity Commission. They are, however, registered with the Prudential Regulation Authority. The rules of a registered society are filed with the PRA.

▶ The form and contents of the constitution must comply with relevant provisions in the 2014 Act.

Royal Chartered body (incorporated by Royal Charter)

▶ Royal Chartered bodies are rare and only a very small number of charities are in this legal form.

▶ The principal governing document of such a charity is its Royal Charter (granted by Her Majesty the Queen using her Royal prerogative powers, based on advice from the Privy Council).

▶ Those appointed to the Privy Council mostly comprise ministers, other parliamentarians and members of the judiciary, although only serving Government ministers are involved in Privy Council matters for the purpose of recommending and granting a Royal Charter.

▶ A Royal Chartered body also usually has rules and bye-laws that provide additional and complementary constitutional provisions (dealing with lower level administrative matters).

▶ Amendments to Royal Charters can be made only with the agreement of the Queen in Council.

▶ Amendments to a Royal Chartered body's bye-laws require the approval of the Privy Council (though not normally of the Queen).

Procedure

Altering the constitution of an unincorporated members' association

▶ Generally the constitution will contain a power of amendment. This is likely to require changes to be approved by resolution of the members, passed at a general meeting of the members. There will usually be detailed additional procedural requirements, such as a particular period of notice. There will also usually be a requirement for a particular majority vote in favour, in order for the resolution to be passed (typically two-thirds of the votes cast or two-thirds of the total number of members in the association).

▶ Note that some alterations will require prior regulatory consent from the relevant charity regulator(s) – for example any alteration to the charitable purposes.

▶ Alterations take effect as the members' resolution is passed. However if the alteration required the prior consent of one or more charity regulators, the resolution has no effect if that consent has not been obtained.

▶ If there is no power of amendment, the statutory powers of alteration in the Charities Act may be available.

Altering a trust deed

▶ Generally the deed will include a power of amendment, which will specify the procedures to be followed. That will provide for at least some changes to be made by decision of the trustees (provided certain formalities are followed, for instance execution of a deed of amendment).

▶ Certain alterations, including any change to the charitable purposes (i.e. the charitable trusts themselves) will require the prior consent of relevant charity regulator(s).

▶ If the trust deed does not contain a suitable power of amendment, the statutory powers of alteration in the Charities Act may be available. However if not, the alteration will require a Charity Commission scheme.

Charities Act 2011 power to alter constitutions (unincorporated charities)

▶ Where the constitution of an unincorporated charity does not provide a power of amendment (or the power is inadequate to enable the proposed change to be made), it may be possible for the trustees to use one of the statutory powers of amendment provided by the Charities Act 2011 (sections 275 and 280).

Small charity – alteration of purposes (ss. 275–279)

▶ The power is available to an *unincorporated* charity if:

▷ its gross income in the last financial year did not exceed £10,000; and

▷ the charity does not hold any designated land.

▶ 'Designated land' means land held on trusts which stipulate that it is to be used for the purposes of the charity (or some particular purposes amongst its purposes).

▶ The trustees must be satisfied that:

▷ it is expedient in the interests of the charity for its current purposes to be replaced; and

▷ so far as reasonably practicable, the proposed new purposes are similar to those they will replace.

▶ If the charity has a membership, the trustees would need to obtain approval from the members (a vote in favour by two-thirds of the total number of members is required).

▶ A copy of the relevant trustees' resolution (and members' resolution, if applicable) and a statement from the trustees providing their reasons for making the changes must be provided to the Charity Commission.

▶ The Commission can require the proposed changes to be advertised or, if it does not think the proposed changes are appropriate, it can prevent them from becoming effective. Otherwise, the changes will take effect 60 days after the documents are provided to the Commission.

Alteration of administrative powers and procedures (s. 280)

▶ The trustees of an *unincorporated* charity may alter its constitution in relation to their administrative powers and procedures (for example the quorum at trustees' meetings). No income threshold applies.

▶ If the charity has members, the trustees must obtain approval from the members (a vote in favour by two-thirds of the total number of members is required).

▶ The change takes immediate effect as the relevant resolution of the trustees (or the members, in a membership charity) is passed.

▶ The change must be notified to the Charity Commission.

Altering the rules of a registered society

▶ Any changes to the rules of a charitable registered society must be made in accordance with that legislation and in accordance with relevant provisions of the particular organisation's rules. The procedures will include the passing of a resolution of the members and the filing of required forms and documents with the Prudential Regulation Authority.

Amending a Royal Charter

▶ Proposed changes to administrative provisions in a Royal Charter should be sent to the Clerk to the Privy Council. The Charity Commission does not need to be notified.

▶ The Privy Council Office will then evaluate the amendments proposed and consult with appropriate advisers, chosen according to the nature and functions of the Charter body, to establish if they have any comments on the proposed changes.

▶ The Office will raise any queries directly with the applicant charity.

▶ If a draft of proposed amendments can be agreed with the Privy Council Office, the organisation then presents a Petition to the Sovereign in Council for a Supplemental Charter. The Petition should state the authority under which it is submitted (for example a resolution passed at a meeting of the members) and should contain sufficient information to enable the Privy Council to make a recommendation to Her Majesty.

▶ The Petition should be submitted in the name of the body concerned and be under its corporate seal, duly attested.

▶ The applicant must pay fees to the Crown Office with regard to the sealing of the Supplemental Charter.

▶ Note that if any *regulated changes* are proposed, such as changes to the name, charitable purposes, powers to pay trustees (other than re-imbursement of out-of-pocket expenses) or the dissolution provisions, the Privy Council Office will consult with the Charity Commission.

The process of change may only proceed if the Commission provides confirmation it has no objections to the proposed changes.

Filing requirements

▶ The relevant charity regulator(s) should be notified of all changes to the constitution of a charity. A copy of the relevant resolution (not the meeting minutes) and a copy of the altered constitution should be provided.

Scotland

▶ There is a specific formal notification procedure to the OSCR that must be followed when a charity on the Scottish Charity Register alters its constitution. A three-month time limit applies.

More information

▶ For information on the articles of CLGs, the constitutions of CIOs and alteration of articles or CIO constitutions see checklists: 'CIOs – constitutions general', 'Articles – alteration (CLGs)' and 'CIOs – alteration of constitutions'.

Data protection and GDPR

Introduction

Organisations that handle personal data about individuals have legal obligations to protect that data under the Data Protection Act 2018 and the General Data Protection Regulation (GDPR).

An organisation that is a data controller processing personal data must pay a fee to the Information Commissioner's Office (ICO) unless they are exempt from that requirement.

Whether or not an organisation is obliged to pay the fee, it has a range of other obligations under the legislation.

Checklist

▷ Is there an obligation to pay a fee to the ICO, or does an exemption apply?

▷ See the online self-assessment on the ICO website: ico.org.uk/for-organisations/data-protection-fee/self-assessment.

Data – format

▷ The legal rules apply to personal data whether it is held and processed electronically or on paper or in mixed media.

Data controllers

▷ There are legal obligations on those who control data, i.e. those who determine the purpose and means of processing personal data. These include requirements about keeping records of personal data and processing activities.

▷ Data controllers are required to ensure that any data processors they use comply with data protection requirements.

Data processors

▷ There are also legal obligations for data processors, who process personal data on behalf of, or at the direction of, a data controller.

▷ These provisions are intended to regulate independent contractors engaged to deal with data on behalf of another organisation. They can be relevant, for example, where a charity buys data processing services from a third party (e.g. in relation to a donor database or appeals).

International dimension

▷ The data protection requirements apply to data processing with the EU and also to data processing outside the EU when it is done by organisations that offer goods or services to individuals in the EU.

Data protection principles

▷ The statutory data protection principles are:

1. Personal data shall be processed lawfully, fairly and transparently.
2. Personal data shall be obtained only for one or more specified, explicit and legitimate purposes, and shall not be further processed in any manner incompatible with that purpose or those purposes.
3. Personal data shall be adequate, relevant and limited to what is necessary for the purpose or purposes for which they are processed.
4. Personal data shall be accurate and, where necessary, kept up-to-date.
5. Personal data shall be kept in a form which permits identification of individuals for no longer than is necessary for that purpose or those purposes.
6. Personal data shall be processed in a manner that ensures the appropriate security of the personal data, including protection against unauthorised or unlawful processing, accidental loss destruction or damage, using appropriate technical or organisational measures.

Retention periods

▷ An organisation should only hold personal data for as long as is necessary. An appropriate retention policy and procedures should be adopted (including procedures for removal and secure destruction of data no longer needed).

Enforcement powers and penalties

▷ There are significant enforcement powers and substantial financial penalties for major breaches of the legal requirements on data protection. There are also some criminal penalties.

Areas of risk for charities

▷ Particular areas of risk for charities may include:

▷ data security breaches (for example the loss of unencrypted laptops, tablets, other mobile devices or portable IT memory/ storage devices, or the loss of paper-based material);

▷ improper or insecure disposal of old data;

▷ engaging third party contractors to collect and/or use personal data; and

▷ reputational risks and/or financial risks if there are breaches of data protection law or poor data protection practice.

Protective actions

▶ Charities should adopt a suitable data protection policy and associated procedures. These should be reviewed on a regular basis.

▶ Read ICO guidance, in particular the ICO's charity sector guidance.

▶ Ensure the charity's staff and appropriate volunteers receive relevant training and carry out regular refresher training. This should aim to raise awareness, ensure the right culture is established, encourage appropriate behaviour and ensure that required procedures are being followed in practice.

Filing requirements

Fees

▶ There is an annual registration fee for organisations obliged to register with the ICO.

More information

▶ The ICO publishes a wide range of data protection guidance, checklists and self-assessment tools on its website, including some specifically for charities: ico.org.uk.

Disclosure obligations – communications and documents

Introduction

There are various disclosure obligations that affect documents and communications issued or made by or on behalf of charities. Some of these obligations arise from charity law and apply generally to charities or specifically to registered charities or particular legal forms of charities (e.g. CIOs).

Company disclosure obligations apply to charitable CLGs and the trading subsidiaries of charities.

For details of the disclosure obligations relevant to charitable CLGs and trading subsidiaries and premises, see checklist: 'Disclosure obligations – premises (company law)'.

Checklist

England and Wales – charity law requirements

▶ All charities registered in England and Wales with annual income exceeding £10,000 must state that they are registered charities on these items:

　▷ Notices, advertisements or other documents issued by or on behalf of the charity that solicit money or property for the charity's benefit.

　▷ Bills of exchange, promissory notes, endorsements, cheques and orders for money or goods purporting to be signed on the charity's behalf.

　▷ Bills, invoices, receipts and letters of credit.

▶ Best practice is to state 'Registered charity in England and Wales number XXXXXXX'.

▶ The statement must be in English, except for Welsh charities which can use Welsh.

▶ If the charity normally uses another language, the statement can appear in both English and that other language.

s. 39 Charities Act 2011

▶ The printing must be in legible characters.

▶ Anyone who issues, or authorises the issue of, a non-compliant item is liable to a criminal penalty whether or not they did so knowingly (it is a strict liability offence).

▶ CIOs have these obligations:

▷ To disclose their names in the same items and communications in which a company is obliged to disclose its name.

s. 211 Charities Act 2011

▷ To disclose their names in conveyances (defined for these purposes as any instruments that create, transfer, vary or extinguish an interest in land).

▷ To disclose the fact they are CIOs on documents and in communications (including emails, websites and hard copy documents).

s. 212 Charities Act 2011

Scotland – charity law requirements

▶ The disclosure requirements apply to:

▷ Letters.

▷ Emails.

▷ Advertisements.

▷ Notices and official publications.

▷ Items soliciting money or property.

▷ Invoices.

▷ Receipts.

▷ Accounts.

▷ Campaign and educational documentation.

▷ Documents relating to land transactions.

▷ Documents relating to contracts.

See Charities References in Documents (Scotland) Regulations 2007

▶ The required disclosures are:

▷ The Scottish charity registration number.

▷ The name by which the charity is recorded on the Scottish Charity Register.

▷ An indication of the organisation's charitable status (if the word 'charity' or 'charitable' is not part of the name).

▶ The requirements apply to all charities in the Scottish Charity Register (including English charities that are registered).

Company disclosure requirements

▶ Charitable CLGs and trading subsidiaries of charities are subject to these disclosure obligations. Note that for charitable CLGs this is in addition to their charity law disclosure obligations.

▶ For the purposes of the tables below, 'company name' means the name of the company as on the company's certificate of incorporation, including 'Limited' or 'Ltd' (or their Welsh equivalents) and 'where registered' means 'England & Wales', 'Scotland' or 'Northern Ireland' according to the location of the registered office.

▶ Whether on stationery, websites or premises, all disclosures must be in characters which can be read with the naked eye.

STATIONERY, WEBSITES, ETC.

	Company name	Where registered	Registered office address	Company name
Business letters	✓	✓	✓	✓
Order forms	✓	✓	✓	✓
Orders for goods, services or money	✓	✓	✓	✓
Cheques	✓			
Invoices and receipts	✓			
Notices and official publications	✓			
Bills of exchange, promissory notes, endorsements, bills of parcel and letters of credit	✓			
Written demands for payment of debts	✓			
Websites, order forms, emails and other electronic documents	✓	✓	✓	✓
Applications for licences to carry on a trade or activity	✓			

▶ At premises, details must be positioned so they can be seen easily by visitors.

Statement of limited liability status

▶ A charitable company that has been granted permission to omit 'limited' from its name under the Companies Act 2006 (or the previous Companies Act 1985 rules) must state that it is a limited company on all business letters and order forms. The statement must be in English and in legible characters; the usual form is 'A company limited by guarantee'.

Notes

▶ Company disclosure obligations arise from s. 82 Companies Act 2006, The Companies (Trading Disclosures) Regulations 2088, SI 495 of 2008 and The Companies (Trading Disclosures) (Amendment) Regulations 2009, SI 218 of 2009.

More information

▶ See checklist: 'Disclosure obligations – premises (company law)'.

Disclosure obligations – premises (company law)

Introduction

Charitable CLGs and trading subsidiaries of charities are subject to company law disclosure obligations in relation to premises.

Checklist

▶ The key company law disclosure obligation in relation to premises is to disclose the company name. This means its formal legal name (as shown on its certificate of incorporation or, if the name has been changed since incorporation, the name as shown on the relevant certificate of incorporation on change of name).

PREMISES

	Company name
The company's registered office (unless the company has always been dormant)	✓
Any 'inspection place', i.e. any location (other than the registered office) where the company keeps any company record available for public inspection (unless the company has always been dormant)	✓
Every location in which the company carries on business that is not the registered office or an 'inspection place' (unless primarily used for living accommodation or unless every director is protected from disclosure of their residential address to a credit reference agency)	✓

Procedure

▶ At premises, details must be positioned so they can be seen easily by visitors. The company's registered name must be displayed continuously unless the premises are shared by six or more companies. In that case, each company's name only needs to be displayed for at least 15 continuous seconds at least once in every three minutes – for example, where names are displayed electronically, in rotation.

Notes

▶ If the company uses a trading or operating name, its full legal name must be shown at its premises. If the operating or trading name is also shown, the necessary statement indicating that the company uses that other name must be made.

▶ There is no legal requirement for a company to display its certificate of incorporation at its registered office or any other premises.

More information

▶ See checklist: 'Disclosure obligations – communications and documents'.

Electronic communications

Introduction

Electronic communications are in widespread everyday use in charities for general communication (internal and external). The general law on electronic communications applies to such communications.

This checklist addresses electronic communications in the specific contexts of communications with regulators and formal communications between charities and their members.

Checklist – regulators

Charity Commission

▶ The Charity Commission strongly encourages charities to deal with formal notifications or consent applications to, and filing of documents with, the Commission by electronic communications. Notifications, applications and filing are carried out via the Charity Commission's website.

▶ It also strongly encourages all other communications to the Commission to be made electronically. There is an online email facility on the Commission's website.

Charity annual returns (England and Wales)

▶ The charity annual return must be filed online via the Commission's website (there is no paper equivalent).

The OSCR

▶ The OSCR also encourages charities to use electronic filing and communicate with the OSCR electronically.

▶ Paper-based filing options remain available (e.g. for filing of the charity annual return or the annual accounts).

Charity annual returns (Scotland)

▶ The online charity annual return is shorter, so quicker and easier to complete.

▶ A charity on the Scottish Charity Register may still opt to file the longer paper version of the charity annual return.

Companies House

▶ Companies House strongly encourages companies to deal with their filing obligations online.

▶ Most items and forms that may need to be filed by a company can be filed electronically via Companies House website. Alternatives include using commercial software that offers an electronic filing facility or developing bespoke software (the latter is unlikely to be attractive for a charity, due to the technical complexities and the associated costs).

▶ Paper-based alternatives remain available, though few companies now use them.

Checklist – electronic communications with members

Non-company charities

▶ Charities that are not companies need to have provisions in their constitutions if they wish to use electronic communications for formal communications with their members.

Companies – Companies Act 2006

▶ A company may communicate with its members electronically, regardless of the provisions of its articles, provided it does so in accordance with schedules 4 and 5 of the Companies Act 2006. Those provisions are both detailed and somewhat complex.

Companies – articles

▶ It is important that the articles 'fit' as certain other provisions of the Act do override the articles. In addition, there are some practical areas where the Companies Act provisions need to be supplemented by provisions in the articles. Updating and modernisation of the articles is therefore advisable to give a company full flexibility to take advantage of the company law electronic communications options.

Companies – documents and information

▶ Under the rules in the Companies Act, any document or information may be sent or supplied electronically to its members by the company.

Companies – key definitions

▶ The relevant Companies Act rules provide key definitions as follows:

▷ 'Hard copy form' means that the document or information is supplied in a paper copy or similar form capable of being read.

▷ 'Electronic form' means that the document or information is sent or supplied by electronic means (e.g. email or fax) or by any other means in electronic form (e.g. a CDROM sent by post).

▷ 'Electronic means' – a document or information is sent by electronic means if it is sent and received by means of electronic equipment for the processing or storage of data and transmitted, conveyed or received by wire, radio, optical means or other electromagnetic means.

▶ A document or information sent by electronic means must also be sent in such a form that the sender reasonably considers will enable the recipient to read it and retain a copy of it. In this context, 'read' means that the document or information can be read with the naked eye, or, if it consists of images, pictures, plans etc. it can be seen by the naked eye. The retained copy can be electronic (e.g. an email or text message).

Procedure

Electronic communications by individual members to their company

▶ The member may send or supply information and documents in electronic form (e.g. by email or via a website) if the company has:

▷ *expressly agreed* (generally or specifically) to that means of communication;

▷ provided an electronic address *to be used for that purpose*; and

▷ not revoked that agreement.

Member consent pre-Companies Act 2006

▶ Any agreement provided by a member, under pre-Companies Act 2006 rules, to the sending or supply of documents or information electronically can be treated as an agreement made under the Companies Act 2006 rules.

▶ An electronic address supplied under those earlier rules can continue to be used under the current rules.

Deemed agreement *by company*

▶ A company is deemed to have agreed to receive documents in electronic form:

▷ for any document or information relating to proceedings at a
meeting, if the notice of meeting includes an electronic address
(e.g. email address);

▷ for any document or information relating to proxies, if the form of
proxy or proxy invitation includes an electronic address (e.g. email
address); and

▷ for any document or information relating to a written resolution
of the members, if it includes an electronic address (e.g. email
address).

▶ This is subject to any conditions or limitations set out in the
document.

▶ So if companies include email addresses in such documents, they
should make it clear if they do *not* intend to indicate deemed
agreement to receipt of documents electronically.

Electronic communications by a company to its members

▶ A company may send or supply information and documents to a
member in electronic form (e.g. by email or via a website) if the
member has:

▷ indicated their *express agreement* (either generally or specifically)
to that means of communication;

▷ provided an electronic address *to be used for that purpose*; and

▷ not revoked that agreement.

▶ Where there is *express* agreement from members to receiving
documents and information electronically, the address to be used for
the communications is that supplied for this purpose by the intended
recipient (individuals). In the case of a company that is the intended
recipient, the address is the one deemed to have been provided by
that company.

Publication of documents or information on a website

▶ A company can send or supply documents electronically by making
them available on a website. Members may expressly agree to this
or, where the required conditions are met, the company can deem
members to have agreed.

▶ For the *deeming provisions* to apply (schedule 5 Companies Act
2006), either:

▷ the members must pass an ordinary resolution that the company
may communicate with its members through a website (the
resolution must be filed at Companies House within 15 days); or

▷ the company's articles must contain a provision to that effect.

▶ *In addition* each member must be asked individually by the company to consent to communications by means of a website (either generally or in relation to specific documents). If a member fails to respond within 28 days, starting with the date on which the request is sent, that member is deemed to have agreed that the company may send or supply documents or information to that member by making them available via a website.

▶ The request must:

▷ clearly state the effect of a failure to respond (i.e. explain that the member will be deemed to have given consent); and

▷ be sent not less than 12 months after any previous request made to that member in respect of a similar class of documents.

▶ Note that if a member replies stating that he or she does *not* agree, the company may not send or supply documents or information to that member via a website. It must also wait 12 months before it can ask that member for such consent again.

Notification that a document or information has been made available via a website

▶ When a document or information is made available via a website, the company must notify the intended recipient of:

▷ the presence of the item on a website;

▷ the website address;

▷ the place on the website where the item may be accessed; and

▷ how to access the item.

▶ Note that in order to send this notification electronically (e.g. by email) the company needs the member's express agreement to the sending of the notification by electronic means. Otherwise it has to provide the notification in hard copy form (e.g. by letter).

Notice of general meeting on a website

▶ The above rules regarding making documents and information available on a website apply and must be observed. In addition, the notification sent by the company to the member to advise him or her that the item is available on a website must specify:

▷ that it concerns a notice of a general meeting; and

▷ the place, date and time of the meeting.

Further rules and requirements for communication via a website

▶ As well as obtaining all the necessary consents from members, a company wishing to communicate with its members via a website must also comply with these further rules and requirements:

▷ The document or information is taken to be sent or supplied on the date on which the notification is sent or, if later, the date on which the document or information first appears on the website.

▷ The document or information on a website must be made available in a form, and by a means, that the company reasonably considers will enable the recipient to read it and retain a copy of it.

▷ The company must make the item available on the website throughout the period specified by any applicable provisions in the Companies Act (e.g. notice period for a general meeting). If no such period is specified, the item must be available for a period of 28 days beginning with the date on which the notification is sent to the intended recipient.

▷ A failure to make the document or information available on the relevant website for the required period is disregarded if it is available for part of the period and the failure is wholly attributable to circumstances that it would not have been reasonable to have expected the company to prevent or avoid.

Member's right to request hard copy

▶ Regardless of any consents to electronic communications that have been given, or deemed given, a company must provide a hard copy of any document sent by electronic means, or made available on a website, if a member requests a copy.

▶ The copy must be provided within 21 days of receipt of the request.

▶ It must be provided free of charge.

Authentication of documents sent to the company

▶ Electronic form documents are sufficiently authenticated if the identity of the sender is confirmed in a manner specified by the company.

▶ If none is specified, the authentication will be sufficient if the communication contains, or is accompanied by, a statement of the sender's identity and the company has no reason to doubt the truth of that statement.

▶ Where an item is provided by one person on behalf of another, the company may require reasonable evidence of the authority of the provider to act on behalf of that other person.

Deemed service of documents sent or supplied *by a company*

▶ The Companies Act specifies these rules for items sent *by a company*:

▷ If the item was sent by electronic means and the company can show that the item was properly addressed, that item is deemed to have been received 48 hours after it was sent (only working days are counted).

▷ If the item was made available on a website, it is deemed to have been received when the material was first made available on the site or, if later, when the recipient received, or is deemed to have received, notice the item was available on the website.

▶ These provisions apply subject to any contrary provision in the company's articles or any contrary agreement between the company and the intended recipient.

Members' written resolutions (companies)

▶ A written resolution, or a statement relating to one, may be sent to a member electronically, or by means of a website, provided the member has consented or is deemed to have consented (see above).

▶ The resolution must be made available for a period beginning on the date on which it is made available electronically and ending on the date on which the written resolution lapses if not consented to. (The lapse date is 28 days unless the articles provide a different period for members to indicate their consent to the resolution.)

▶ A company may provide an electronic address so that the resolution can be consented to by a member emailing consent to that address.

Filing requirements

Charity Commission

▶ To provide online notifications to the Charity Commission or file documents online via the Commission's website you need to be a registered online presenter, with your own password, and to use the relevant charity's own unique password. You will generally also need to provide the relevant charity's name and its registered charity number.

▶ If the charity's password is lost, it is possible to apply for a new password online on the Commission's website: www.charitycommission.gov.uk.

Companies House online WebFiling

▶ The straightforward sign-up process, to become an authorised user, is set out on Companies House website. The website also provides helpful online guidance about WebFiling for users.

Companies House – Registrar's Rules

▶ Detailed technical requirements for more complex methods of electronic filing at Companies House, including requirements applicable to bespoke software that companies may decide to develop for use with electronic filing, are set out in the Registrar's Rules:

▷ www.companieshouse.gov.uk/about/policyDocuments/ registrarsRules/infoRegistrarsRules.

Notes

▶ Key relevant legal provisions are:

▷ Electronic Communications Act 2000;

▷ the Electronic Commerce (EC Directive) Regulations 2002 SI 2012 of 2002;

▷ Companies Act 2006, in particular ss. 308–309, 333, 1143–1148, 1168, 1173;

▷ Schedule 4 [communications *to* a company *by an individual member*]; and

▷ Schedule 5 [communications *by* a company, including a corporate member of another company that wishes to communicate electronically with the company of which it is a member].

▶ Further legal requirements, beyond those summarised in this checklist, apply to the use of electronic communications with members by public companies (they are rarely relevant to charities).

More information

▶ ICSA guidance note 'Electronic Communications with Shareholders' provides guidance on best practice. The note principally deals with law and practice in relation to companies limited by shares. However it is also a useful reference point for CLGs wishing to widen electronic communication with their members, especially CLGs with large memberships. The guidance note is available to ICSA members at: www.icsa.org.uk.

Electronic voting

Introduction

In the membership context, electronic voting can be very useful administratively in charities that have large memberships. It can also help encourage members' participation in members' decisions.

Checklist

▶ There are no statutory rights for directors or trustees of non-company charities to have access to electronic voting at meetings. The matter largely depends on the individual charity's constitution.

▶ However, note the Companies Act provisions regarding the use of electronic communications between companies and their members. They include the possibility of electronic provisions of notices and documents for general meetings or written resolutions of the members and the possibility of electronic communications for the lodgement of proxies by members.

Procedure

Companies – members

▶ Note the provisions of the Companies Act with regard to electronic proxy lodgement, written resolutions and electronic communications and the general rules and requirements regarding electronic communications between companies and their members.

▶ Any other form of electronic voting at members' general meetings is only permissible if the company's articles provide for it.

Companies – directors

▶ Electronic voting at board meetings may be permitted and facilitated by a company's articles. If so, the board will usually have adopted a formal policy and procedures to supplement the provisions of the articles and address practical matters, including security and privacy issues, as well as verifications and record-keeping.

Other charities

▶ Electronic voting at members' meetings and/or board meetings may be permitted by the individual charity's constitution. If so, the board will usually have adopted a formal policy and procedures to supplement the provisions of the constitution and address practical matters, including security and privacy issues, as well as verifications and record-keeping.

Good practice guidance

▶ It is good practice to address these areas in a charity that wishes to provide electronic voting options:

▷ For members, ensure they also have a right to submit a postal vote (as well as the option to vote in person at the meeting and any proxy rights they have under the charity's constitution or, for companies, under the provisions of the Companies Act).

▷ Allocate a unique identifying number to each member, as part of the identification and security process for electronic voting.

▷ Where a secret ballot is to be conducted, ensure the unique identifying number cannot be used to identify the member casting a particular vote (e.g. do not use their general membership number as the identifier).

▷ The unique identifying number should only be usable once (to ensure only one vote is recorded).

▷ For a secret ballot, arrange voting via a secure website, with appropriate encryption, to ensure the vote is not traceable to the member casting that vote. Also ensure the software used prevents any record of the vote being kept on the computer terminal used.

▷ Ensure there are adequate general safeguards against fraud, to protect the integrity of the voting process and to maintain security and privacy.

▷ Consider using external specialists to advise and assist, which may include independent scrutineers.

More information

▶ Helpful advice, guidance and services are available to support charities in relevant areas – see, for example: www.icsa.org.uk and www.electoral-reform.org.uk.

Execution of documents – companies

Introduction

A CLG or any other company (for example the trading subsidiary of a charity) is subject to company law rules and requirements when it executes formal documents.

The individual company's articles are also important for some aspects, such as the number of countersignatories required when the company seal is used and who can be authorised to be a countersignatory for that purpose.

Checklist

▶ Is the document being executed under the law of England and Wales?

▶ Is any other territorial law relevant to the particular document and/or the transaction to which it relates?

▶ Do legal procedures, regulatory requirements or local expectations in any other territory need to be considered (e.g. if the document will be used overseas or a relevant party to it is an organisation constituted under the law of another territory)?

▶ Does the company have a seal?

▶ If so, is it appropriate to use the seal in the execution of this document or will an alternative method of execution be acceptable and appropriate?

▶ If the seal is to be used, what do the articles provide with regard to authorising its use and the countersignatories?

▶ If the company does not have a seal, or it does but the seal is not to be used for executing this document, which of the alternative execution methods can or must be used?

Companies Act provisions

▶ Companies Act provisions state that a company can execute a document under the law of England and Wales by:

▷ fixing the company seal on the document; or

> ▷ executing without use of a seal, in accordance with the Companies Act procedures.

Execution of documents by companies without a seal under the law of England and Wales

▶ The Companies Act permits execution of a document by a company, without a seal, if it is signed on behalf of the company by:

> ▷ two directors;
>
> ▷ one director and the secretary; or
>
> ▷ one director in the presence of a witness, who attests the director's signature.

▶ Note that non-directors (i.e. non-trustees) may not be authorised for this purpose. These decisions should be carefully recorded in the minutes of the relevant board meeting. The company may also choose to keep a non-statutory register of executions.

Execution of deeds – companies

▶ For certain legal transactions and arrangements under the law of England and Wales it is appropriate or necessary to enter into a deed. A document is validly executed as a deed by a company, for the purposes of section 1(2)(b) of the Law of Property (Miscellaneous Provisions) Act 1989, and for the purposes of the law of Northern Ireland, if it is:

> ▷ duly executed; and
>
> ▷ delivered as a deed.

▶ Delivery is presumed on execution unless the contrary is proved. A deed must contain appropriate wording, including in its execution clause.

Execution of documents under the law of Scotland

▶ The law of Scotland makes different provision for the execution of documents. The key provisions are in the Requirements of Writing (Scotland) Act 1995 and, in the context of companies, section 48 of the Companies Act 2006. Specific legal advice should be taken where appropriate.

Procedure

Execution using the company seal

▶ Check the provisions of the particular company's articles with regard to procedures, in particular the number of countersignatories required and who can be authorised as a countersignatory for the use of the seal.

▶ Use of the seal should be formally authorised by the board.

▶ The countersignatories for the sealing also need to be authorised by the board.

▶ These decisions should be recorded in the minutes of the relevant board meeting.

▶ The minutes should also clearly identify the relevant document that is to be sealed.

▶ Records should be kept of all items sealed. A register of sealings is useful (though not a statutory requirement).

▶ The seal itself should be kept in safe custody.

Execution without the seal

▶ The decision to execute is a matter for the whole board, as is the authorisation of the chosen signatories.

▶ These decisions should be recorded in the minutes of the relevant board meeting.

▶ The minutes should also clearly identify the relevant document that is to be sealed.

▶ If the document is a deed, ensure the wording of the minutes describes it as a deed and refers to execution of the document as a deed.

▶ Records should be kept of all items formally executed by a company. A register of executions of documents is useful (though not a statutory requirement).

Filing requirements

▶ Execution of certain documents may be part of a transaction that causes the company to have a filing obligation at Companies House (e.g. execution of a charge) or elsewhere (e.g. a land transaction that has to be filed with HM Land Registry or the Land Registers of Scotland).

Notes

▶ A company may choose to have a company seal but is not obliged to do so. Initial adoption of a seal should be by formal resolution of the board. Subsequently, the company has a choice of executing documents with its seal or using the Companies Act alternative methods of execution for the particular item.

▶ Many items, including many contracts, do not need formal execution. Instead, an authorised person signs the relevant document 'for and on behalf of' the company.

▶ The Companies Act 2006 uses the term 'authenticated' widely in relation to documents and information sent to a person by a company or supplied by a person to a company. It does so for both hard copy and electronic formats. The legal rules specify:

▷ A hard copy item is authenticated if it is signed by the person sending or supplying it.

▷ An item in electronic form is authenticated if:

> the identity of the sender is confirmed in a manner prescribed by the company; or
> where no such manner has been specified, if the communication contains or is accompanied by a statement of the identity of the sender and the company has no reason to doubt the truth of that statement.

[See Companies Act 2006 s. 1146.]

Execution of documents – other charities

Introduction

The general rules and procedures for execution of documents by charities that are not companies vary according to the alternative legal form of the particular charity, the terms of its constitution and, in some cases, applicable statutory provisions.

Checklist

▶ Charities that are incorporated bodies but not companies, for example Royal Charter bodies, execute documents in accordance with relevant statutory provisions applicable to that type of corporate body and in accordance with the provisions of their own constitutions (e.g. provisions relating to the use of a seal).

▶ CIOs or SCIOs must follow the procedures required by their own constitutions to execute documents.

▶ Unincorporated charities execute documents (including deeds) in accordance with their own constitutions (usually by signature of all the trustees).

▶ There is a useful statutory power for the trustees of an unincorporated charity to authorise any two or more of the trustees to execute documents in the names of, and on behalf of, the trustees to give effect to a transaction to which all the trustees are a party. The authority conferred may be general or limited as specified in the relevant trustees' decision (e.g. authority to execute a specific document, rather than documents in general). A further advantage of this procedure is that it avoids having to join in new trustees to a deed previously signed by all the former trustees.

s. 333 Charities Act 2011

CIOs – regulations

▶ CIOs may execute documents under their seal or by the alternative method specified in the CIO general regulations.

Regulation 20 of the General Regulations

CIOs – contracts

▶ CIOs may make contracts in writing under their seals or by a person acting for the CIO under express or implied authority.

Regulation 19 of the General Regulations

CIOs – execution using a seal

▶ If a CIO has a seal it may choose to execute documents using that seal.

Regulation 20 of the General Regulations

▶ When using the seal, the relevant provisions of the specific CIO's constitution should be checked and observed.

CIOs – execution without use of a seal

▶ Whether or not a CIO has a seal, it may execute documents in accordance with the relevant provisions of the General Regulations, which are:

a) a CIO that has more than one trustee can validly execute a document with the signatures of at least two of its trustees; or

b) a CIO with just one trustee can validly execute a document with the signature of that one trustee; and

c) the document is expressed as being executed by the CIO (in whatever form of words).

CIOs – execution of deeds

▶ A CIO may execute a deed with signatures as stated in the immediately preceding section, with the document itself making it clear on its face that it is intended by the persons making it to be a deed.

Regulation 21 of the General Regulations

Procedure

▶ The detailed procedure will depend on the legal nature of the charity involved, the type of document and the relevant transaction to which it relates. The procedure may also be affected by particular provisions in the charity's constitution.

▶ CIOs are subject to the statutory provisions in the general regulations regarding execution of documents, including contracts.

▶ Usually, the trustee board will authorise execution of the most important documents on behalf of a charity.

▶ It is likely that at least two signatories will be required in relation to major transactions and certain important legal documents.

Filing requirements

▶ Execution of certain documents may be part of a transaction that causes the charity to have a filing obligation (e.g. a land transaction that has to be filed with HM Land Registry or the Land Registers of Scotland).

Notes

▷ A CIO may choose to have a seal (however this is not a legal obligation).

Regulation 23 of the General Regulations

▷ If it does have a seal, the CIO's name must be engraved in legible characters on the seal.

More information

▷ The detailed requirements relating to CIOs are set out in the Charitable Incorporated Organisations (General) Regulations 2012, SI 3012 of 2012.

Financial controls

Introduction

Financial controls are a key part of a charity's wider risk management and controls framework.

Checklist

Financial controls

▶ Everyone in the charity should take financial controls seriously and follow the charity's established procedures at all times.

▶ Segregation of duties is a key element of financial controls. No one person should have sole responsibility for the entirety of a transaction.

▶ No one person should have too influential a role in the day-to-day financial activities of the charity.

▶ Delegation of particular financial activities and functions should be properly authorised and clearly documented. The limits of the authority of both individuals and groups (e.g. committees of the board) need to be both clear and well understood.

▶ The use of any delegated authority in financial matters should be monitored. There should also be appropriate internal reporting to the board.

▶ For the smallest charities, with few people available, the full range of normal segregation controls may not be practicable. If this is the case, the trustees should find alternative mechanisms, such as the board periodically reviewing transaction reports and/or arranging periodic independent checks, to be undertaken by different people to those who are customarily involved in processing transactions.

Key areas – financial controls

▶ Some of the key areas to address in the charity's internal financial controls framework include:

▷ custody and security of cash;

▷ processing, recording and application of funds received from public collections, appeals and fundraising activities;

▷ receipt, recording and application of both general donations and restricted purpose donations;

▷ Gift Aid donations, declarations, records and claims;

▷ banking transactions, including authorisation of cheques and other forms of funds transfers;

▷ authorisation of purchases and payments;

▷ payroll and other employee-related transactions (including tax, National Insurance and pension contributions); and

▷ processing of expense claims.

Financial information

▶ Accurate financial information is needed to:

▷ facilitate good decision making;

▷ facilitate the effective operation of the charity;

▷ help manage cash flow;

▷ monitor performance, costs and expenditure; and

▷ assist the correct management and use of the charity's resources.

Internal financial records

▶ Charities are required by law to keep internal financial records which:

▷ record and explain all transactions, including receipts and expenditures, and the reasons for those transactions;

▷ disclose the charity's current financial position with reasonable accuracy; and

▷ enable the trustees to ensure the annual accounts meet the applicable financial reporting standards.

▶ These internal financial records should be kept for at least six years. Some records may need to be kept longer because of particular legal or regulatory requirements relevant to the specific charity.

Management accounts

▶ Good quality, accurate, management accounts are an essential financial management tool. Generally they are produced either monthly or quarterly.

▶ The management accounts should enable the trustees to:

▷ monitor performance against budget;

▷ identify any key discrepancies in that performance;

▷ understand the real costs of major activities;

▷ identify key areas of expenditure and the reasons for the expenditure; and

▷ ensure the charity's resources are being deployed in accordance with the priorities set by the board and within the terms of the charity's purposes, powers and constitution.

Expenses

▶ The charity should adopt a formal written expenses policy.

▶ The policy should establish clear parameters about what expenses can be refunded, in what circumstances and the restrictions that apply (e.g. standard mileage payment rates, caps on permitted travel and accommodation expenses).

▶ The policy should specify appropriate procedures to be followed to claim and verify expenses and the reasons for those expenses.

▶ It should also specify the procedures by which claims are verified and authorised for payment. Those procedures should include these features:

▷ A standard expense claim form.

▷ Provision of evidence of the reasons for the expenditure and the amounts (including receipts and verification of any VAT paid).

▷ Any mileage payable should be within HMRC limits, so that tax and National Insurance issues will not arise.

▷ The claimant should play no part in verifying or authorising their own expenses (or those of anyone connected to them, such as a family member).

▷ Cash payments should be avoided, with BACS transfers or cheques used instead.

▷ Adequate records should be kept to provide an audit trail.

▶ The policy and associated procedures should apply to anyone making expense claims (including staff, trustees and volunteers).

▶ It is best practice to avoid charity expenses being paid personally by staff, trustees and volunteers and then reclaimed. The charity should pay its own expenses directly whenever possible.

International transactions

▶ There are particular risks of loss or misappropriation when funds and other assets are moved between different territories.

▶ Trustees have a responsibility to safeguard charitable funds and assets, to ensure they are used for legitimate purposes and that they are used within the charity's own charitable purposes.

▶ Verification of the correct end use of funds transmitted overseas is essential.

▶ Where possible it is best to move funds through formal banking systems. If alternative financial systems are to be used the trustees must consider what additional measures are needed to ensure security of transfer, verification of delivery and the verification of end use of those funds.

Fraud, theft, bribery, terrorist abuse and other criminality

▶ Good financial controls, along with diligent management and effective trustee oversight, are important tools in managing these risks.

Serious incident reporting

▶ Where incidents or fraud or other financial crime are identified, or suspected, a charity should act immediately to minimise the risks of serious and irrecoverable losses and to protect its reputation and good standing.

▶ Consideration should always be given to:

  ▷ informing the police or other investigatory authorities (in some circumstances this is an absolute legal duty for the trustees and others in, or connected with, the charity);

  ▷ making a serious incident report to the Charity Commission (and/ or informing other charity regulators such as the OSCR or the Charity Commission for Northern Ireland); and

  ▷ notifying the charity's independent examiner or auditors.

▶ The Charity Commission expects a diligent approach to be taken by trustees, so if in any doubt it is best to make a report of any incident that may be considered serious.

Procedure

▶ Document internal financial procedures and controls.

▶ Provide guidance to staff and any volunteers involved in relevant activities.

▶ Provide appropriate training for new staff and new volunteers.

▶ Address the training needs of the trustees in relation to financial management of the charity.

Filing requirements

▶ Note the filing obligations relating to annual accounts and the annual trustees' report under charity law and, for CLGs, also under company law. For further details see checklist: 'Annual accounts and annual trustees' report'.

More information

▶ Charity Fraud – A Guide for the Trustees and Managers of Charities (Charity Finance Group, NCVO, ACEVO, Institute of Fundraising, Charity Commission, National Fraud Authority, ICAEW and others) www.cfg.org.uk/resources/Publications.

▶ Internal Financial Controls for Charities (CC8) (Charity Commission).

▶ Charity Commission guidance on serious incident reporting (available on the Commission's website).

▶ A range of useful guidance, reference material and training events are available from the principal charity sector support bodies, including:

  ▷ Charity Finance Group: www.cfg.org.uk.

  ▷ The Honorary Treasurers Forum: www.honorarytreasurers.org.uk.

  ▷ Association of Church Treasurers and Accountants: www.acat.uk.com.

  ▷ NCVO: www.ncvo.org.uk.

▶ Charities should also make good use of the expertise and support available from their independent examiner or auditors in relation to effectiveness of financial controls and systems.

Financial year-end

Introduction

A charity's financial year-end marks the end of an accounting period.

The financial year-end date is the date to which the annual accounts for that period are made up.

Checklist

Companies

▶ A company's financial year-end is its 'accounting reference date' for the purposes of the Companies Act 2006.

▶ The accounting reference date determines the end date for the financial year (the 'accounting reference period') and the period within which accounts have to be laid before the members in general meeting (if applicable).

▶ It also determines the deadline by which when the accounts must be delivered to Companies House.

▶ There is a leeway of seven days on either side of the accounting reference date for the actual date to which the accounts are made up, to accommodate, for example, an exact 52-week year which some companies find more convenient. This is unlikely to be used by a charitable company or a charity's trading subsidiary.

▶ For a new company, the accounting reference date is the last day of the month in which the company was incorporated. The directors may resolve to alter this to a more convenient date (subject to the additional Companies Act rules about length of accounting period etc.).

Unincorporated charities

▶ The constitution may provide rules regarding the financial year. It may also specify how the financial year-end can be altered.

Procedure

Companies – altering financial year-end

▶ A company's accounting reference date can be altered for any accounting reference period and all subsequent periods provided:

▷ the directors resolve to alter the date;

▷ the required form is filed at Companies House (AA01 or electronic equivalent); and

▷ the notice is given to Companies House within the period being altered or, if after it has ended, within the period allowed for filing the annual accounts for that period.

▶ In addition, an accounting reference date cannot be altered:

▷ so as to make an accounting reference period longer than 18 months; or

▷ so as to extend the period beyond 12 months more than once in every five years (there are exceptions for aligning the dates of subsidiary undertakings and parent undertakings).

Other charities – altering financial year-end

▶ Consider what, if any, legislative requirements and restrictions apply (e.g. industrial and provident society law).

▶ Check the provision of the constitution and follow any required procedures.

Filing requirements

Registered charities England and Wales – Charity Commission

▶ The annual accounts and annual trustees' report must be filed within 10 months of the financial year-end (unless a filing exemption applies, for example the exemptions for small charities).

Other charities England and Wales

▶ Exempt and excepted charities are not obliged to file their annual accounts with the Charity Commission. However, a particular exempt or excepted charity may be obliged to file its accounts with some alternative principal regulator or with another regulator because of the legal form of the charity (especially if it is incorporated) or because of other regulatory regimes to which the charity is subject due to its particular activities.

Charities on the Scottish Charity Register

▶ Charities on the Scottish Charity Register must file their annual accounts with the OSCR within nine months of their financial year-end.

Companies

▶ Notice of a change of accounting reference date must be filed with Companies House (form AA01 or electronic equivalent).

▶ Companies must file their annual accounts with Companies House within nine months of their accounting reference date.

Fundraising – charity sector self-regulation

Introduction

There is some compulsory legal regulation of charity fundraising but it is not a comprehensive legal regime applicable to all charity fundraising. Rather, there are areas of charity law and areas of other law that apply to certain kinds of fundraising activity and/or particular relationships where charity fundraising is undertaken.

The so-called 'self-regulation' of charity fundraising relies on a mix of voluntary compliance with good practice and on some charities opting to oversight by the non-statutory Fundraising Regulator. The Fundraising Regulator is a 'not-for-profit' company limited by guarantee.

The Charity Commission recognises the importance of fundraising as a source of income for charities and acknowledges that public generosity to charities is an enduring feature of our society. However, the Commission points out that the public expect charities to raise money in a considerate and responsible way and then to use the funds raised effectively. The Commission's fundraising guidance reminds charities and their trustees that the public's trust and generosity should not be taken for granted. It also emphasises that the trustees have overall responsibility and accountability for their charity's fundraising. The regulator expects them to exercise diligent oversight in this area.

Checklist

▶ Ensure trustees, all senior staff and key volunteers involved in overall management of the charity, as well as involved specifically in its fundraising activities, are aware of key principles (in particular see the key principles in the Code of Fundraising Practice).

▶ Trustees should familiarise themselves with the Charity Commission's guidance 'Charity Fundraising: A Guide to Trustee Duties' CC20 (available on the Commission's website).

▶ Ensure compliance with all legal requirements applicable to the types of fundraising carried out by the charity.

▷ Adopt relevant good practice where appropriate and practicable (in particular the good practice recommendations in the Code of Fundraising Practice).

▷ Trustees should adopt a fundraising policy suitable for their charity and ensure it is followed. The policy should be periodically reviewed and updated.

▷ Consider whether it is appropriate for the particular charity to join the *optional* charity sector fundraising 'self-regulatory' scheme operated by the Fundraising Regulator. An annual fee is payable (known as a 'levy'); the amount depends on the charity's annual fundraising costs. A formal registration process must be followed. The Fundraising Regulator accepts applications from any organisation based in England and Wales or Northern Ireland that carries out charitable fundraising.

Procedure

▷ Follow the overarching principles that underpin the Code of Fundraising Practice:

1. Legal.
2. Open.
3. Honest.
4. Respectful.

▷ Adopt relevant good practices, especially good practices recommended by the Code of Fundraising Practice and its supporting rulebooks (street fundraising, door-to-door fundraising, private site fundraising).

▷ Follow the core principles on fundraising, set out in the Charity Commission's guidance (CC20):

1. Effective planning.
2. Supervision of fundraisers.
3. Protection of the charity's reputation, funds and other assets.
4. Compliance with relevant law and regulation.
5. Identifications and adherence to appropriate codes of practice.
6. Commitment to openness and accountability.

▷ Trustees should take an active leadership role and exercise diligent and effective oversight of the charity's fundraising.

▷ Ensure any funds raised for restricted purposes are properly applied only to those purposes for which the funds were raised.

Notes

▷ The Charity Commission's principal role, in the context of funds raised for charities, is a protective one in the context of funds raised for charities, including their safe custody and correct application. Where necessary it can use some of its intervention powers to achieve this.

More information

▶ www.gov.uk/government/organisations/charity-commission.

▶ www.fundraisingregulator.org.uk.

Fundraising – commercial participators

Introduction

Fundraising ventures by commercial participators, in the course of which representations are made that contributions will be given to one or more charitable institutions, are subject to the legal and regulatory requirements set out in Part II of the Charities Act 1992 and the Charitable Institutions (Fundraising) Regulations 1994 (as amended by the Charities (Protection and Social Investment) Act 2016).

These provisions are very widely drawn and apply in many different situations, for example commercial catalogue merchandising that has a charity fundraising element involved, charity promotions of services by third parties or charity promotions of sales of particular goods by retailers such as supermarkets.

Checklist

Commercial participators – meaning

▶ A *commercial participator* is someone who carries on a non-fundraising business and, in the course of that business, carries out a promotional venture representing that contributions will be given to, or applied for the benefit of, a charitable institution.

Charitable institution

▶ For these purposes, a *charitable institution* is a charity or another institution established for charitable, benevolent or philanthropic purposes.

Promotional venture

▶ For these purposes, a *promotional venture* is any advertising or sales campaign or any other venture undertaken for promotional purposes. The word 'venture' is not specifically defined in the legislation. The Oxford English dictionary defines it as 'that which is ventured or risked in a commercial enterprise or speculation'.

Representations

▷ The relevant regulations define 'to represent' very widely, as meaning to represent:

'In any manner whatever, whether expressly or impliedly, whether done by speaking directly . . . or by means of a statement published in any newspaper, film or radio or television programme or otherwise.'

Charitable contributions

▷ In relation to any representation made by a commercial participator or any other person, charitable contributions means:

a) the whole or part of:
    i) the consideration given for goods or services sold or supplied by him or her; or
    ii) any proceeds (other than such consideration) of a promotional venture undertaken by him or her; or
b) sums given by him or her by way of donation in connection with the sale or supply of such goods or services (whether the amount of such sums is determined by reference to the value of such goods or services or otherwise).

Services

▷ Services includes facilities and in particular:

a) access to any premises or events;
b) membership of any organisation;
c) provision of any advertising space; and
d) provision of any financial facilities.

Charities trading companies

▷ A trading company owned by a charitable institution is not a commercial participator for the purposes of these particular regulations.

▷ However, charities should operate their trading companies within all applicable legal provisions and in accordance with relevant parts of the Code of Fundraising Practice (available on the Fundraising Regulator's website).

Procedure

Agreement between charity and commercial participator

▷ It is *unlawful* for a commercial participator to make representations that charitable contributions are to be given or applied for the benefit of a charitable institution unless it does so in accordance with an agreement that meets the requirements of the relevant regulations (see 'Introduction' above).

▶ Those requirements are detailed, they oblige the commercial participator and the charity to enter into a *written* agreement and specify matters that the agreement must address. Further details can be found in the Code of Fundraising Practice and the Legal Appendices to the Code, available on the Fundraising Regulator's website.

Solicitation statements

▶ Recent changes have been made to the detailed requirements for the solicitation statements that must be provided by commercial participators when making representations about contributions to charitable institutions.

▶ Care should be taken to consider both the revised legislative provisions and the relevant sections of the Code of Fundraising Practice (appendices to the Code provide further detail about the requirements for solicitation statements).

Other requirements

▶ Additional requirements apply to the records that must be kept, access rights for the relevant charitable institutions to those records, the payment of money across to the institutions and the time limit for that (28 days after receipt unless the charitable institution has agreed some other period).

Penalties

▶ Breaches of these requirements by any commercial participator are criminal offences and penalties apply (fines).

More information

▶ Code of Fundraising Practice and model agreement available from the Institute of Fundraising: www.fundraisingregulator.org.uk.

▶ CC20 Charity Fundraising: A Guide to Trustee Duties (Charity Commission) available on the Commission's website.

Fundraising – professional fundraisers

Introduction

Fundraising for charities by professional fundraisers and fundraising consultants is subject to the legal and regulatory requirements set out in Part II of the Charities Act 1992 and the Charitable Institutions (Fundraising) Regulations 1994 SI 3024 of 1994 (as amended by the Charities (Protection and Social Investment) Act 2016).

Checklist

Professional fundraisers – meaning

▶ A *professional fundraiser* is:

a) any person (apart from a charitable institution or a company connected with such an institution) who carries on a fundraising business; or

b) any other person (apart from a person who falls within the exceptions – see below) who for reward solicits money or other property for the benefit of a charitable institution if he or she does so otherwise than in the course of any fundraising venture undertaken by a person falling within (a) above.

▶ The *exceptions* are:

▷ any charitable institution or any company connected with a charitable institution;

▷ any officer or employee of such an institution or company, or any trustee of such an institution, acting (in each case) in his or her capacity as such;

▷ any person acting as a collector in respect of a public charitable collection (apart from a person who is to be treated as the promoter of that collection);

▷ any person who in the course of a relevant programme makes any solicitation at the instance of the charitable institution or company; and

▷ any commercial participator.

▶ A *relevant programme* is a radio or television programme in the course of which a fundraising venture is undertaken by:

▷ a charitable institution; or

▷ a company connected with such an institution.

Additional exceptions to the definition of professional fundraiser

▶ The definition of 'professional fundraiser' does not apply to a person if he or she does not receive:

▷ more than £10 per day or £1000 per year by way of remuneration in connection with the soliciting of money or other property for the benefit of the charitable institution; or

▷ more than £1000 by way of remuneration in connection with any fundraising venture in the course of which he or she solicits money or other property for the benefit of the charitable institution.

▶ These amounts are effective from 1 April 2009.

Charitable institution

▶ For these purposes, a *charitable institution* is a charity or another institution established for charitable, benevolent or philanthropic purposes.

To solicit

▶ The relevant regulations define 'to solicit' very widely. It means to solicit in any manner whatever, whether expressly or impliedly, or whether done:

a) by speaking directly to the person or persons to whom the solicitation is addressed (whether in his or their presence or not);

b) by means of a statement published in any newspaper, film or radio or television programme; or

c) otherwise.

References to a solicitation shall be construed accordingly.

Fundraising business

▶ A fundraising business means any business carried on for gain and wholly or primarily engaged in soliciting or otherwise procuring money or other property for charitable, benevolent or philanthropic purposes.

Procedure

Agreement between charity and professional fundraiser

▶ It is unlawful for a professional fundraiser to solicit money or other property for the benefit of a charitable institution unless it does so in accordance with an agreement that meets the requirements of the relevant regulations (see 'Introduction' above).

▶ Those requirements are detailed; they oblige the fundraiser and the charity to enter into a *written* agreement and specify matters that the agreement must address. Further details can be found in the Code of Fundraising Practice and the Legal Appendices to the Code, available on the Fundraising Regulator's website.

Solicitation statements

▶ Recent changes have been made to the detailed requirements for the solicitation statements that must be provided by professional fundraisers when making representations about contributions to charitable institutions.

▶ Care should be taken to consider both the revised legislative provisions and the relevant sections of the Code of Fundraising Practice (appendices to the Code provide further detail about the requirements for solicitation statements).

Telephone solicitations

▶ If a solicitation is made by telephone, the fundraiser must notify the donor of their cancellation rights.

Other requirements

▶ Additional requirements apply to the records that must be kept, access rights for the relevant charitable institutions to those records, the payment of money across to the institutions and the time limit for that (28 days after receipt unless the charitable institution has agreed some other period).

Penalties

▶ Breaches of these requirements by any commercial participator are criminal offences and penalties apply (fines).

More information

▶ Code of Fundraising Practice and its appendices, available from the Fundraising Regulator's website: www.fundraisingregulator.org.uk.

▶ CC20 Charity Fundraising: A Guide to Trustee Duties (Charity Commission) available on the Commission's website.

Fundraising – public collections

Introduction

The regulation of public collections for charitable causes is governed by a mix of statutory regulation, local bye-laws, good practice and the charity sector's various self-regulatory initiatives.

Checklist

Public collections – England and Wales

▶ Public collections such as door to door and street collections of cash are largely subject to a local authority-based licensing regime.

▶ For door-to-door fundraising, with very few exceptions, it is usually necessary for the promoter of the collection to obtain a licence from the local authority responsible for the area in which the collection will be carried out.

▶ Collectors must carry a certificate of authority signed by the licenced promoter. They must also wear an official badge (also signed by the promoter). These items must be shown to any member of the public who requests to see them. They must be handed back to the promoter at the end of the collection.

▶ Collectors must be at least 16 years of age.

National collections exemptions

▶ There are special national exemptions from the local licensing regime, issued by the Home Office. Such exemption orders are rare (they are used only for the principal nationwide charity collections, such as the Poppy Appeal for the Royal British Legion).

Public collections – Scotland

▶ A public charitable collection in Scotland is subject to the equivalent requirements under the law of Scotland.

Northern Ireland

▶ A public charitable collection in Northern Ireland is subject to the equivalent requirements under the law of Northern Ireland.

Procedure

▶ Consider and comply with all applicable legal and regulatory requirements.

▶ Also consider and comply with relevant parts of the Code of Fundraising Practice and the supplementary rulebooks to the Code (there are rulebooks for street fundraising, door-to-door fundraising and private site fundraising). The Code is available on the Fundraising Regulator's website.

Notes

▶ The main legislation in England and Wales is the House to House Collections Act 1939, the Police, Factories etc. (Miscellaneous Provisions) Act 1916 and associated regulations.

Static collection boxes

▶ There are currently no specific regulations governing static collection boxes, although the usual charity disclosure requirements would of course apply.

▶ Good practice recommendations in the Code of Fundraising Practice and guidance available from the Institute of Fundraising should be considered and followed where appropriate.

More information

▶ Institute of Fundraising: www.institute-of-fundraising.org.uk.

▶ Fundraising Regulator: www.fundraisingregulator.org.uk.

Fundraising – Scotland

Introduction

Fundraising on behalf of charities or other benevolent bodies in Scotland is subject to the requirements of Scottish charity law (see sections 79–83 of the Charities and Trustee Investment (Scotland) Act 2005 and the Charities and Benevolent Fundraising (Scotland) Regulations 2009 SSI 121 of 2009.)

It is important to recognise that these provisions are not restricted solely to fundraising for charities on the Scottish Charity Register. Rather, fundraising for any charity or any 'benevolent body' is subject to the requirements.

Checklist

Who is subject to the regulatory regime

▶ The regulatory regime extends to benevolent fundraisers, professional fundraisers and commercial participators.

Benevolent body

▶ For these purposes, a *benevolent body* is a body set up for benevolent or philanthropic purposes.

Professional fundraiser

▶ For these purposes, a *professional fundraiser* is a person who carries on a fundraising business or who, in return for a financial reward, seeks money or other property for a benevolent body or for general charitable, benevolent or philanthropic purposes.

Commercial participator

▶ For these purposes, a *commercial participator* is an organisation carrying on a business, other than a fundraising business, who, in the course of the business, takes part in a promotional venture where some or all of the proceeds are to be given to benevolent bodies or used for charitable, benevolent or philanthropic purposes.

Benevolent fundraiser

▶ A benevolent fundraiser includes benevolent bodies and companies. It also extends to individuals in either of those who are:

▷ in management or control;

▷ acting as employees or agents; or

▷ in some situations, acting as a volunteer.

Protections for charities – unauthorised fundraising

▶ There are some useful protections in the regulations for charities in relation to unauthorised fundraising. Initially they can seek to challenge and obtain prohibitions on such activities themselves. If that fails, it is possible to make application to the court (though in practice this may be a rather costly and unattractive option).

Procedure

Agreements with professional fundraisers and commercial participators

▶ The regulations require a written agreement between the fundraiser or participator and the organisations for which he is raising funds. This must address particular areas.

Statements to donors

▶ There are detailed requirements about the statements that must be made to donors during such fundraising.

▶ This must include information about the intended beneficiary organisations (if more than one organisation is involved, details must be provided about the proportions in which each is to benefit) and the remuneration of and expenses for the fundraiser/participator.

▶ Other detailed requirements vary, depending on whether the solicitation is oral or written.

Other requirements

▶ Additional requirements apply to the records that must be kept, access rights for the relevant charitable institutions to those records and the payment of money across to the institutions.

Penalties

▶ Breaches of these requirements are criminal offences and penalties apply (fines) – usually to the fundraiser rather than the charity.

More information

▶ The OSCR has issued guidance:
Benevolent Fundraising – A Guide to the Charities and Benevolent
Fundraising (Scotland) Regulations 2009.
See: www.oscr.org.uk.

▶ Additional guidance is available from the Institute of Fundraising:
www.institute-of-fundraising.org.uk.

Funds and assets

Introduction

All charitable funds and assets are held by a charity in order to pursue its charitable purposes.

Some funds and assets may be subject to additional legal restrictions, particularly with regard to how they may be spent or otherwise used.

Checklist

All charities

▶ Every charity must ensure its funds and assets are correctly applied to its own charitable purposes and within the powers of the particular charity.

Funds and assets – trustees' responsibilities

▶ Trustees have prime responsibility for the care and correct application of the charity's funds and assets.

Correct application of funds and assets

▶ The charity's resources must not be used for any non-charitable purpose or for any charitable purposes beyond the charity's own charitable purpose.

▶ Charitable funds and assets must not be used to provide private or commercial benefits to third parties (except to the extent that benefit is purely necessary and incidental to the carrying out of the charitable purposes).

▶ Charitable funds and assets must not be used to further the interests of a commercial organisation.

Charitable companies

▶ A charitable CLG is the absolute owner of its assets.

▷ Of course in practice they can only be used within its charitable purposes (objects) and in accordance with the powers set out in the articles of the company (and any restrictions on the use of those powers).

Charitable incorporated organisations

▷ There is a statutory obligation for a CIO to use and apply its assets in furtherance of its charitable purposes and in accordance with its constitution. Effectively this creates a statutory trust over all the CIO's assets.

Types of funds

▷ *Unrestricted funds* are the funds held by a charity that are not subject to any special trusts and restrictions, controlling how they may be spent. Unrestricted funds may be applied for any activities that are within the charity's charitable purpose.

▷ *Restricted funds* are funds that are held by the charity for a specific, restricted purpose. Typically the restrictions arise because the donor specified the restricted purpose when making the donation, or the funds were provided as a grant for a specific purpose, or the charity appealed for funds for a specific project or activity.

▷ In older charities, the restriction may relate to particular legal conditions imposed when the charity was originally established or at the time it acquired a particular piece of property (this is relatively common in relation to some historic gifts of property for charitable purposes).

▷ The restrictions on any restricted funds must be carefully observed. The trustees must ensure that relevant liquid funds or assets are used only within the terms of the particular restrictions. If in any doubt legal advice should be taken.

▷ Restricted funds should not be spent on the charity's general running costs.

▷ A restricted fund should not be in deficit.

Reporting restricted funds

▷ Restricted funds (including assets purchased with such funds, for example land and buildings) should be clearly identified and reported on in the charity's annual accounts.

▷ Notes should explain the nature of the relevant restriction.

Altering restrictions on restricted funds

▷ If it becomes impossible to use the funds within the terms of the original restriction, the charity may seek the original donor's permission to redeploy the funds (effectively either relaxing or entirely removing the restriction).

▷ Where that is not possible (for example the donor is dead) there are usually other routes by which restrictions may be altered. However, these will often be somewhat complex and are likely to involve legal changes and the consent of the Charity Commission. Legal advice should be taken.

Permanent endowment

▷ Permanent endowment is capital funds that must be retained to generate future income. Only that income (not the capital value) may be spent in pursuing the charity's charitable purposes.

▷ Generally the assets representing the capital can be changed from time to time (e.g. investments altered).

▷ Older unincorporated charities are more likely to have permanent endowment. It is less common in newer charities (and not possible in a charitable CLG).

▷ There are various legal mechanisms that can sometimes be used to remove permanent endowment restrictions, enabling the former non-spendable capital (or part of it) to be spent in the future. These procedures are subject to arrange of conditions and safeguards. Charity Commission consent may be required. Legal advice should be taken.

Functional permanent endowment

▷ Functional permanent endowment is non-spendable capital that must be used for a particular limited charitable purpose (for example as an almshouse or school). It usually takes the form of land and buildings.

▷ Functional permanent endowment is more common in older unincorporated charities. It is rare in newer charities (and not possible in a charitable CLG).

▷ It is difficult and sometimes impossible to remove such restrictions, however it may be possible to relax them in particular situations. There may be several different legal procedures involved and Charity Commission consent is likely to be required.

Misuse of funds and assets

▷ Misuse of charitable funds and assets is likely to be a breach of trust.

▷ Trustees can incur personal liability for a breach of trust, whatever legal form the charity takes (including a limited liability legal form).

Procedure

Safeguarding funds and assets

▷ The charity's total resources must be safeguarded against harm. Areas of particular importance to consider are:

▷ appropriate risk management;

▷ suitable insurance cover;

▷ protecting resources from incorrect use; and

▷ safeguarding against fraud, theft and other forms of misappropriation of funds and assets.

More information

▶ CC25 Charity Finances: Trustee Essentials (Charity Commission) is available on the Commission's website.

General meetings – conduct and voting

Introduction

The individual charity's constitution must also be considered in relation to the conduct of general meetings of the members and voting at those meetings. In addition, charities in certain legal forms are subject to some relevant statutory rules – in particular this is the case for CLGs, CIOs, SCIOs and registered societies.

Checklist

Pre-meeting preparations

▶ Ensure any required prior regulatory consents have been obtained (e.g. from the Charity Commission or the OSCR).

▶ Make practical arrangements with the venue (e.g. IT/audio, refreshments, appropriate accessibility arrangements for people with special access needs).

▶ Check the provisions of the constitution regarding who chairs the meeting and with regard to other key matters, such as the quorum and voting methods and rights.

▶ Brief the meeting chair as appropriate.

▶ Ensure all relevant reference documents and other papers are ready and will be available at the meeting.

▶ Ensure proxy forms and written notifications of the appointment of corporate representatives (by corporate members) have been checked and validated in advance of the meeting.

▶ Arrange any signing in procedures and any necessary verifications of identity (e.g. of appointed proxies or authorised representatives of corporate members).

▶ Prepare voting arrangements. If a poll is or may be required, prepare voting papers and arrange independent scrutineers.

Procedure

Quorum

▶ The charity's constitution should specify the quorum.

▶ The quorum is the number of participants with voting rights who must be present before the meeting can validly conduct business.

▶ If a quorum is not present the meeting cannot validly proceed. Decisions should not be purported to be taken at an inquorate meeting.

▶ *Companies* – if the articles are silent, the Companies Act default rule is that two qualifying persons are a quorum. A 'qualifying person' is:

   ▷ an individual who is a member of the company;

   ▷ an authorised representative of a corporation that is a member; or

   ▷ a proxy for a member

s. 318 Companies Act 2006

▶ There is a special rule for single member companies which can have a valid quorum of one (regardless of the provisions of their articles). It is rare for a charitable company to be a single member company.

Chair

▶ Usually there is a regular office holder who takes the chair (often the chair of the board). However it may be necessary to make an appointment of meeting chair at the beginning of the meeting (e.g. if the relevant regular office holder is not present).

Chair's powers

▶ The constitution is likely to set out some powers for the chair of a members' general meeting. Otherwise, consider and follow general good practice and underlying legal principles (such as the need to deal fairly with all members, ensuring their rights are respected and can be exercised effectively – for example their voting rights).

Chair's role

▶ The essential role of the meeting chair is to ensure the meeting is conducted in an orderly fashion and that the business is properly dealt with.

▶ For charities in a legal form to which statutory rules apply to general meetings (see 'Introduction') the chair should ensure those rules are properly observed.

Proxies – companies

▶ Members of companies have an absolute statutory right to appoint a proxy if they wish to do so. The company's articles may not override this right and any clause that is at odds with them is ineffective.

s. 324 Companies Act 2006

▶ The proxy can be anyone chosen by the appointing member.

▶ The proxy has the right to speak and to vote at the meeting (whatever voting method is being used on a particular matter).

▶ The appointing member may choose to instruct the member how to vote on particular matters or may authorise the proxy to make their own decision.

Proxies – other charities

▶ Whether members of CIOs, SCIOs and unincorporated members' associations have proxy rights depends on the individual charity's constitution.

Proxy voting

▶ If members have the right to vote by proxy at the meeting they must be allowed to exercise that right.

Voting rights

▶ Voting rights of the members largely depend on their class of membership and the provisions of the individual charity's constitution.

▶ Usually a member has one vote on any matter, though in some charities there may be non-voting membership classes.

▶ Note that a voting member of a company has an absolute statutory right to vote by proxy if the member wishes to do so.

▶ Corporate members can exercise their voting rights by proxy or by appointing an authorised representative to attend and vote at the meeting.

▶ For corporate members of CLGs this is a statutory right.   **s. 324 Companies Act 2006**

Voting methods

▶ Generally voting is conducted by show of hands.

▶ Voting can also be by poll (effectively a written ballot). This is most often used:

  ▷ if the particular charity's constitution requires poll voting on certain matters (e.g. a secret ballot for voting on candidates proposed for appointment to the board); or

  ▷ if the vote is expected to be close or the matter being decided is likely to be contentious.

▶ Usually the constitution enables the chair of the meeting to decide that a poll vote should be taken on a particular matter.

▶ For companies, the Companies Act provides minimum rights for members to demand a poll. In a CLG these rights are: **s. 321 Companies Act 2006**

▷ not less than five members having the right to vote on the resolution; or

▷ a member or members representing not less than 10% of the total voting rights of all the members having the right to vote on the resolution.

Prior written ballots

▶ A charity's constitution may provide for prior written ballots, enabling members to submit their votes in advance of the meeting on particular matters (e.g. proposed appointments to the board). This is relatively rare.

Types of resolution – companies

▶ The Companies Act provides for ordinary resolutions and special resolutions of the members of a company. If the articles are silent as to which type must be used and there is no statutory rule applicable to the particular proposed decision, an ordinary resolution can be used.

▶ The Companies Act (or other legislation) specifies the use of a special resolution for the most important decisions, in particular:

▷ changing the company's name;

▷ altering its articles; and

▷ voluntary winding up.

Ordinary resolution (company)

▶ At a general meeting, an ordinary resolution is passed by a simple majority *of votes cast*. (Abstentions are not relevant.)

Special resolution (company)

▶ A special resolution must be proposed as a special resolution (and identified as a special resolution on the meeting notice).

▶ At a general meeting, a special resolution is passed by a 75% majority *of votes cast*. (Abstentions are not relevant.)

Types of resolution – other charities

▶ The types of resolution that can be passed at a general meeting of other types of charity, and when a particular type may or must be used, will often be specified in the individual charity's constitution.

▶ In certain circumstances there may also be relevant statutory provisions (e.g. registered societies).

Amendment of resolutions

▶ There is usually very limited scope to amend a resolution at a meeting. Each item of business must normally be dealt with on the basis of the meeting notice.

▶ No alteration should be considered that materially alters the scope of the resolution or might in any way prejudice the rights of members (including those who, on the basis of the wording set out in the meeting notice, chose not to attend).

▶ The chair should rule in relation to any proposed alteration (noting any applicable rules in the charity's constitution and also good practice principles).

Filing requirements

▶ Some members' resolutions may trigger a filing or notification requirement to charity regulators and/or other regulators (such as Companies House).

▶ Occasionally a statutory fee may also be payable (e.g. a company change of name resolution).

More information

▶ See checklists: 'General meetings' and 'General meetings – notice periods and short notice'.

General meetings – notice periods and short notice

Introduction

Notice periods for general meetings may be set out in the individual charity's constitution. In certain legal forms of charity there are also statutory requirements to consider (in particular for companies).

Checklist

Notice period – companies

s. 307(1) Companies Act 2006

▶ A private company must give at least 14 clear days' notice of a general meeting.

▶ Note that if the individual company's articles provide for a longer notice period that requirement must be observed. This is particularly likely to be the case in the articles of a company incorporated prior to 1 October 2009.

Notice period – other charities

▶ Check the provisions of the individual charity's constitution.

Clear days

▶ Usually notice periods must be 'clear days' periods. This means the day on which the notice is received (or deemed received if sent by post or by electronic communications) is not counted, nor is the day of the meeting. Check the provisions of the individual charity's constitution and consider any applicable statutory provisions (especially those applicable to companies under the Companies Act).

Deemed delivery

▶ The constitution usually specifies when a notice sent by post is to be deemed delivered. It may also specify a deemed delivery rule for notices sent by electronic communication.

▶ In the case of a company, consider relevant Companies Act provisions as well as the articles (especially in relation to electronic delivery of a meeting notice).

Consent to short notice – companies

▶ Shorter notice may be given if the necessary majority of the members agree – i.e. the majority in number of members who have the right to attend and vote at the meeting who together hold not less than 90% of the total voting rights at the meeting.

▶ The company's articles can alter that percentage to a higher percentage (but it must not exceed 95%). Any such higher figure required must be observed. Note that the articles of many older companies do impose a higher percentage requirement (particularly companies incorporated before 1 October 2009).

▶ Note that a resolution to consider the removal of a trustee/director or the removal of an auditor *cannot* be considered at a meeting held on short notice.

Consent to short notices – other charities

▶ Check the provisions of the individual charity's constitution.

Methods of service of notices

▶ Normally hard copies may be given in person or sent by post to the members.

▶ A charity's constitution may also enable members to opt for electronic service of notices.

▶ For companies, the Companies Act makes detailed provision regarding possible electronic delivery of notices of general meetings (see checklist: 'Electronic communications').

▶ Subject to the detailed provisions in the Companies Act, a CLG may in principle serve notice of a general meeting on its members:

▷ in hard copy form;

▷ in electronic form;

▷ by means of a website; or

▷ by a combination of these methods.

Entitlement to notice

▶ Usually all members are entitled to notice of general meetings. However, check the provisions of the individual charity's constitution and the rights of different membership classes as, rarely, there may be a non-voting class of membership that is not entitled to receive notices of general meetings.

▶ Usually the trustees are entitled to receive copies of the notice (regardless of whether they are also members).

▷ Auditors of a company are entitled to receive a copy of any notice of a general meeting. In other types of charity the auditors may have a similar right arising from provisions of the individual charity's constitution.

Procedure

Notice of meeting

▷ Trustees' meeting approves the calling of a general meeting.

▷ The meeting may approve the draft notice or authorise the secretary to prepare the notice.

▷ The issue of the notice formally convenes the meeting.

▷ Ensure all relevant information is included in the notice, especially practical details (such as date, time and place of the meeting) and any details required to be included under statutory provisions (e.g. the required proxy rights statement on a notice of a general meeting of the members of a company).

▷ Check service methods permitted by the charity's constitution.

▷ Check any service method preferences that have been indicated by particular members (e.g. electronic service).

▷ Ensure that notices are sent out in accordance with the permitted methods and members' notified choices.

▷ Ensure that the relevant contact address (postal or email) as recorded in the register of members is used.

▷ Calculate the notice period carefully, noting that it is likely to be a 'clear days' notice period.

▷ Keep a copy of the notice as issued to the members and appropriate records of despatch date and particular despatch methods used.

▷ Enclose with the notice any other relevant or required documents (e.g. proxy forms, instructions on how to return completed proxy forms and relevant time limit, copies of any other documents that need to be circulated prior to the meeting).

Consent to short notice

▷ If the members' consent to short notice is to be sought, the trustees will usually instruct the secretary, or some other suitable person, to circulate a draft written consent to short notice to the members. This is usually sent with the notice of meeting but it can be circulated in advance of the notice.

Filing requirements

▶ Neither a copy of the meeting notice nor any consent to short notice need to be filed with any regulator. However, they should be retained in the charity's own records.

Notes

Special notice – companies

▶ Special notice of the intention to move certain resolutions must be given *to the company* by the person proposing to move that resolution.

▶ This applies to resolutions proposing the removal from office of a trustee/director or an auditor. (Note also that such resolutions cannot be considered at a meeting held on short notice.)

▶ The special notice must be served at least 28 clear days before the meeting at which the resolution will be proposed.

▶ The person affected by the proposal has various statutory rights (including the right to be provided with a copy of the meeting notice and a right to make representations).

▶ Legal advice should be taken before attempting to follow any forcible removal procedure.

More information

▶ See checklists: 'General meetings' and 'General meetings – conduct and voting'.

General meetings

Introduction

General meetings are meetings of a charity's members (not its trustees). Therefore charities in a legal form without a membership, for example unincorporated charitable trusts, do not hold general meetings.

Checklist

Extraordinary general meeting (EGM)

▶ An EGM is essentially any meeting of the members other than the annual general meeting. It is usually arranged because there is a particular matter that requires a members' decision or the authority of a formal resolution of the members.

AGM

▶ Some charities must hold an annual general meeting of their members. This usually arises because of provisions in the individual charity's constitution – a specific obligation to hold an AGM and/or requirements to deal with certain matters at an AGM each year (such as presentation of annual accounts and reports or appointments and retirements of trustees and/or officers).

AGM – companies

▶ There is no company law obligation to hold an AGM, a private company can choose whether or not it wishes to do so. This is subject to the terms of the individual company's articles – if they require the holding of an AGM the company must ensure it meets that requirement each year.

AGM – CIOs

▶ A CIO may be obliged to hold an AGM under the terms of its own constitution.

▶ A CIO that uses the Charity Commission's 'Association' model constitution is obliged to hold an AGM. (The Commission's 'Foundation' model does not include this provision.)

Members' meeting obligation – SCIOs

▶ SCIOs have a statutory obligation to hold a meeting of their members at least once in every 15 months. At least 14 days' notice of the meeting must be given to both the members and the trustees.

▶ This is not technically an AGM although in practice the business dealt with at these meetings is usually the normal business of a typical AGM.

Legal form

▶ Check what legal form the organisation takes. Note that:

▷ Charitable CLG or trading subsidiary company – general meetings are governed by the Companies Act 2006 and the individual company's articles.

▷ CIO – general meetings are governed by the CIO provisions of the Charities Act 2011, the supplementary CIO regulations and the individual CIO's constitution.

▷ SCIO – general meetings are governed by the SCIO provisions of the Charities and Trustee Investment (Scotland) Act 2005, the supplementary SCIO regulations and the individual SCIO's constitution.

▷ Unincorporated members' association – general meetings are governed by the individual UMA's constitution.

▷ Royal Charter body – general meetings are governed by the terms of its rules and any bye-laws (both of which will have been made pursuant to the Charter).

▷ Registered society – general meetings are governed by the relevant legislation and the individual society's own constitution.

Procedure

▶ Procedures relating to general meetings are usually partly governed by applicable statutory provisions and partly by the terms of the individual charity's own constitution (see the checklist above).

Prior regulatory consents

▶ Note that prior regulatory consents will be needed *before* some members' decisions can be taken. For example, this will be the case if a charity is seeking to alter its charitable purposes (objects).

Statutory procedural requirements – companies

▶ For companies, there are a range of statutory procedural requirements relevant to general meetings of the members of a company, including:

▷ the contents of and permissible delivery methods for notices;

▷ notice periods and whether shorter periods are permissible in particular circumstances;

▷ variation of the rights of membership classes; and

▷ proxy rights.

▶ In many cases these apply regardless of the provisions of the individual company's articles.

Typical outline procedure

▶ Subject to specific statutory or constitutional requirements, the typical outline procedure is as follows:

▷ Convene a board meeting to determine what business is to be proposed at the general meeting, approve the notice of meeting and authorise the issue of the notice to convene the meeting.

▷ Issue of notice and any accompanying documents (usually dealt with by the secretary, if there is a secretary).

▷ Make the practical arrangements for the meeting (e.g. IT/audio, disability access, arrangements for minutes to be taken).

▷ Ensure chairship and conduct of the meeting is dealt with in accordance with the provisions of the individual charity's constitution and any applicable statutory provisions (for example, companies must allow validly appointed proxies to vote).

▷ Complete minutes as soon as practicable after the meeting.

▷ Deal with any other record-keeping, notification or filing requirements that arise in consequence of the decisions taken at the meeting (e.g. appointment of new trustees, alterations to the constitution of the charity, etc.).

Filing requirements

▶ There may be various filing or official notification requirements to be dealt with depending on the nature of the business that was dealt with and the regulatory and registration regimes to which the particular charity is subject (Charity Commission, the OSCR, the Charity Commission for Northern Ireland, Companies House, Care Quality Commission, Homes and Communities Agency etc.).

▶ Note that time limits may apply.

▶ Occasionally, a statutory fee may also be payable.

More information

▶ See checklists: 'General meetings – conduct and voting' and 'General meetings – notice periods and short notice'.

Governance – Charity Governance Code

Introduction

Governance is about how organisations are governed by their most senior leadership group. In a charity that leadership group is the board of trustees.

The key pillars of governance are:

▷ direction (provision of top level leadership and the setting of strategy);

▷ effectiveness (making good use of financial and other resources to achieve desired outcomes);

▷ supervision (establishing and overseeing effective controls and monitoring); and

▷ accountability.

The Code aims to help charity trustees develop high standards of governance because good governance is fundamental to the health and effectiveness of a charity.

The Code is intended for use by registered charities in England and Wales. However some aspects of it are helpful to other charities. The principles are of general relevance and many of the recommended practices are applicable or can be easily adapted to suit an individual non-registered charity.

Checklist

▶ A steering group comprising the leading charity sector bodies is responsible for the content and periodic review of the Code (during review periods the group seeks views and comments from across the charity sector). The organisations represented on the steering group are ICSA: The Governance Institute, NCVO, Small Charities Coalition, WCVA, ACEVO and the Association of Chairs.

▶ The Charity Governance Code is a voluntary code for the charity sector. Compliance with the Code is strongly encouraged by the Charity Commission but it is not a legal requirement.

- The Charity Commission recommends that charities that choose to adopt the Code should state publicly on their website and in their annual trustees' report that they have done so.

- The Code sets principles and recommended good practice. Some aspects are deliberately aspirational, as the Code aims to encourage a culture of continuous improvement.

- There are two versions of the Code, the larger charities version for charities with annual income over £1 million and the smaller charities version.

- The core principles of the Code focus on:

  ▷ organisational purpose;

  ▷ leadership;

  ▷ integrity;

  ▷ decision making, risk and control;

  ▷ board effectiveness;

  ▷ diversity; and

  ▷ openness and accountability.

Procedure

- Governance procedures and processes must comply with applicable provisions of charity law and other relevant legal provisions (for example company law if the charity is a charitable company).

- The procedures and processes must also comply with relevant aspects of the charity's constitution, for example rules and requirements about trustee eligibility, appointment and terms of office and provisions relating to board meetings and trustee decision making.

- Subject to the above, charities are strongly encouraged to adopt the Charity Governance Code and reflect its principles and its good practice recommendations in their governance procedures and processes.

Notes

- Registered and non-registered charities (for example exempt charities) operating in some sectors, such as social housing, health or education may need to consider one or more other codes of governance or codes of conduct and/or competency frameworks.

More information

- Both versions of the Code and other resources can be accessed on the Code website: www.charitygovernancecode.org.uk.

Governance – principles and key areas

Introduction

In the context of a charity, governance is the means by which a charity is directed and controlled by its governing body (i.e. the board of trustees).

Governance is not an end in itself. Rather it is a means towards ensuring the charity's well-being and success, particularly successful charitable impact of its activities.

Governance is not the same as day-to-day operational management and delivery of activities. It is at a higher, more strategic level, creating a vision for the organisation that helps deliver lasting social impact.

Checklist

Underlying aim of governance in charities

▶ The underlying aim of governance in charities is to add long-term value in the charitable context. In particular this is about improving the quality of the charitable outcomes for which the charity was set up and the charitable impact of the charity's activities.

Key aspects of governance

▶ Key aspects of governance are:

▷ providing direction;

▷ enhancing effectiveness; and

▷ ensuring accountability.

Governance – role of the board of trustees

▶ The fundamental role of the board of trustees is to be the governing body of the charity, providing strong strategic leadership, clear direction and diligent, effective, oversight to the charity.

▶ The trustees should govern the charity in accordance with legal requirements, applicable statutory provisions, the terms of the particular charity's constitution and good governance practices and principles.

▶ Truly good governance needs a healthy culture within the charity that is genuinely 'lived' by everyone in that charity – trustees, officers, staff and volunteers. Trustees must embrace the charity's values, as part of this healthy culture.

Independence in governance

▶ It is vital that trustees maintain independence in governing the charity and in making decisions about the charity. They must be, and be seen to be, independent, acting at all times in what they honestly believe to be the best interests of the charity's charitable purposes.

▶ Trustees must not allow themselves to be unduly and improperly influenced by personal interests or the interests of individuals and organisations with which they are connected or the interests of third parties (such as funders, donors, partner organisations or the charity's founders). In addition, it is important that trustees are not unduly influenced by any loyalties they have to others.

▶ Any trustee appointed directly by a particular individual or an appointing body (for example a local authority) must act independently and not as a representative of that individual or appointing body.

Conflicts of interest

▶ Trustees have a fiduciary duty of undivided loyalty to their charity.

▶ Their most fundamental duty as trustees is to act in what they honestly believe to be the best interests of their charity's charitable purposes.

▶ It is essential that trustees have appropriate awareness of potential conflicts of interest (including conflicts of loyalty arising because of any loyalty a trustee may feel (or duty of loyalty a trustee may owe) to any other party).

The Code principles

▶ The Charity Governance Code sets out fundamental, high level, principles for the provision of good governance and leadership by an effective board. These principles are supported by good practice recommendations.

▶ Charities are strongly encouraged to adopt the Charity Governance Code and use both its principles and good practice recommendations in their governance.

Governance systems and practices

▶ Governance systems and practices vary considerably, to reflect the particular circumstances and the individual needs of each organisation as well as the particular legal form the organisation takes.

Procedure

▶ Governance procedures will in part be set by the legal form of the particular charity and the provisions of its constitution.

▶ In addition, standards of good governance and best practice should be considered and followed as far as practicable in the particular circumstances.

More information

▶ See checklist 'Governance – Charity Governance Code' and the two versions of the Charity Governance Code, for larger charities and for smaller charities, available on the Code website: www.charitygovernancecode.org.uk.

Health and safety

Introduction

Like any other organisation, a charity has health and safety responsibilities towards people who might potentially be harmed on its premises or through its activities or the use of any of its assets (for example vehicles and equipment).

Checklist

▶ Consider health and safety issues in relation to volunteers and visitors to the charity's premises, participants at its events, the charity's staff, any contractors it may engage and the general public.

▶ Ensure health and safety matters are embedded in the charity's risk assessment and risk management processes.

▶ Provide awareness training both to new staff and volunteers and as 'refreshers' for existing team members.

▶ Encourage a positive and responsible organisational culture towards health and safety matters.

▶ Reasonable precautions should be taken at all times, above all to protect individuals from harm and also to protect the charity, its trustees and its senior managers from potential legal penalties and liabilities.

▶ Employers have a general responsibility to provide a safe place of work. Specific obligations apply in a number of areas, including fire safety awareness and training.

▶ Workers also have a duty to take care of their own health and safety and that of others who may be affected by their actions at work.

Procedure

RIDDOR

▶ RIDDOR (Reporting of Injuries, Diseases and Dangerous Occurrences Regulations) 2013 require employers, and other people in charge of work premises, to report and keep records of:

▷ work-related accidents that cause deaths;

▷ work-related accidents which cause certain serious injuries (reportable injuries);

▷ diagnosed cases of certain industrial diseases; and

▷ certain 'dangerous occurrences' (incidents with the potential to cause harm).

▶ Note that accidents to members of the public, as well as staff, may require reporting.

▶ The Health and Safety Executive provides a useful guidance note which can be accessed on the HSE website (see 'More information' below).

COSHH

▶ The Control of Substances Hazardous to Health Regulations set out a wide range of health and safety related obligations and requirements.

▶ The COSHH Regulations deal with potentially hazardous materials and processes such as asbestos and silica, gas and oil extraction, storage and supply, stone working, welding and other hot processes and agricultural activities.

▶ Their potential application is very wide-ranging and charities should be careful that they identify all situations where the requirements are applicable and do follow those requirements.

▶ There is useful guidance on the HSE website (see 'More information' below).

Notes

▶ The principal legislation is the Health and Safety at Work etc. Act 1974 and associated regulations. However, there are many other Acts of Parliament and a considerable body of supplementary regulations that relate to particular activities, industries or processes, particular hazards etc.

More information

▶ The Health and Safety Executive has a range of responsibilities relating to the promotion and, where necessary, enforcement of compliance with health and safety legislation. It also seeks to encourage good practice and preventative health and safety activities.

▶ HSE provides a wealth of helpful reference and guidance material on its website: www.hse.gov.uk.

Independent examination of accounts – general

Introduction

The thresholds for external scrutiny of charity annual accounts in England and Wales (audit, independent examination or complete exemption from compulsory scrutiny obligations) has largely been harmonised for all registered charities, regardless of the legal form they take.

An independent examination is a form of external scrutiny of the annual accounts.

Checklist

▶ Independent examination offers an assurance that nothing has been found that needs to be brought to the attention of the trustees (a negative assurance). It is less rigorous than an audit.

▶ For charities in England and Wales, the trustees must take a positive decision to opt for independent examination instead of audit.

▶ A charity in Scotland that meets the relevant thresholds has an automatic right to independent examination instead of audit. This is subject to any requirement for audit in the charity's own constitution. Note also the requirement in a charitable company for a resolution of the board that audit is not likely to be needed (see further below).

▶ The independent examiner's report is addressed to the trustees (not the members of the charity).

▶ The report is a matter of public record and is attached to the publicly filed copy of the charity's annual accounts.

▶ If the charity's gross annual income exceeds £250,000 the independent examiner must be suitably qualified in accordance with applicable regulations.

▶ For a charitable company, if the trustees wish to claim audit exemption and have the annual accounts of the charity independently examined, instead of audited, they must pass a resolution that appointment of an auditor is not necessary on the ground that audited accounts are unlikely to be required.

s. 485 Companies Act 2006

Thresholds (England and Wales)

▶ A charity in England and Wales may usually opt to have its annual accounts independently examined, rather than audited if:

▷ annual income does not exceed £500,000; and

▷ assets do not exceed £3,260,000.

▶ The smallest charities, with income under £25,000 can opt not to have any external scrutiny on their accounts.

Constitution

▶ The relevant statutory provisions regarding independent examination scrutiny, as an alternative to audit, are permissive not overriding. If the individual charity's constitution requires the appointment of auditors and audit of the annual accounts, those requirements *must* be observed.

Smallest charities

▶ The smallest charities, with gross income under £25,000, may choose not to have any external scrutiny of their accounts. However, note that Church of England Parochial Church Councils are required to arrange independent scrutiny of their accounts under church accounting regulations, regardless of income level.

Procedure

▶ The independent examination must be carried out in accordance with the Charity Commission's directions and guidance for independent examiners (CC32) and in accordance with appropriate professional standards.

▶ The directions are made by the Commission under powers given to it by the Charities Act 2011. The directions must be followed by an independent examiner.

▶ The directions address:

▷ eligibility for independent examination;

▷ independence of the prospective examiner – whether any conflicts of interest prevent them acting;

▷ recording the examination;

▷ planning the examination;

▷ checking that the accounting records are kept to the required standard;

▷ checking that the accounts are consistent with the accounting records;

▷ checking whether related party transactions have been properly disclosed (in accruals accounts);

▷ checking the reasonableness of significant estimates, judgements and accounting policies;

▷ checking whether the trustees have considered the financial position of the charity at the end of the reporting period. If the accounts are accruals accounts, also checking whether the trustees have made an assessment of the charity's position as a going concern in approving the accounts;

ss. 156 and 159 Charities Act 2011

▷ checking the form and content of the accounts;

▷ identifying items from the analytical review of the accounts that need to be followed up for further explanation or evidence;

▷ comparing the trustees' annual report with the accounts;

▷ writing and signing the independent examiner's report;

▷ the examiner's duty to report matters of material significance to the Charity Commission; and

▷ the examiner's discretion to report relevant matters to the Charity Commission.

Examiner's duty to report matters to Charity Commission

▶ An independent examiner is under a statutory duty to report certain matters of material significance to the Charity Commission.

▶ This applies where, in the course of the examination, the examiner identifies a matter which relates to the activities or affairs of the charity, or of any connected institution or body, which the examiner has reasonable cause to believe is likely to be of material significance for the purpose of the exercise by the Charity Commission of its statutory functions.

▶ The Commission's statutory functions are set out in s. 156(3) of the Charities Act 2011.

▶ Examples of such matters, given in the Charity Commission's guidance for examiners, include:

▷ matters suggesting dishonesty or fraud, involving a significant loss or major risk to the charity;

▷ failures of internal controls (including governance failures) that have resulted in a significant loss or misappropriation of charitable funds, or which lead to significant charitable funds being put at major risk;

▷ suspicions of money-laundering or the involvement of funds that are the proceeds of organised crime;

▷ that the charity is a conduit for criminal activity;

▷ that the charity, its trustees or employees, or its assets, have been involved in, or used for, terrorism or proscribed organisations (inside or outside the UK);

▷ that the way the charity carries out its work relating to the care and welfare of beneficiaries does (or has) put those beneficiaries at significant risk of abuse or mistreatment; and

▷ significant breaches of trust or of legislative requirements.

Scotland

▶ Charity law in Scotland applies its own thresholds for the independent examination of the accounts of unincorporated charities and SCIOs. For charitable companies, the UK Companies Act thresholds apply.

▶ The overall thresholds in Scotland for opting to have annual accounts independently examined, rather than audited, are:

▷ annual income does not exceed £500,000; and

▷ assets do not exceed £3,260,000.

▶ Note that there is no complete exemption from independent scrutiny for the smallest charities (unlike the position in England and Wales).

▶ Independent examiners must meet the relevant criteria set out in the applicable regulations.

▶ Independent examiners have notification obligations to OSCR if, during the course of their examination, they come across any matters of relevance to the exercise of OSCR's statutory functions.

▶ The main statutory provisions applicable to the independent scrutiny of charity accounts in Scotland are set out in the following:

▷ Charities and Trustee Investment (Scotland) Act 2005.

▷ Charities Accounts (Scotland) Regulations 2006 SSI 218 of 2006.

▷ Charities Accounts (Scotland) Amendment Regulations 2007 SS1 136 of 2007.

▷ Charities Accounts (Scotland) Amendment Regulations 2010 SSI 287 of 2010.

▶ Guidance on independent examination and the qualifications required under Scottish charity law for independent examiners is published by the OSCR: www.oscr.org.uk.

Northern Ireland

▶ Relevant provisions in the Charities (Northern Ireland) Act 2008 and regulations made under it address the requirements for charities in Northern Ireland.

Filing requirements

▶ A copy of the independent examiner's report must be included with the publicly filed copy of the charity's annual accounts.

▶ A copy of the report should also be included when any copy of the accounts is issued to third parties and members of the public.

▶ There are other filing and notification obligations which may apply when independent examiners are appointed or cease to hold office and various reporting obligations to the charity regulators, should an independent examiner become aware of a notifiable matter.

Notes

▶ Some major funders may demand independent scrutiny or full audit of a charity's annual accounts (particularly public bodies that provide funds).

More information

▶ For charities:
CC15d Charity Reporting and Accounting: The Essentials
(Charity Commission).

▶ For independent examiners:
CC32 Independent Examination of Charity Accounts: Examiners
(Charity Commission).

▶ See also the relevant professional guidance issued by bodies such as the Institute of Chartered Accountants in England and Wales and the Institute of Chartered Accountants for Scotland and the Association of Charity Independent Examiners:

▷ www.icaew.com.

▷ icas.org.uk.

▷ www.acie.org.uk.

▶ In relation to Scotland, see: Scottish Charity Accounts: An Updated Guide to the 2006 Regulations: www.oscr.org.uk.

Independent examiner – appointment

Introduction

An independent examiner must be independent of the charity. The trustees must also ensure the examiner:

▷ has the requisite ability and practical experience to carry out a competent examination of the charity's annual accounts; and

▷ holds any required qualifications.

Checklist

▶ Is there a current auditor in office?

▶ If so, consider when that period of office will expire or whether early cessation of office (by voluntary resignation) is appropriate and permissible.

▶ Does the charity's constitution *require* the appointment of an auditor or the carrying out of an audit? If so, those provisions must be observed (or changed).

▶ Does a funder or any other interested party require an audit of the annual accounts?

▶ Do the trustees consider that an optional audit would be appropriate for any reason?

▶ Does the charity meet applicable thresholds for independent examination of its annual accounts?

▶ How will the charity identify and assess possible candidates for the role of independent examiner?

▶ What procedure does the constitution require (if any) for the formal appointment of an independent examiner? (For example, a resolution of the members at an AGM may sometimes be required.) If it is silent, the board can make the formal appointment.

▶ Are there any formalities to deal with regarding the cessation from office of a previous auditor or any previous independent examiner?

Qualifications (England and Wales)

▶ If the income level is over £250,000, the independent examiner must be qualified in accordance with the provisions of the Charities Act. This requires membership of one of the listed professional bodies set out in the Act and holding the qualifications and having the relevant experience required by the professional regulations of that body for charity independent examiners.

Qualifications (Scotland)

▶ An independent examiner who is examining accruals based accounts must hold one of the relevant professional qualifications specified in the applicable regulations.

▶ If the accounts to be examined are receipts and payments accounts, it is not a requirement to appoint an examiner within the above categories. However, the trustees must ensure that whoever they do appoint has the necessary skills and competence to carry out a proper examination.

Procedure

▶ The appropriate procedures to identify a suitable candidate vary from one charity to another. Some charities opt for a competitive tendering and formal interview process to select an independent examiner while others use more informal ways to discern suitable candidates (such as recommendation).

▶ Steps should be taken to ensure both the competence and the independence of the proposed examiner (ensure there are not conflicts of interest).

▶ The independent examiner is likely to ask the charity to follow some formal procedures relating to his or her engagement (such as signature of an engagement letter).

▶ The formal appointment process usually involves a decision of the trustees. However, the constitution of some charities may require a decision of the members (for example at the AGM).

▶ Ensure the decision is recorded in the minutes of the relevant meeting.

Companies – resolution that audit unlikely to be required

▶ Note that if the trustees of a charitable company wish to claim audit exemption and have the charity's annual accounts independently examined, instead of audited, they must pass a resolution that appointment of an auditor is not necessary on the ground that audited accounts are unlikely to be required.

s. 485 Companies Act 2006

Companies – auditor ceasing to hold office

▶ If an auditor of a company ceases to hold office for any reason, a statement must be given to the company by the outgoing auditor setting out any circumstances relevant to the cessation of office that should be brought to the attention of members or creditors of the company (or stating that there are none).

ss. 519–520
Companies Act 2006

▶ If matters are specified, the company must circulate a copy of the statement within 14 days to all those entitled to receive copies of the annual accounts.

▶ The auditor must send a copy of the statement to Companies House (within seven days after the expiry of the 21 days' period following the date of deposit of the statement, which is the period allowed for a potential application to court by the company not to have to circulate the statement).

▶ An auditor who ceases to hold office before that term of office expires must notify the appropriate audit authority.

ss. 522–525
Companies Act 2006

Filing requirements

▶ Consider what, if any, formal or informal notifications may need to be made to the charity regulator(s) or other parties.

Notes

▶ Relevant Scottish legislation specifies the categories of persons eligible to be appointed as independent examiners for charities on the Scottish Charity Register. The OSCR publishes guidance for both charities and examiners: www.oscr.org.uk.

More information

▶ See the various relevant professional guidance issued by bodies such as the Institute of Chartered Accountants in England and Wales and the Institute of Chartered Accountants for Scotland and the Association of Charity Independent Examiners:

▷ www.icaew.com.

▷ icsa.org.uk.

▷ www.acie.org.uk.

Independent examiner – qualifications

Introduction

In most cases, the independent examiner for a charity's annual accounts must hold particular qualifications.

In all cases, the examiner must be genuinely independent and have the requisite ability and practical experience to carry out a competent examination.

Care should be taken to check that there are no direct or indirect connections between the proposed examiner and the charity, or its trustees, or anyone else closely involved in the administration of the charity, which could prejudice the examiner's capacity to be truly independent.

Checklist

Charities in England and Wales gross income under £250,000

▶ It is not compulsory for the examiner to hold particular qualifications.

Charities in England and Wales gross income over £250,000

▶ The examiner must be a member of one of the bodies listed in the Charities Act 2011 and permitted by the rules of that body to undertake the role of independent examiner.

▶ The relevant bodies are:

▷ Institute of Chartered Accountants in England and Wales.

▷ Institute of Chartered Accountants of Scotland.

▷ Institute of Chartered Accountants in Ireland.

▷ Association of Chartered Certified Accountants.

▷ Association of Authorised Public Accountants.

▷ Association of Accounting Technicians.

▷ Association of International Accountants.

▷ Chartered Institute of Management Accountants.

▷ Institute of Chartered Secretaries and Administrators.

▷ Chartered Institute of Public Finance and Accountancy.

▷ Fellow of the Association of Charity Independent Examiners.

Charities on the Scottish Charity Register

▶ An independent examiner carrying out an examination of accruals accounts for a charity on the Scottish Charity Register must be a member of one of these bodies:

▷ Institute of Chartered Accountants of Scotland.

▷ Institute of Chartered Accountants in England and Wales.

▷ Institute of Chartered Accountants in Ireland.

▷ Association of Chartered Certified Accountants.

▷ Association of Authorised Public Accountants.

▷ Association of Accounting Technicians.

▷ Association of International Accountants.

▷ Chartered Institute of Management Accountants.

▷ Institute of Chartered Secretaries and Administrators.

▷ Chartered Institute of Public Finance and Accountancy.

Or

▷ A full member of the Association of Charity Independent Examiners.

Or

▷ A person appointed by the Accounts Commission for Scotland.

Or

▷ The Auditor General for Scotland.

▶ If the charity prepares receipts and payments accounts, it is not a requirement that the examiner holds one of the above qualifications. However, the trustees must ensure that the person appointed as examiner has the necessary knowledge and skills to carry out a competent examination.

Notes

▶ The individual may be required by the relevant professional body to hold a current practising certificate in order to be eligible to accept appointment as an independent examiner. Note this is likely to be the case even where the examiner acts on a voluntary basis.

More information

▶ CC15d Charity Reporting and Accounting: The Essentials.

▶ CC32 Independent Examination of Charity Accounts: Examiners.

▶ Independent Examination – OSCR Guidance for Charities and Independent Examiners.

▶ These are available on the regulators' websites.

Independent examiner – removal

Introduction

Removal of an independent examiner should be distinguished carefully from other reasons for the cessation of office of an independent examiner (for example, voluntary resignation).

Forcible removal of an examiner is a serious matter (and a rare event). It is likely to signify there are major problems in relation to the charity.

Where a forcible removal is being considered the charity should seek professional advice.

Checklist

▷ Obtain professional advice before proceeding with a forcible removal.

Procedure

▷ There is no specific statutory procedure.

Filing requirements

▷ Some disclosure, reporting or notification obligations may arise, depending on the circumstance (for example, if there is anything that the trustees or the outgoing examiner should report to the charity regulators).

Notes

▷ Note that there will normally be a professional adviser/client contractual relationship between the examiner and the charity. Consideration should be given to the correct steps to end that relationship and to deal with any outstanding issues (e.g. unpaid fees to the outgoing examiner).

More information

▶ Charity Commission guidance for trustees on reporting serious incidents is available on the Commission's website.

▶ For guidance on the duty of independent examiners to report certain matters to the Commission, see CC32 Independent Examination of Charity Accounts: Examiners (also available on the Commission's website).

Independent examiner – resignation

Introduction

An independent examiner may choose to resign from office voluntarily. This should be distinguished from cessation of office for any other reason.

Checklist

▶ Consider the reason for cessation of office (e.g. voluntary resignation) and the applicable procedures.

▶ Consider the appropriate process for appointing a new independent examiner and follow appropriate procedures.

▶ A voluntary resignation can usually be reported to the next board meeting; however, if that will not be held for some considerable period it may be necessary to convene an additional meeting (e.g. to deal with the appointment of a new examiner).

Procedure

▶ Ensure any outstanding matters with regard to the final examination by the outgoing examiner are properly dealt with.

▶ Obtain signed letter of resignation from the outgoing examiner.

▶ Arrange any required meetings.

Filing requirements

▶ It is unlikely that there will be any immediate filing/notification obligations on the charity.

▶ The outgoing examiner should address any required notifications to their relevant professional body etc. and whether there are any matters of concern that may require reporting to the charity regulator(s) (this is rarely the case but might occur).

▶ The change will be identified in public when the next set of independently examined accounts are filed.

▶ However, there may be some practical notifications to consider (e.g. ensuring relevant people within the charity are notified of the change and the contact details for the new examiner).

Notes

▶ If the charity becomes subject to compulsory audit under applicable thresholds, it should arrange for any serving independent examiner to leave office (by voluntary resignation) and take the necessary steps to appoint an auditor.

Insolvency

Introduction

Acting promptly and seeking appropriate professional advice as soon as financial difficulties arise, rather than waiting until the charity is financially doomed, will reduce the risks of personal liabilities for the trustees.

The trustees should take immediate steps to deal with matters properly as soon as there is any risk of insolvency, in order to minimise the risks of losses to creditors and protect the interests of other stakeholders, so far as possible in the circumstances.

For companies, the insolvency legislation applies to both solvent and insolvent winding up of companies (also known as 'liquidation') [Insolvency Act 1986 as amended and relevant regulations].

Checklist

▶ There are two principal tests of solvency, the cash flow test and the balance sheet test.

Solvency – cash flow test

▶ The test centres on whether the organisation can pay its debts in full (including any interest) as they fall due over the next 12 months.

Solvency – balance sheet test

▶ This centres on whether the realisable value of the assets continues to exceed the value of the charity's liabilities. It can only be relied on, in the 'going concern' context, if the trustees can reasonably assume that the charity will continue to operate.

▶ If the trustees are not confident that the charity will continue to operate, they must make their calculation on the basis that activity will stop and so they must also include all liabilities that would crystallise on a winding up when they assess whether the balance sheet solvency tests can be met.

Solvent winding up

▶ If the charity is able to pay its debts in full, together with the costs of the winding up, a solvent winding up is available.

▶ For a company, a members' voluntary winding up is available provided that the directors of the company can give the required declaration of solvency. This is a formal legal assurance that the company can meet its debts in full, with interest, during 12 months from the date of commencement of the winding up.

Insolvent winding up

▶ If the charity is not able to pay its debts in full, together with the costs of the winding up, an insolvent winding up will be necessary.

Trustees' liabilities

▶ If the assets of an unincorporated charitable trust or unincorporated members' association are insufficient to meet the charity's debts and liabilities, the trustees are at risk of personal liability.

▶ There may be some relevant insurance or, in the case of a members' association, the committee members may have an indemnity from the charity's members. This is rare and, even if it does exist, it may not in fact protect the trustees.

▶ The trustees of incorporated charities, such as charitable CLGs or CIOs are less likely to incur personal liability. However, especially in an insolvent winding up there are particular risks associated with:

  ▷ breaches of trust (which amounts to a breach of a trustee's fiduciary duties to the charity);

  ▷ any personal guarantees that may have been given; and

  ▷ wrongful or fraudulent trading.

Procedure

Companies – commencement of winding up

▶ There are a number of methods by which the winding up of a company might begin (outlined below). Some are only available if the company is solvent, some only if it is insolvent and others are potentially available in either situation.

  ▷ Members' voluntary winding up, commenced by special resolution of the members (this is typically used if the company is solvent).

  ▷ Creditors' voluntary winding up (this is relevant where a declaration of solvency cannot be given by the directors).

▷ Winding up by petition to the court. This can occur if:

> a person with the required legal standing can bring the petition on the grounds that it is just and equitable that the company should be wound up; or

> a judgement creditor for a debt of not less than £750 has not been paid within 21 days of service of a demand for payment in the prescribed form.

Procedure – conduct of the winding up (companies)

▶ The Insolvency Act and relevant regulations provide the detailed procedures to be followed.

▶ A licenced insolvency practitioner will be appointed as the liquidator (most IPs are chartered accountants who have gained specialist qualifications and have relevant experience as IPs).

CIOs and SCIOs

▶ Specific winding up regulations apply to charitable incorporated organisations and Scottish charitable incorporated organisations, which specify the procedures to be followed.

Other charities

▶ Procedures will depend on the legal form of the particular charity and, in some situations, may also be affected by the charity's constitution.

Filing requirements

▶ Public notification of formal winding up is normally required (via the Charity Commission and/or the OSCR and, for companies, also via Companies House).

▶ During the course of the winding up of any limited liability organisation, such as a company, CIO or SCIO, there will be a number of additional public filing requirements.

▶ The liquidator will deal with relevant obligations.

Notes

▶ Once a liquidator has been formally appointed the powers of the trustees immediately cease. However, the winding up of the charity does not relieve them of any potential liabilities – for example, for breaches of trust, breaches of duty or failure to meet statutory obligations.

▶ In some circumstances, receivership or administration may be a possible option for charities that are facing financial difficulties.

▷ Administration is a rescue mechanism that is an alternative to liquidation of a company. Once an administration order is made there is a moratorium which prevents the creditors from taking action against the company without the consent of the appointed administrator.

▷ A company voluntary arrangement is another rescue mechanism that can avoid liquidation of a company. It involves the directors of a company making a proposal to the creditors as to how the company's debts will be repaid in a more favourable way than would be the case if the company was liquidated.

More information

▷ See CC12 Managing a Charity's Finances, available on the Charity Commission website.

▷ For additional information about licenced insolvency practitioners and the range of services they can offer to a charity experiencing financial difficulties, see the Insolvency Practitioners Association website: www.insolvency-practitioners.org.uk.

Inspection of registers – companies

Introduction

Companies are required to keep statutory registers.

The Companies Act provides detailed rules on the format in which registers can be kept and where they can be kept.

There are rights of access to these registers for certain people and, for most of the registers, also for the general public.

Checklist

Location of registers

▶ Registers must be available at the registered office or at the SAIL (single alternative inspection location) that the company has notified to Companies House as the location of its registers, where inspections may be carried out.

▶ In order to use a SAIL a company must ensure these statutory criteria are met:

▷ The SAIL must be situated in the part of the UK in which the company is registered.

▷ The company must notify Companies House that it is using a SAIL and supply details of that location (form AD02).

▷ The company must notify Companies House which records are kept at the SAIL (form AD03).

▶ All records of a given type (e.g. registers) must be kept together at one location, they cannot be split between the registered office and a SAIL.

Request from business contact for location information

▶ If a person with whom the company deals in the ordinary course of business makes a written request to the company for disclosure of its registered office address and any other address where it keeps company records for inspection, and which records are kept there, the company must provide that information. The company must also state the address of any SAIL it is using and indicate which records are kept there.

▷ A time limit of five working days applies for the company's response.

Registers open to public access

▷ These registers are open to public access:

▷ register of members;

▷ register of directors; and

▷ register of secretaries.

▷ Note that the register of directors' residential addresses is not open to public inspection.

Inspection – access hours

▷ The registers of a private company must be available for inspection for at least two hours between 9am and 3pm on business days.

Procedure

Inspection request – notice period

▷ A person wishing to inspect a company's registers must give at least 10 days' notice.

▷ (Two days if the request is made during the notice period for a general meeting or during the circulation period for a written resolution of the company's members.)

Inspection fees

▷ Members may inspect the registers without charge as can the auditors or independent examiner.

▷ Members of the public can be required to pay an inspection fee for an inspection of the register of members (although in practice this is rarely imposed by companies). The fee rate is prescribed by regulations at £3.50 per hour (or part thereof) during which the register is inspected.

Inspection request – register of members

▷ The access request must provide the name and address of the person making that request.

▷ The request must state what the information will be used for, whether it will be shared with anyone else and, if so who and for what purpose.

▷ The company has five days to comply with the request or make an application to court.

▶ If the company does not consider the request is made for a proper purpose it may, within five days, apply to the court for an order to that effect, which enables it to deny the access request. This is extremely rare in practice.

▶ The Companies Act 2006 does not specify what is, or is not a 'proper purpose'. The Institute of Chartered Secretaries and Administrators has issued guidance for commercial companies, which may be a useful reference point for the boards of charitable companies and the subsidiaries of charities.

Filing requirements

▶ If the company chooses to use a SAIL as the location for its statutory registers, it must notify Companies House (see above).

Notes

▶ The Companies Act requires various other documents to be available for public inspection. However, most of these relate to commercial companies limited by shares so they will not be relevant to a charity (e.g. a director's service contract or a contract for the purchase of a company's own shares from a shareholder).

More information

In addition to the Companies Act provisions, there are detailed regulations in:

▷ the Companies (Company Records) Regulations 2008 SI 3006 of 2008; and

▷ the Companies (Fees for Inspection of Company Records) Regulations 2008 SI 3007 of 2008.

Investments – general

Introduction

Unlike private investors managing their own monies, charity trustees do not have complete freedom to make whatever decisions they wish in relation to the investment of charitable funds. Their general duties require them to exercise due caution in making investment decisions. Indeed, the Charity Commission suggests that trustees must 'minimise risk' to their charity's funds (e.g. by having a mix of investments).

Some investments are made purely for financial return; these are financial investments.

Some are made in order to achieve charitable outcomes, directly relevant to the charity's charitable purposes. These are social impact investments, sometimes called 'programme related investments'.

Other investments are 'mixed motive' investments, made with the deliberate intention of achieving both a financial return and a charitable outcome. Provided they meet the relevant statutory criteria, these investments may be 'social investments' for the purposes of the Charities (Protection and Social Investments) Act 2016. See checklist: 'Investments – social investments (Charities (Protection and Social Investment) Act 2016)'.

Checklist

▶ What are the motivations for making the proposed investment? How does that affect the kind of investment – for example, does it indicate this would be a financial investment?

▶ Consider the charity's powers to make investments.

▶ Are those inhibited in any way? For example, by provisions of the charity's own constitution.

▶ What investment powers do the trustees have authority to exercise?

▶ Do the provisions of the Trustee Act 2000 apply? (This is of particular relevance to unincorporated charitable trusts in England and Wales.)

▷ Consider the charity's investment policy and any relevant criteria of that policy to the matter under consideration (this is of particular relevance where a financial return is being sought).

▷ Address risk management issues.

Procedure

▷ The procedures required to deal with charity investment matters will depend on the legal form of the charity, as well as applicable statutory or constitutional powers, rules and restrictions.

▷ Where matters relating to the delegation of discretionary investment decisions or the use of nominees to hold charity investments are involved, additional legal, regulatory and procedural requirements will apply.

▷ Ensure appropriate documents and evidence are retained.

▷ Make appropriate records of investment decisions.

Filing requirements

▷ A range of public disclosures must be made in the charity's annual trustees' report and accounts in relation to charity investments, to comply with the Charities SORP.

Notes

Investment

▷ 'Investment' has a very wide meaning in relation to charitable funds. In its broadest sense it can cover financial investments, made with the intention of growing capital or generating income (or a mix of both). It can also mean investments made with a view to achieving charitable outcomes and a financial return, which are usually called 'social investments'.

Charity investment regulation under English law

▷ Specific charity law provisions relating to social investments by charities are set out in the Charities (Protection and Social Investment) Act 2016. See checklist: 'Investments – social investments'.

▷ In addition, English charity law has specific provisions relevant to the investments of unincorporated charities (in the Trustee Act 2000). See checklist: 'Investments – unincorporated charities'.

Reserves, investment policies and performance

▷ Charity reporting standards require charity trustees to include in their annual trustees' report:

▷ Details of the charity's reserves policy and of the performance against that policy, with an explanation of the actions the trustees are taking to address any shortfall or deal with any excess of reserves held.

▷ Information about the charity's investment policy, its main objectives and performance against those objectives.

▶ The standards also require reporting of sums held in investments, income received on investments and investment fund balances at the beginning and end of a financial year.

▶ These obligations extend to all kinds of investments aimed at producing a financial return, whatever investment funds or other assets those may be invested in (for example, investment land).

Ethical investment

▶ The 'norm' for investments is that the best return must be sought on the funds invested. It is generally recognised that trustees have some scope for departing from that, to allow an ethical stance to inform their investment strategy. However, trustees do not have 'carte blanche', nor may they follow their own personal ethical preferences, as if they were private investors.

▶ Board members, collectively and individually, are subject to the overriding trustee duty to pursue the charity's charitable purposes. When deciding on their investment stance, they can:

▷ take into account that investment in a particular type of business would entail conflict with those purposes; and

▷ balance the risks of potentially losing support against the risks of potential financial underperformance.

▶ An investment strategy informed by moral considerations should not be allowed to create a risk of significant financial detriment to the charity.

Scotland

▶ The Charities and Trustee Investment (Scotland) Act 2005 provides a general investment power for charities. The relevant provisions impose duties on the charity trustees to obtain and consider proper advice about the way in which this investment power should be used and, also, to have regard to:

▷ the suitability to the charity of the proposed investment; and

▷ the need for diversification of the charity's investments, as appropriate to the circumstances.

▶ The legislation specifies that 'proper advice' means the advice of a person who is reasonably believed by the trustees to be qualified, through that person's ability and practical experience of financial and other matters relating to the proposed investment.

▶ Further restrictions and obligations apply in relation to the use of investment nominees and the delegation of investment management.

More information

▶ See Charity Commission guidance CC14 Charities and Investment Matters: A Guide for Trustees and the Commission's interim guidance Social investment by Charities (which relates to the Charities (Protection and Social Investment) Act 2016). Both are available on the Commission's website.

Investments – social investments (Charities (Protection and Social Investment) Act 2016)

Introduction

A social investment is an investment made by a charity with both of these aims:

▷ to obtain a financial return; and

▷ to achieve charitable outcomes appropriate to the charity's charitable purposes.

A pure financial investment, made only with the aim of achieving a financial return, is not a social investment for the purposes of the 2016 Act.

There are specific charity law rules and requirements relating to social investments by charities, specified by the Charities (Protection and Social Investment) Act 2016.

The 2016 Act also provides a statutory power to make social investments that is available to most (but not all) legal forms of charity.

Checklist

▶ For the purposes of the 2016 Act, a social investment is a 'relevant act' of charity that is made with a view to:

▷ directly furthering the charity's charitable purposes; and

▷ achieving a financial return for the charity.

▶ The motivation for making the investment is therefore key in determining whether an investment is a social investment for these particular legal purposes.

▶ A financial return means that the financial outcome for the charity is better than would have been the case if the charity had spent the relevant amount.

▶ The Act specifies that a 'relevant act' is either:

▷ the application or use of funds or property by the charity; or

▷ a commitment relating to another party's liability that puts the charity's funds or other property at risk (for example, a guarantee given by the charity on behalf of another party).

▶ The general duties of charity trustees apply to social investment matters. In addition the specific statutory duties of charity trustees, under the 2016 Act, also apply.

▶ Permanent endowment cannot generally be used to make social investments (there are some limited exceptions).

▶ The statutory power to make social investments, provided by the 2016 Act is not available to statutory charities (i.e. charities established by statute or whose purposes are specified by statute) or to Royal Charter body charities.

Procedure

▶ When making decisions about the exercise of the statutory power to make social investments, the trustees' statutory duties (under the 2016 Act) require them to:

▷ consider whether they should obtain advice about the proposed investment;

▷ obtain and consider that advice if necessary; and

▷ satisfy themselves that it is in the interests of the charity to make the investment, having regard to the benefit they expect it to achieve for the charity. This must be in relation to both the expected charitable outcomes and the expected financial returns.

▶ The trustees should ensure they believe the adviser to be competent to give the relevant advice (the law requires them to make a reasonable judgement on that competency).

▶ The trustees must comply with their statutory duties under the 2016 Act themselves, they cannot delegate matters to others.

▶ It is clearly prudent to ensure any advice taken is provided in writing and any verbal discussions with the adviser are also properly documented. In addition, discussions and decisions of the trustees at board meetings should be properly recorded in the meeting minutes.

▶ Trustees are also required to review the charity's social investments from time to time. No set period is specified by the Act for such reviews.

▶ In carrying out a review, the trustees must:

▷ consider whether any advice about the charity's social investments in general, or any of its specific social investment(s), should be taken; and if so

▷ obtain and consider appropriate advice.

▶ Note that these statutory duties apply in relation to social investments and trustees' decisions about them in general, not just to the use of the statutory social investment power by the trustees.

Filing requirements

▷ Relevant investment reporting requirements must be met, in particular the investment reporting standards set by the Charities SORP.

Notes

▷ The usual public benefit rules and the usual restrictions on private benefits apply and must be observed.

More information

▷ See the Charity Commission's interim guidance 'Social Investments by Charities' and CC14 'Charities and Investment Matter: A Guide for Charity Trustees'. Both are available on the Commission's website.

Investments – unincorporated charities

Introduction

English charity law has specific provisions relevant to investments of *unincorporated* charities (in the Trustee Act 2000).

Checklist

▶ Although the Act provides a general investment power and a further power to invest in land, there may be additional limitations on a particular charity because of the terms of its own constitution.

Trustees' statutory duties

▶ The Trustee Act 2000 imposes statutory duties on the trustees of unincorporated charities.

▶ In relation to *financial investments* the trustees must:

▷ adopt an investment policy, measure performance of the charity's investments against that and report on these matters in their annual trustees' report;

▷ observe their general statutory duty to exercise reasonable skill and care in relation to investment matters;

▷ obtain and consider proper independent investment advice before using their investment powers; and

▷ have regard to the standard investment criteria.

Standard investment criteria

▶ The standard investment criteria are:

▷ the suitability to the charity of the type of investment being considered;

▷ the suitability of the particular investment as an investment of that type; and

▷ the need for diversification of the charity's investments, as appropriate to the charity's circumstances.

Delegation of discretionary investment management powers, use of nominees

▶ Further restrictions and obligations apply to the use of investment nominees and the delegation of investment management.

Procedure

▶ The procedures required to deal with charity investment matters in an unincorporated charity will depend on the legal form of the charity, as well as applicable statutory or constitutional powers, rules and restrictions.

▶ Where matters relating to the delegation of discretionary investment decisions or the use of nominees to hold charity investments are involved, additional legal, regulatory and procedural requirements will apply.

▶ Ensure appropriate documents and evidence are retained.

▶ Make appropriate records of investment decisions.

Filing requirements

▶ A range of public disclosures must be made in the charity's annual trustees' report and accounts in relation to charity investments, to comply with the Charities SORP reporting standards.

Notes

▶ *Incorporated charities* are not specifically subject to the Trustee Act provisions but their trustees are subject to the general duties of charity trustees. It is clearly wise for them to adopt an investment policy, with clear objectives, and to measure actual investment performance. There should also be transparent reporting to the Charities SORP standards.

▶ Specific statutory provisions apply to social investments, under the Charities (Protection and Social Investment) Act 2016.

More information

▶ See checklists: 'Investments – general' and 'Investments – social investments (Charities (Protection and Social Investment) Act 2016)'.

▶ See also CC14 'Charities and Investment Matters: A Guide for Trustees' and the further Charity Commission interim guidance on 'Social Investment by Charities'. Both are available on the Commission's website.

Land transactions

Introduction

Land transactions involving charities should be dealt with carefully, as they involve important and sometimes complex issues. There are potential risks for trustees if such matters are not dealt with correctly. Appropriate specialist professional advice should be taken.

Checklist

▶ A full board decision is normally needed for any substantive land transaction (acquisition or disposal) (i.e. the matter cannot be dealt with by a sub-committee).

▶ Consider the charity's powers (constitutional and statutory).

▶ Check the transaction will further the charitable purposes and be in the best interests of the charity.

▶ Ensure any conflicts of interest are identified and managed correctly.

▶ Is a 'connected party' involved? If so, additional legal restrictions apply, including the need for Charity Commission prior consent.

▶ Consider if the transaction requires prior Charity Commission consent for any reason and/or any other regulatory consent(s).

▶ Ensure trustees have considered relevant Charity Commission guidance, in particular:

　▷ CC28 Sales, leases, transfers or mortgages: What charity trustees need to know about disposing of charity land.

　▷ CC33 Acquiring land.

Scotland

▶ Land law in Scotland differs significantly to land law in England and Wales. Specialist legal advice should be taken.

▶ Note also that there is Scotland specific tax legislation that is relevant to charity land transactions in Scotland. Specialist tax advice should be taken.

Procedure

▶ The procedures involved will depend on the nature of the charity and the nature of the transaction.

▶ If any connected party is involved, further procedures must be observed, in addition to those required because a charity is one of the parties.

▶ Various special statements must be made in the relevant documents.

▶ For transactions in relation to land in Scotland, procedures differ substantially from those applicable in England and Wales.

Filing requirements

▶ The usual land registration requirements will apply.

▶ Companies must file required details of charges they create at Companies House. Note the changes to the legal rules and procedures introduced by the Companies Act 2006 (Amendment of Part 25) Regulations 2013 SI 600 of 2013.

▶ There is no requirement or option for CIOs to register charges with the Charity Commission.

▶ Where Charity Commission consents are required there will also be relevant applications and notifications to be made to the charity regulator.

Notes

▶ Incorporated charities can usually hold the title to land and buildings directly, in their own capacity.

▶ Unincorporated charities, which lack legal capacity, cannot usually do so. Instead, individual nominees (often some of the charity trustees) or a professional nominee body will hold the title as custodians, on behalf of the charitable purposes of the charity.

More information

▶ See the Charity Commission guidance notes mentioned above.

▶ Land Registry for England and Wales: www.landregistry.gov.uk.

▶ Registers of Scotland: www.ros.gov.uk.

Loans

Introduction

Charities may be involved in borrowing money, for a particular project, such as the acquisition of land or the refurbishment of a building, or to secure a contract or a grant funding arrangement.

Where a charity borrows funds it may also be giving security to the lender over some of its assets.

Charities may also be involved in lending funds. While this is not common, it is perhaps most likely to occur where the lending is in direct pursuit of the charitable purposes. For example, some anti-poverty charities and charities involved in addressing social inequalities and fair trade issues make low interest or interest free loans to some of their beneficiaries.

Checklist

Loan funding for charities – general

▶ Loan funding is a potential source of temporary income for charities, for example, as part of the funding package to acquire or refurbish a building.

▶ Loans create an outstanding liability, as they are debts that must be repaid in accordance with the loan terms (they are not grants or donations).

▶ The borrower charity must manage its finances sufficiently well to generate enough unrestricted income to meet the repayments (including interest) as they fall due.

Borrowing – charitable purposes and powers

▶ A charity may borrow money to further its charitable purposes (but not for non-charitable purposes or for anything beyond the charity's own purposes and its powers).

▶ There may be an express borrowing power in the constitution.

▶ A power to borrow in direct pursuit of the charitable purposes can normally be implied, unless the constitution specifically prohibits or limits borrowing (such limits or restrictions are more common in older unincorporated charities).

▶ A CLG that is a charity benefits from the Companies Act presumption that a company may do anything lawful, unless its articles contain restrictions.

▶ A CIO has statutory power to do anything which is calculated to further its charitable purposes. In relation to borrowing (or lending), particular consideration should be given to the statutory trust over a CIO's assets, which places an obligation on the CIO to use and apply its assets in furtherance of its charitable purposes.

Granting security – powers

▶ Power to grant security may arise from provisions in the charity's constitution or be implied.

▶ CLGs and CIOs – note the comments above.

▶ Unincorporated charities generally need to check their constitutions for a specific power.

▶ If the trustees of an unincorporated charity hold, or have held, land, they may be able to rely on the statutory power to mortgage land set out in section 6(1) of the Trusts of Land and Appointment of Trustees Act 1996 (specialist advice should be taken if in any doubt).

Borrowing – trustees

▶ Major borrowing decisions should be taken by the full board (not a sub-committee). This also applies to any decision to grant security.

▶ The trustees should be mindful of their general duties and of any particular duties and responsibilities that apply to the proposed transaction or arrangement.

▶ Careful risk assessment and financial prudence are essential.

Security – CIOs

▶ A CIO cannot register any charge it creates on its public record as the Charity Commission does not operate a register of charges. This causes some legal and practical difficulties for CIOs that need to give security against their borrowings or other purposes.

▶ If the security relates to land, there will be relevant public registration requirements at the Land Registry (or, for land in Scotland, in the Registers of Scotland).

Statutory restrictions on mortgages (ss. 124–129 Charities Act 2011)

▷ If a charity intends to mortgage land held by, or on trust for that charity, it must comply with these statutory provisions.

▷ They relate to the granting of a mortgage as security for a loan (or grant).

(Note these provisions do not apply to exempt charities.)

▷ The trustees may authorise the granting of a mortgage, without prior Charity Commission consent or a court order, provided that:

    a) they have obtained and considered written advice from a suitable person; and

    b) advice has addressed particular matters, specified in the Charities Act.

▷ The person must be someone:

    a) the trustees reasonably believe to be qualified by their ability in, and practical experience of, financial matters; and

    b) who has no financial interest in the making of the loan (or grant) to be secured.

▷ The advice must be provided in writing and considered by the trustees before they commit to the charity giving the mortgage. The advice must address:

    a) whether the loan (or grant) to be secured is necessary in order for the trustees to pursue a particular course of action in connection with which they are seeking the loan (or grant);

    b) whether the loan (or grant) terms are reasonable, having regard to the status of the charity as a prospective borrower (or grant recipient);

    c) the charity's ability to repay the relevant sum, on the proposed terms; or, in the case of any other obligation being secured (e.g. in relation to a grant); and

    d) whether it is reasonable for the trustees to undertake to discharge the obligation, having regard to the charity's purposes.

▷ It is best practice to ensure the adviser is entirely independent and has adequate professional indemnity insurance in place, in case of any future legal issue.

(Reliance for this advice on a senior staff member, while not strictly prohibited, is therefore unwise.)

Trading subsidiaries

▷ Charitable funds should not be put at risk through the making of unsecured loans by a charity to its trading subsidiary.

▷ A trading subsidiary usually has normal commercial borrowing powers. However, caution should be exercised in relation to borrowings by a subsidiary from normal commercial lenders (or other sources), in order to protect the charity from any risks (including financial risks and risks to the charity's reputation).

▶ Care must be taken about any potential related party transactions or proposed financial dealings with trustees or organisations or individuals who are connected to trustees.

Procedure

▶ The procedures involved will depend on the nature of the charity and the nature of the transaction(s).

▶ If any connected party is involved, prior Charity Commission consent will be required and further procedures must be observed (in addition to those required because a charity is one of the parties).

▶ Various special statements must be made in the relevant documents.

▶ For transactions in relation to land in Scotland, procedures differ substantially from those applicable in England and Wales.

Filing requirements

▶ The usual land registration requirements will apply to transactions relating to land.

▶ Companies must file required details of charges they create at Companies House. Note the changes to the legal rules and procedures introduced by the Companies Act 2006 (Amendment of Part 25) Regulations 2013 SI 600 of 2013.

▶ Where Charity Commission consents are required there will also be relevant applications and notifications to be made to the charity regulator.

More information

▶ Land Registry for England and Wales: www.landregistry.gov.uk.

▶ Registers of Scotland: www.ros.gov.uk.

Members' associations

Introduction

A members' association is one of a number of optional different legal forms that charities may take.

Checklist

Legal nature

▶ A members' association is a group of individuals associating together for a common purpose (i.e. the charitable purpose).

▶ The association does not have its own independent legal identity (it does not exist in its own right in law, separate to its members, trustees and officers).

▶ It does not have the capacity to hold property directly nor to enter into contracts or other legal agreements. This means individuals have to act in their own capacities on its behalf (with attendant liability risks).

Governing law

▶ The relevant law governing unincorporated members' associations is almost entirely common law (there is no specific statute governing unincorporated members' associations).

▶ Members' associations and their trustees are, of course, subject to the general law. Some areas are of particular importance (and carry the greatest risks) – for example, health and safety and employment law.

Liability

▶ The association's funds and assets are at risk in relation to the debts and other liabilities incurred in the association's activities.

▶ There is no limited liability protection for the members or trustees of the association.

Constitution

▶ A members' association will have a constitution. This is normally approved by the first members shortly after or as the association comes into being.

▶ Members' associations are heavily dependent on their own constitutions, as there are no fall-back statutory provisions. It is therefore essential that the constitution:

▷ deals adequately with all key areas; and

▷ is up-to-date and compliant with the general law (for example, equalities legislation).

▶ It is advisable to review the constitution regularly and update it whenever appropriate.

Alteration of constitution

▶ A power to alter the constitution is usually set out in a clause within the constitution. The provision is likely to require various formalities to be observed and to require a resolution of the members (for further details see checklist: 'Constitutions – other types of charity').

▶ Note that various alterations will require prior consent from relevant charity regulators – for example, any proposed alteration to the charitable purposes (objects).

Registration

▶ There is no public register of members' associations.

▶ A members' association that is a charity in England and Wales will be registered with the Charity Commission (unless an exemption or exception applies).

▶ In Scotland, any members' association that is a charity will be registered on the Scottish Charity Register held by the OSCR (there are no exemptions or exceptions from the registration requirement).

Members

▶ Of necessity, there must be at least two members in order for there to be a members' association. There may, or may not, be some commonality (or complete commonality) between the membership and the trustees.

▶ As stated above, the members do *not* have limited liability protection.

▶ There is a potential risk of personal liability for the members, particularly if the funds and assets prove insufficient to meet the debts and liabilities incurred as a result of the association's activities.

Charity trustees

▷ The members of the governing body (which is often called a committee) are the charity trustees.

▷ Officers are usually also trustees but this is not always the case.

Trustees' liabilities

▷ Since a members' association is unincorporated and does not offer limited liability protection, the trustees are at personal risk in its day-to-day activities. While in theory they can look to the association's funds and assets to indemnify them, this will not always provide sufficient protection. There are particular liability risks in the event of insolvency and certain other situations – for example, if there have been significant breaches of the constitution or if the trustees or officers have acted beyond the scope of their authority.

▷ It should be noted that the association itself cannot be held liable for wrongful acts committed by its representatives while they were acting on its behalf. The liability risks rest with the individuals in question. It is somewhat unclear as to the extent this liability could reach beyond the particular at fault individuals to all the officers or even to the members of the association. Again, the greatest risks arise if the funds and assets are insufficient to meet a claim.

Property trustees and custodian trustees

▷ Some members' associations appoint property trustees to hold the title to land that is held for the charitable purposes of the association.

▷ There may sometimes be custodian trustees holding other assets.

▷ When there are changes amongst such trustees it is necessary to transfer the title of the relevant property or other assets to the incoming trustees. This is administratively inefficient and involves some level of legal formalities and practical steps, with attendant costs.

▷ Care should be taken as to the exact role of such individuals and their legal responsibilities, powers and potential liabilities. Legal advice may be appropriate.

Officers

▷ Typically a members' association will appoint some officers – at least a chair of the trustees, possibly others such as a treasurer, secretary or membership officer.

▷ The role and responsibilities of the officers depends in part on the constitution of the particular charity. Otherwise it is a matter of the role and responsibilities and the levels of authority that have been given to each specific officer post by decision of the trustees.

- There are no statutory provisions to fall back on (as would be the case for many other legal forms, including CIOs and charitable CLGs).

- Any delegated authority should be very carefully documented and its exercise monitored by the trustees.

- It is strongly advisable to have written officer role descriptions.

Procedure

- Procedures largely depend on the terms of the constitution of the specific association.

Filing requirements

- A charitable members' association is subject to the usual charity filing obligations.

Notes

- The Scottish Law Commission has proposed a range of reforms to the law on unincorporated associations in Scotland, particularly to address the most significant problems (including issues of lack of capacity and concerns about the liability of trustees, officers and members).

- Very similar difficulties are acknowledged to apply to members' associations under the law of England and Wales and the Law Commission has proposed reforms.

Members' rights, duties and liabilities – companies

Introduction

A company limited by guarantee is one of the most common legal forms used by charities. It is, inherently, a membership organisation that has both members and trustees.

Checklist

Requirement to have members

▶ There must be members in any company.

▶ Typically, the articles of a charitable company will require a minimum of three members.

Duties – statutory

▶ Company members do not have specific statutory duties.

Legal responsibilities

▶ Members are bound by the terms of the company's articles and must observe the provisions of those articles.

▶ The articles may require certain specific things of members – for example, payment of an annual membership subscription applicable to their particular class of membership.

Rights – general

▶ Members of a company have a range of rights. Some are statutory (arising from the Companies Act), others arise from the company's articles.

▶ Many of the members' statutory rights cannot be overridden and any attempt to do so (for example, a contradictory clause in the articles of the company) will be ineffective.

▶ Other rights depend on the terms of the particular company's articles.

▶ There may be several membership classes, with some differences between the rights of those classes.

Members' statutory rights (Companies Act 2006)

▶ Some of the most important statutory rights of company members are:

1. to attend and vote at general meetings of the members (unless the particular membership class held does not have these rights);
2. to appoint a proxy to attend, speak and vote at general meetings of the members (instead of the member attending in person);
3. to vote on written resolutions of the members (providing the member is in a voting class of membership and is an 'eligible member' in respect of that resolution under the Companies Act provisions for written resolutions of the members); and
4. to be provided with copies of the annual trustees' report and accounts.

▶ Items 3 and 4 cannot be restricted or removed by provisions in the articles, they are absolute rights.

▶ Members also have access rights to the company's statutory registers; for further details see checklist: 'Inspection of registers (companies)'.

Matters reserved to the members

▶ In addition to their statutory rights, company members have particular rights in relation to matters reserved to the members. These are matters which the members have a formal legal right to deal with.

▶ Important examples of such matters (which are specified in the Companies Act 2006) are:

a) a special resolution to alter the articles (including an alteration to the charitable purposes [objects]);
b) a special resolution to change the name of the company (including a change to omit the word 'limited') [this applies unless the articles give a specific power to the trustees to alter the name, which is unlikely];
c) removal of a director from office as a director (particular procedures apply and the director has specific rights); and
d) removal of an auditor before the end of the relevant period of office (particular procedures apply and the auditor has specific rights).

Class rights

▶ Members in a particular class of membership have various protections with regard to their membership class rights. Those rights cannot be varied, directly or indirectly, unless the relevant class of members gives its consent to the variation.

Liabilities

▶ Members of a company have limited liability protection, in their capacity as members. This means that, under normal circumstances, they cannot be held liable for the company's debts and its other liabilities.

▷ The guarantee sum is fixed at the incorporation of the company and cannot subsequently be increased. It is not possible to set different levels of guarantee for different classes of members.

▷ Members of a CLG have a theoretical financial liability, under the terms of their members' guarantee. This is the sum each member agrees to pay if the company is ever wound up (typically it is a nominal sum, usually just £1). The guarantee is only payable if a liquidator makes a call for the payment during the course of winding up (this is extremely unlikely in practice).

▷ Members of a company limited by shares are liable to pay the sum they have agreed to pay to the company on their shares (often the nominal value of each share, sometimes the nominal value plus an extra sum of share premium). The members stand to lose that sum, in the event of insolvent liquidation, but they cannot be pursued for any additional contributions to the debts and liabilities of the company.

Procedure

▷ Most procedures relating to the nature, exercise and alteration of members' rights are governed by Companies Act provisions.

Filing requirements

▷ There are filing requirements at Companies House when members exercise some of their rights and when they deal with matters reserved to the members.

Notes

Governance

▷ The members' role in relation to governance of companies is largely passive (governance is a matter for the trustees). In most companies, the only part members play is to appoint some or all of the trustees at the annual general meeting (check the particular charity's articles as the relevant rules and procedures do vary from one company to another).

Trading subsidiaries

▷ Usually the parent charity will be the only member. However, if the charity is unincorporated, the subsidiary's shares will have to be held by individuals acting as nominees.

▷ It is common for the parent charity to have additional rights and powers, beyond the members' rights and powers that apply under the Companies Act. Check the terms of the subsidiary's articles to establish the exact details in each case.

Members' rights, duties and liabilities – unincorporated members' associations

Introduction

An unincorporated members' association is one of the most common legal forms used by charities. It is, inherently, a membership organisation that has both members and trustees.

Note that the association has no independent legal existence of its own, rather it is simply a collection of individuals associating together for an agreed purpose (the charitable purpose) and on agreed terms (as set out in the constitution). This has very important practical and legal implications for the individual members, as well as for the trustees (i.e. the committee).

Checklist

Requirement to have members

▶ There must be at least two members in any members' association. The constitution may specify a higher minimum number of members.

Duties – statutory

▶ There are no specific statutory duties of membership as unincorporated members' associations are essentially governed by common law, there is no specific Act of Parliament (as there is for companies or CIOs).

Legal responsibilities

▶ Members are bound by the terms of the charity's constitution and must observe those provisions.

▶ The constitution may require certain specific things of members – for example, payment of an annual membership subscription applicable to their particular class of membership.

Rights – general

▶ The rights of members of an unincorporated members' association depend on the terms of the particular association's constitution.

Class rights

▷ There may be several membership classes, with some differences between the rights of those classes. If so, the constitution may provide particular procedures that must be followed to alter the rights of any membership class.

Members' statutory rights

▷ The members do not have specific statutory rights.

Matters reserved to the members

▷ Some matters may be reserved to the members by the terms of the particular association's constitution, which may require a formal resolution of the members in particular situations or to deal with particular matters.

▷ Typically, these matters are likely to require a members' resolution:

▷ altering the constitution (including the charitable purposes);

▷ changing the name; and

▷ winding up.

Liabilities

▷ The members of an unincorporated members' association do *not* have the protection of limited liability.

▷ While the greatest risks of personal liability rest with the trustees (i.e. the members of the committee) and the officers of the association, in some extreme situations there can be a risk of members' liability.

Procedure

▷ Procedures required – for example, in relation to members' decision making, annual general meetings or other general meetings of the members, etc. – will depend on the terms of the particular association's constitution.

Filing requirements

▷ A charitable unincorporated members' association is subject to the usual public filing obligations for unincorporated charities.

Notes

▷ There is no separate public register of unincorporated members' associations.

Members' rights, duties and liabilities – CIOs

Introduction

A CIO is one of the legal forms used by charities. It is, inherently, a membership organisation that has both members and trustees.

Checklist

Requirement to have members

▶ There must be at least one member in any CIO (usually there will be more).

▶ The constitution is likely to specify a minimum number of members.

Duty – statutory

▶ A member of a CIO has a specific statutory duty to exercise their membership powers in a way the member decides, in good faith, will be most likely to further the charitable purposes of the CIO.

s. 220 Charities Act 2011

Legal responsibilities

▶ Members of a CIO are bound by the terms of the particular CIO's constitution and must observe the provisions of that constitution.

▶ The constitution may require certain specific things of members – for example, payment of an annual membership subscription applicable to their particular class of membership.

Rights – general

▶ Members of a CIO have a range of rights. Some are statutory (arising from the Charities Act and the CIO regulations); however, most depend on the terms of the particular CIO's constitution.

Class rights

▶ There may be several membership classes, with some differences between the rights of those classes. If so, the constitution may provide particular procedures that must be followed to alter the rights of any membership class.

Members' statutory rights

▶ Members of CIOs do not have the same range of statutory rights as the members of a charitable company have under company law. For example, they do not have a statutory right to appoint proxies to attend members' meetings (they may only do so if the particular CIO's constitution permits this).

▶ CIO members have a statutory right to inspect the CIO's register of members.

Matters reserved to the members

▶ Some matters are reserved to CIO members and so require a formal resolution of the members, in particular:

▷ alteration of a CIO's constitution;

▷ a decision to amalgamate with another CIO;

▷ a decision to transfer the CIO's undertaking to another CIO; and

▷ a decision to dissolve the CIO.

Liabilities

▶ The members of a CIO have the protection of limited liability.

▶ The members may, or may not, have a liability to contribute to the CIO's assets in the event of a winding up. If they do have such a liability the particular CIO's constitution will state this and specify an amount (typically a nominal sum, probably just £1).

Procedure

▶ Some procedures relating to the nature, exercise and alteration of members' rights are governed by the Charities Act and the CIO regulations; however, many depend largely or entirely on the terms of the particular CIO's constitution.

Filing requirements

▶ There may be filing requirements with the Charity Commission when members exercise some of their rights.

▶ There are usually filing requirements when a CIO's members deal with matters reserved to the members.

Notes

▶ There is a public right of access to a CIO's register of trustees (but not to its register of members).

Governance

▶ The members' role in relation to governance of CIOs is largely passive (governance is a matter for the trustees). However, individual members should consider their statutory duty as a CIO member when exercising their membership rights (see above).

▶ In most CIOs, the main role of the members is to appoint some or all of the trustees at the annual general meeting (check the particular CIO's constitution as the relevant rules and procedures do vary from one CIO to another).

Scotland

▶ The position regarding SCIOs is broadly comparable. However, note that the statutory duties are:

   ▷ to act in the interests of the SCIO; and

   ▷ to seek, in good faith, to ensure the SCIO acts in a manner that is consistent with its charitable purposes.

s. 55 Charities and Trustee Investment (Scotland) Act 2005

Members' rights, duties and liabilities – SCIOs

Introduction

A SCIO (Scottish charitable incorporated organisation) is one of the legal forms used by charities in Scotland. It is, inherently, a membership organisation that has both members and trustees.

Checklist

Requirement to have members

▶ There must be at least two members in any SCIO (the English equivalent is permitted to have a sole member, subject to the terms of its own constitution).

▶ The constitution may specify a higher minimum number of members.

Duty – statutory

▶ A member of a SCIO has specific statutory duties:

  ▷ to act in the interests of the SCIO; and

  ▷ to seek, in good faith, to ensure the SCIO acts in a manner that is consistent with its charitable purposes.

s. 55 Charities and Trustee Investment (Scotland) Act 2005

Legal responsibilities

▶ Members of a SCIO are bound by the terms of the particular SCIO's constitution and must observe the provisions of that constitution.

▶ The constitution may require certain specific things of members – for example, payment of an annual membership subscription applicable to their particular class of membership.

Rights – general

▶ Members of a SCIO have a range of rights. Some are statutory (arising from the Charities and Trustee Investment (Scotland) Act 2005 and the associated SCIO regulations); however, most depend on the terms of the particular SCIO's constitution.

Class rights

▷ There may be several membership classes, with some differences between the rights of those classes. If so, the constitution may provide particular procedures that must be followed to alter the rights of any membership class.

Members' statutory rights

▷ Members of SCIOs do not have the same range of statutory rights as the members of a charitable company have under company law. For example, they do not have a statutory right to appoint proxies to attend members' meetings (they may only do so if the particular SCIO's constitution permits this).

▷ SCIO members have a statutory right to inspect the SCIO's register of members.

Matters reserved to the members

▷ Some matters are reserved to SCIO members and so require a formal resolution of the members, in particular:

▷ alteration of a SCIO's constitution (including its charitable purposes);

▷ a decision to amalgamate with another SCIO;

▷ a decision to transfer the SCIO's undertaking to another SCIO; and

▷ a decision to dissolve the SCIO.

Members' meeting

▷ A SCIO must hold a meeting of its members at least once in every 15 months. Note that there is no opt-out available (as would be the case for a charitable CLG which is only obliged to hold an AGM if its own articles specify a requirement for an AGM).

▷ The Charities and Trustee Investment (Scotland) Act 2005 does not specify the business for the AGM, so that will be subject to any relevant provisions in the constitution or, if the constitution is silent, the trustees will determine the business to be dealt with at the meeting.

Liabilities

▷ The members of a SCIO have the protection of limited liability.

▷ The members may, or may not, have a liability to contribute to the SCIO's assets in the event of a winding up. If they do have such a liability the particular SCIO's constitution will state this and specify an amount (typically a nominal sum, probably just £1).

Procedure

▶ Some procedures relating to the nature, exercise and alteration of members' rights are governed by the Charities Act and the CIO regulations; however, many depend largely or entirely on the terms of the particular CIO's constitution.

Filing requirements

▶ There may be filing requirements with the OSCR when members exercise some of their rights.

▶ There are usually filing requirements when a SCIO's members deal with matters reserved to the members.

Notes

▶ There is a public right of access to a SCIO's register of trustees (but not to its register of members).

▶ Note that a SCIO cannot convert to another legal form, amalgamate with another SCIO or seek its own removal from the register of charities without dissolving itself.

Governance

▶ The members' role in relation to governance of SCIOs is largely passive (governance is a matter for the trustees). However, individual members should consider their statutory duties as a SCIO member when exercising their membership rights (see above).

▶ In most SCIOs, the main role of the members is to appoint some or all of the trustees at the annual general meeting (check the particular SCIO's constitution as the relevant rules and procedures do vary from one SCIO to another).

Membership classes and variation of rights

Introduction

Some, though not all, charities have a formal membership. Whether or not there is a membership structure depends on the legal form of the particular charity. Certain legal forms require a membership – for example, charitable companies, charitable incorporated organisations, Scottish charitable incorporated organisations, unincorporated members' associations and charitable industrial and provident societies.

Members' rights will in part depend on the terms of the particular charity's constitution.

In some legal forms of charity there are also some statutory members' rights (for example, charitable companies, CIOs and SCIOs).

A membership charity may have different classes of membership, where the rights and responsibilities of each class differ from those of the other classes.

Checklist

▶ If there are different membership classes, the constitution of the particular charity probably specifies this and sets out the main rights and responsibilities of each membership class.

▶ Some detailed matters, such as the different membership application fees or annual subscriptions for the various membership classes, the members' code of conduct and the disciplinary procedures in relation to members, may be dealt with in subsidiary rules or bye-laws.

▶ As a rule of thumb, the most fundamental rights of membership should be dealt with in the main constitution (e.g. voting rights at general meetings of the members) while lower level matters, such as different annual subscription levels, can be dealt with in subsidiary rules or bye-laws.

▶ Care must be taken to ensure the rights of membership classes are respected and properly observed.

▷ Particular care must be taken when making any changes to membership classes that involve any variation of the rights of that class.

▷ The constitution and/or statutory provisions may specify how changes to membership classes can be made and provide safeguards for membership class rights.

▷ The consent of the members in the class affected is likely to be needed in order to make changes to the rights of a membership class. This will probably apply to indirect, as well as direct, variations of the rights of a membership class.

CIOs

▷ The CIO regulations state that if a CIO has more than one class of membership then the different classes of membership together with their voting rights, *must* be set out in the constitution.

Companies

▷ If a charitable company has more than one class of members, it is strongly advisable to set out details of each membership class and the rights of the classes in the articles.

Procedure

▷ Procedures vary, depending on the legal form of the charity and applicable provisions in its constitution and/or statutory provisions.

▷ A variation of rights often involves changes to the charity's constitution.

Unincorporated members' association

▷ The constitution should set out procedures for varying membership rights and altering membership classes. This may include obtaining a specified majority vote in favour from the membership class affected and/or the membership as a whole.

▷ Some changes to the constitution are likely to be necessary in order to make the changes and/or in consequence of the changes.

CIOs and SCIOs

▷ The constitution should set out procedures for varying membership rights and altering membership classes. This may include obtaining a specified majority vote in favour from the membership class affected and/or the membership as a whole.

▷ Some changes to the constitution are likely to be necessary in order to make the changes and/or in consequence of the changes.

Charitable companies

▶ In a charitable company, the variation of the rights of a class of members requires the prior consent of each membership class affected. This is the case for indirect as well as direct variations of rights.

s. 631 Companies
Act 2006

▶ If the articles provide a written method for variation of membership class rights that must be followed. Otherwise class consents must be obtained either:

▷ in writing from at least three-quarters of the members in the class affected; or

▷ by a special resolution passed at a separate meeting of the members in the class affected.

▶ If the alteration requires any amendment to the articles, a special resolution of the membership as a whole will also be required to make that change.

▶ The courts generally take a wide view of what is a membership class right and what is a variation of a members' class right. It is therefore advisable to err on the side of caution and obtain class consents if there is a possibility that any change amounts to a variation of rights.

Filing requirements

▶ The creation or removal of a membership class or the variations of the rights of a membership class will need to be notified to relevant regulators where changes are made to:

▷ a charitable company;

▷ a CIO;

▷ a SCIO; or

▷ some other legal forms of membership charity (e.g. a charitable industrial and provident society).

Companies House

▶ In a charitable company, the creation of a new membership class, the naming of a membership class or the alteration of the name of an existing class, as well as any change to the rights of a membership class, must be notified to Companies House using the relevant forms (or electronic equivalent). Class consents to the variation of members' rights must also be filed, together with any special resolution to alter the articles and a printed copy of the altered articles.

Notes

Membership records

▶ Care should be taken to ensure records are clear with regard to who the formal members are and what class of membership each member holds (e.g. the register of members or membership list).

▶ Contemporaneous records should be made when new members join and when any members leave, to ensure the record of the formal members is accurate and up-to-date.

▶ The creation of membership classes and the variation of the rights of any class should also be recorded promptly and accurately.

▶ Note the statutory requirements to keep registers of members that apply to charitable companies, CIOs and SCIOs – see checklist: 'Records'.

Informal 'membership'

▶ Some charities have an informal 'membership', that is a group of individuals who, while perhaps described as 'members', are not members in any formal legal sense. Rather they are in a less formal relationship with the charity, perhaps as supporters or practical volunteers. It is important to distinguish any such groups from those who are formal legal members (with rights and responsibilities in respect of the charity).

▶ It is best to avoid use of the term 'member' in such situations, choosing an alternative term instead (such as 'supporter' or 'associate').

▶ The constitution should be carefully worded to avoid confusing genuine formal members with other groups – it is important to draw distinctions clearly.

Memorandum – company incorporation

Introduction

The initial members of a company are its 'subscribers' on incorporation. They automatically become the first members as the certificate of incorporation is issued by the Registrar of Companies.

A charitable company must usually have at least three initial members (i.e. three subscribers).

Checklist

▶ The subscribers must be stated on the memorandum.

▶ The memorandum is one of the various documents required to incorporate a new company.

Procedure

▶ Most new incorporations are filed at Companies House by electronic communication (using an electronic version of the memorandum).

▶ It remains possible to file a paper-based application for incorporation; however, the statutory incorporation fee is significantly higher.

Filing requirements

▶ The names of the subscribers must be provided to Companies House in order to incorporate a new company.

Notes

▶ For a share company, it is not necessary to state in the memorandum how many shares each subscriber is taking (Companies House will reject the document if that information is included).

▶ It is important to distinguish the memorandum required to notify the names of the first members when a new company is incorporated (in accordance with the Companies Act 2006) from the old style 'memorandum' that formed part of an old company's constitution under the Companies Acts 1985–1989. See checklist: 'Memorandum – old companies'.

Memorandum – old companies

Introduction

'Old' companies incorporated prior to 1 October 2009 had a two-part constitution:

▷ memorandum of association, which largely dealt with the external aspects of the company; and

▷ articles of association, which largely dealt with the internal administration of the company.

A new company, incorporated on or after 1 October 2009 under the Companies Act 2006 rules and procedures, simply has articles.

Checklist

▶ The memorandum of an old company (limited by guarantee) contained these provisions:

▷ the name of the company (at incorporation);

▷ a statement of the territory of registration (i.e. that the company was to be registered in England and Wales [or simply 'Wales' if the company intended always to keep its registered office in Wales]);

▷ the objects clause (typically this includes powers in support of the objects);

▷ the limited liability clause; and

▷ the statement of the members' guarantee.

▶ The memorandum remains effective and is now to be treated as part of the company's articles.

▶ Any statement of the company's objects effectively acts as a restriction on the activities that company can undertake.

Procedure

▶ Certain alterations can be made to the memorandum, including alterations to the company's objects and its powers. However, in the case of a charitable company, any alteration to the objects or to the winding up clause, or any relaxation of the restrictions on benefits to trustees, is a regulated alteration that requires the prior consent of the Charity Commission.

▷ In Scotland, the relevant legislation requires the OSCR's prior consent for similar changes.

▷ Some matters cannot be altered (e.g. the amount of the existing members' guarantee).

Filing requirements

▷ A company's original memorandum will be on the public record at Companies House.

▷ Details of all subsequent alterations made to the memorandum should also be filed at Companies House.

▷ A change to the objects does not take effect until the relevant documents and form CC04 have been registered on the company's public record by Companies House. (A copy of the Charity Commission consent to the change must also be filed, if the company is a charity.)

Notes

▷ The list of subscribers attached to the memorandum is a historic record of the initial members of the company at the date of incorporation.

▷ Note that CLGs are not required to notify changes amongst their members to Companies House. So to ascertain the current members of a CLG an access request should be made for an inspection of the relevant company's register of members.

▷ Many old companies choose to undertake a full modernisation of their memorandum and articles, moving all the surviving effective provisions of the old memorandum into one comprehensive modern set of articles. Specialist advice should be taken to ensure such changes are made effectively and in accordance with the provisions of the Companies Act 2006 and the various transitional regulations that apply to such 'old' companies.

▷ It is important to distinguish the memorandum that forms part of an old company's constitution under the Companies Acts 1985–1989 from the 'memorandum' that is used to notify the names of the first members (subscribers) when a new company is incorporated under the Companies Act 2006. See checklist: 'Memorandum – company incorporation'.

Minutes

Introduction

Charities should keep records of formal meetings of the trustees and formal members' meetings, such as an annual general meeting. These are usually kept as minutes.

Checklist

Companies – meeting records (general)

▶ The Companies Act requires companies to keep records of meetings of their directors and meetings of their members.

▶ If the meeting was held on or after 1 October 2008 the record must be kept for at least 10 years. If it was held prior to that date the record should be kept indefinitely.

Companies – location where records are kept

▶ Records of general meetings of the members of a company must be kept at the registered office.

▶ Records of board meetings can be kept wherever the board considers appropriate.

Companies – access to meeting records

▶ The auditors (or independent examiner) may access records of meetings of the members and board meetings.

▶ Members and directors can access records of members' meetings.

▶ Directors can access records of board meetings. There is no statutory right for members to access these records.

CIOs

▶ CIOs must keep certain records, including records of:

▷ meetings of their members; and

▷ meetings of their trustees.

▶ The details required in records of trustees' meetings include the names of the trustees present at the meeting, the decisions made at those meetings and, where appropriate, the reasons for those decisions.

▶ Usually a CIO keeps these records in minutes of the relevant meetings.

▶ CIOs are also obliged to keep records of any decisions made by their trustees otherwise than in meetings (e.g. decisions taken by written resolutions).

▶ All these records must be kept for at least six years from the date of the meeting, decision etc.

Other charities

▶ Check the provisions of the constitution, which may include requirements for minutes of meetings, access rights and other relevant procedures etc.

▶ Consider good practice and adopt appropriate procedures (see 'Procedure' below).

Procedure

▶ Minutes of meetings should be:

▷ accurate;

▷ brief; and

▷ complete.

Minutes of record

▶ Principally meeting minutes are minutes of record – setting out the basic record of the meeting itself (type of meeting, when and where it was held, who participated in a formal capacity [e.g. as a trustee or member], confirmation that a quorum was present and a record of who else was present and in what capacity) and a record of the decisions taken at the meeting.

Minutes of narration

▶ Sometimes it is appropriate to include minutes of narration – for example, the principal elements of a discussion that preceded a key or complex decision, the board's reasons for determining a particular course of action (e.g. the financial evidence of the need for, or consequences of, a particular decision).

Authentication of minutes – general

▶ It is common practice for minutes to be authenticated by the signature of the chair of the board, who will usually have chaired the meeting that the minutes record.

Authentication of minutes – companies

▶ If the minutes of a meeting of a company's members or directors are 'authenticated' by the chair of the meeting in question, or the chair of the next meeting, they are *prima facie* evidence of the matters that they record.

▶ The Companies Act 2006 permits electronic authentication methods or signature of a traditional hard copy of the minutes.

Custody and security

▶ Charities should ensure that authorisation procedures, storage and access arrangements ensure the integrity and security of minutes of meetings. Consider in particular:

  ▷ fire, flood, theft and accidental loss; and

  ▷ ensuring that access is only granted to appropriate and authorised people (whether in person or via remote electronic access).

Documents

▶ Copies of any key documents referred to in the minutes should be kept with the minutes.

▶ If the meeting authorises signature or execution of a document by or on behalf of the charity, a copy of the signed/executed document should be kept with the minutes (e.g. a cash flow forecast or budget, bank mandate or contract).

Filing requirements

▶ Minutes do not need to be filed with the charity regulators or any other relevant regulators (e.g. Companies House). They are internal records.

▶ However, some decisions and certain types of resolutions will need to be notified to or certified copies filed with, the charity regulators and/or Companies House.

▶ In the case of companies, some members' resolutions that must be filed with Companies House need to be accompanied by relevant statutory company forms.

Notes

▶ All charities will hold periodic meetings of their board of trustees.

▶ SCIOs (Scottish charitable incorporated organisations) have a statutory obligation to hold a meeting of their members at least once in every 15 months.

▶ There is no comparable statutory requirement for CIOs (although some CIOs have a constitutional requirement to hold regular meetings of their members).

Name change

Introduction

Charities can change their formal legal names. There are, however, various restrictions on the use of particular words (including 'charity' and 'charitable') and the use of other words may need justification or the permission of a third party.

Care should be taken to ensure a proposed new name does not breach any applicable restrictions or infringe the legal rights of any other organisation (including trademarks or service marks, rights in relation to domain names, company names or trading names).

A range of searches and enquiries may be appropriate to establish if there are existing similar or identical names (e.g. the registers held by Companies House, the Charity Commission, the OSCR, Charity Commission for Northern Ireland, Intellectual Property Office [trademarks, service marks, patents etc.])

Checklist

▶ Check availability of the proposed name.

▶ Make appropriate searches and enquiries in relation to names and name-related rights of third parties. In some circumstances it may be appropriate to obtain specialist professional advice.

▶ Consider whether there are restrictions on the use of all or part of the proposed name, or whether justification is required or any third party permissions or consents are needed.

▶ Ascertain and follow the correct procedures required for a name change given the legal form of the particular charity.

Companies – general

▶ The name of a private company must end in 'Limited' or 'Ltd' unless the company has formal permission to omit that from its name.

▶ There are various other restrictions relating to company names; see checklists: 'Names – restrictions' and 'Business names'.

CIOs

▶ The name must end in CIO or Charitable Incorporated Organisation.

SCIOs

▶ The name must end in SCIO or Scottish Charitable Incorporated Organisation.

Procedure

Companies

▶ A company may change its name by:

s. 77 Companies Act 2006

▷ special resolution of its members (which must be filed at Companies House – see 'Procedure' below); or

▷ any other means provided for by the company's articles.

▶ Note that the change does not become effective until the necessary items have been filed with Companies House and the Registrar of Companies has placed them on the company's public record.

CIOs, SCIOs, UMAs and other membership charities

▶ A resolution of the members will be required. The constitution is likely to specify relevant procedures such as notice periods or the majority vote required to pass the resolution.

Unincorporated charitable trusts

▶ The trustees may have a specific power to alter the charity's name. Check the trust deed/document as it may provide such a power and/or set out relevant procedures.

Filing requirements

Companies

▶ A copy of the special resolution and the required form (NM01 Notice of Change of Name by Resolution) must be filed at Companies House. A statutory change of name fee is payable to Companies House.

▶ A copy of the articles, showing the proposed new name, should also be filed.

▶ If the change was made by some other method permitted by the articles, the required form is form NM04 (Notice of change of name by means provided for in the articles).

▶ A certificate of incorporation on change of name will be issued by Companies House which will include the date on which the change took effect.

Notes

▷ The relevant charity regulator(s) should be notified of any change of name.

▷ Ensure all relevant documents and other items are altered, including website, email footers and other relevant disclosures.

▷ Change notices and signs at the charity's premises.

▷ Ensure the bank is notified and any procedures the bank requires are followed.

▷ Ensure the charity's name is altered on cheque books etc.

▷ Notify relevant official agencies (e.g. HMRC) and other relevant regulators.

▷ Notify suppliers, customers and any partner organisations that the charity works with.

▷ If the charity has an official seal, adopt a new seal and arrange safe disposal of the old seal.

More information

▷ Companies House: www.companieshouse.gov.uk.

▷ Intellectual Property Office: www.gov.uk/government/organisation/intellectual-property-office.

▷ Domain names and accredited domain name registrars: ICANN (Internet Corporation for Assigned Names and Numbers): www.icann.org.uk.

Names – restrictions

Introduction

There are various legal restrictions relevant to charity names. The use of particular words is restricted (including 'charity' and 'charitable') and the use of other words may need justification or the permission of a third party.

Care should be taken to ensure a name does not breach any applicable restrictions or infringe the legal rights of any other organisation (including trademarks or service marks, rights in relation to domain names, company names or trading names).

Checklist

▶ Consider:

▷ the general restrictions relevant to charity names;

▷ restrictions that apply because of the particular legal form of the charity (CLG, CIO etc.); and

▷ intellectual property rights and other legal rights of third parties.

Companies – omission of 'Limited'

▶ A company can apply for permission to omit 'Limited' or 'Ltd' (or the Welsh equivalent) from its name provided it complies with these conditions:

a) it is a private company; and

b) it is a charity; or

s. 60 Companies Act 2006

c) it is limited by guarantee, its objects are the promotion or regulation of commerce, art, science, education, religion, charity or any profession, and anything incidental or conducive thereto, *and* the company's articles:

    i. require the company's income to be applied in promoting those objects;

    ii. prohibit the payment of dividends, or any return of capital, to its members; and

    iii. require all the assets that would otherwise be available to its members generally on a winding up to be transferred to another body with similar objects (or another body the objects of which are the promotion of charity and anything incidental or conducive thereto).

▶ If an existing company that uses 'Limited' or 'Ltd' wishes to seek this permission it must follow a formal change of name procedure and submit the required documents, fee and form NE01 (Exemption from requirement as to use of 'limited' or 'cyfyngedig' on change of name).

Companies – general names restrictions

ss. 66(1) and 53
Companies Act 2006

▶ A private company's name must end in 'Limited', 'Ltd' or the Welsh equivalent of either, unless the company has permission to omit that (see above).

▶ A name cannot be registered if:

  ▷ it is the same as another name already registered on the index of company names at Companies House;

  ▷ its use would constitute an offence; or

  ▷ the name itself is offensive.

▶ There are statutory provisions that govern how a name is considered 'the same as' another name. They require certain words to be disregarded when names are compared by the Registrar of Companies.

s. 1099 Companies
Act 2006

▶ There are also regulations that prescribe the letters, signs and symbols that can be used in a company name.

Companies – approvals

▶ Approval is required for the registration of a name that would be likely to give the impression that the company is connected with:

  ▷ Her Majesty's Government, any part of the Scottish administration, the Welsh Assembly Government or Her Majesty's Government in Northern Ireland;

  ▷ a local authority; or

  ▷ any public authority specified in regulations (see Company, Limited Liability Partnership and Business Names (Public Authorities) Regulations 2009 SI 2982 of 2009).

Companies – sensitive words

▶ Regulations prescribe a list of words and expressions that are considered 'sensitive'. Approval is required for their use in a company name.

▶ The restrictions include the plural and possessive forms of the words and expressions and, where relevant, the feminine forms.

▶ See the Company, Limited Liability Partnership and Business (Sensitive Words and Expressions) Regulations 2014 which merge and reduce previous sets of regulations (in force from 1 May 2014).

Companies – 'too like' names and directions for change

ss. 67 and 68
Companies Act 2006

▶ Within 12 months of a company name being registered the Secretary of State may order the company to change its name if the name is 'too like' a name already registered on the index of companies at Companies House.

▶ There is a formal objection procedure which commences with an application to the New Companies Section of Companies House.

▶ The Secretary of State has discretion and will consider each case on its own merits. Successful objections are relatively rare.

Companies – similarity to another name in which a person has goodwill

ss. 69–74
Companies Act 2006

▶ A person may apply for a company to be directed to change its name on the grounds that it is the same as a name in which the applicant has goodwill, or that it is so similar that its use in the UK would be likely to mislead by suggesting a connection with the applicant.

▶ In this context, 'goodwill' includes reputation of any description.

▶ The legal provisions are intended to address previous problems relating to 'squatting' on company names (often described as opportunistic company name registrations).

▶ Company names adjudicators, based at the Intellectual Property Office, deal with such applications and regulations specify procedures, fees, the process for each side to provide evidence etc. See the Company Names Adjudicator Rules 2008 SI 1738 of 2008.

Companies – power of Secretary of State to order a change of name

ss. 64, 75 and 76
Companies Act

▶ The Secretary of State may order a company to change its name:

▷ within five years of registration of the name, if it appears to the Secretary of State that misleading information has been given for the purposes of registration of a particular name, or that an undertaking or assurance given for that purpose has not been fulfilled;

▷ if it is a company whose name does not include 'Limited' and it appears to the Secretary of State that the company is no longer entitled to the exemption; or

▷ at any time, if the company name gives so misleading an indication of the company's activities as to be likely to cause harm to the public.

CIOs

▶ There are specific legal rules regarding the names of CIOs. They include that the name must end in CIO or Charitable Incorporated Organisation.

▶ The Charity Commission will not accept a name that would be misleading, offensive or too similar to the name of an existing charity, unless the CIO is replacing that charity.

▶ It also has powers to require a CIO to change its name if the name is misleading, offensive or too similar to another charity.

▶ There are also legal restrictions on a CIO using the same name as:

▷ an existing company, unless it is a charitable company that is converting to a CIO; or

▷ a former company or CIO that underwent insolvent liquidation.

SCIOs

▶ There are similar legal rules regarding the names of SCIOs. They include that the name must end in SCIO or Scottish Charitable Incorporated Organisation.

Business names

▶ The business names restrictions and requirements extend to companies and to partnerships or individuals that use a business name.

▶ A business name is a name other than the formal legal name (i.e. for a company its registered name) that is used by the company in connection with the company's activities.

▶ The relevant regulations:

▷ require approval for a business name that suggests connection with government or a public authority;

▷ require approval for the use of various prescribed sensitive words or expressions in a business name;

▷ require comments to be obtained from government departments or other relevant bodies in certain cases;

▷ enable approvals to be withdrawn subsequently, in some circumstances;

▷ ban the use of names that give an inappropriate indication that an organisation is a particular type of company or has a particular legal form; and

▷ ban the use of names that give a misleading indication of activities.

Charities – general

▶ 'Charity', 'charitable' and 'trust' (used in the context of a charity) may only be used in the names of bona fide charities.

▶ The charity names restrictions and charitable status disclosure requirements of charity law must be met by all charities. These are set out in the Charities Act 2011 (England and Wales) and the Charities and Trustee Investment (Scotland) Act 2005 and associated regulations.

Filing requirements

▶ A charity's formal name, any previous names, and any operational name it does use, or has used in the past, are recorded on the public register of charities held by the relevant charity regulator(s).

▶ Company names and any previous names, are recorded on the public register of companies held by Companies House.

▶ There is no register of business names.

Notes

▶ Note that there are various statutory requirements that require charities to disclose, on a wide range of documents and communications made by or on behalf of the charity:

  ▷ their full formal names;

  ▷ their charitable status; and

  ▷ various other information and details.

▶ See checklists: 'Disclosure obligations – communications and documents' and 'Disclosure obligations – premises (company law)'.

More information

▶ Companies House: www.gov.uk/government/organisations/companies-house.

▶ Charity Commission: www.gov.uk/government/organisations/charity-commission.

▶ Intellectual Property Office: www.gov.uk/governments/organisations/intellectual-property-office.

▶ Domain names and accredited domain name registrars: ICANN (Internet Corporation for Assigned Names and Numbers): www.icann.org.uk.

Notices (general meetings) – contents

Introduction

A general meeting is a formal meeting of the members of a charity.

In most membership charities, such meetings will be held from time to time because they are required by law (e.g. the statutory general meeting of the members of a SCIO) or by the charity's constitution (e.g. the constitution may require the holding of an annual general meeting of the members). A general meeting may also be held because there is a particular decision or authorisation needed that must be dealt with by resolution of the members (rather than by a decision of the trustees).

As such a meeting is a formal meeting, there will normally be a formal written notice of the meeting.

Checklist

▶ A general meeting is usually convened at the decisions of the trustees, who will approve the draft notice of the meeting and authorise issue of the notice to the members and any other persons entitled to receive notice of members' meetings.

▶ Notice periods may be specified in the charity's constitution; however, note that for companies there are also statutory rules in the Companies Act regarding minimum notice periods.

Notice contents – general

▶ State the type of meeting (for example, annual general meeting or extraordinary general meeting) and:

▷ date;

▷ location; and

▷ start time.

▶ Provide any relevant details of the practical arrangements, such as disability access to the venue, special facilities that will be available at the meeting to assist participants who have special needs (e.g. hearing difficulties).

▶ Enclose any relevant accompanying documents (such as a proxy form).

▶ If proxies can be used, ensure the notice or accompanying documents set out how to return completed forms and specify the deadline for their return.

Notice contents – companies

▶ Notices of a general meeting of the members of a company must comply with relevant Companies Act requirements with regard to contents (see 'Procedure' below).

Procedure

Companies

▶ The trustees normally decide to convene the meeting.

▶ The board approves the contents and the issue of the notice of the meeting.

▶ Include the appropriate basic details (see 'Notice contents – general' above).

▶ The general nature of all ordinary business should be specified.

▶ Where formal resolutions will be proposed, it is best practice to set out the full texts of each resolution, in numbered order.

▶ If a special resolution is to be considered, the notice must indicate that the relevant resolution is to be proposed as a special resolution and set out the full text of that resolution.

▶ The notice must state the full address of the registered office.

▶ A statement must be included regarding proxy rights. This must indicate that members can appoint proxies and that proxies do not have to be members of the company themselves.

▶ Information should also be given as to any prescribed form of proxy to be used, how proxies can be submitted for the meeting and the deadline for their submission. This can be set out in the notice or in accompanying documents (for example, within a specimen form of proxy that is sent out with the notice).

Other charities

▶ The trustees normally decide to convene the meeting.

▶ The board approves the contents and the issue of the notice of the meeting.

▶ Include the appropriate basic details (see 'Notice contents – general' above).

▶ The general nature of all ordinary business should be specified.

▶ Where formal resolutions will be proposed, it is best practice to set out the full texts of each resolution, in numbered order.

▶ Proxy rights depend on the terms of the individual charity's constitution. Depending on the details of that constitution, it may be appropriate or necessary to include information regarding proxy rights in the meeting notice.

Filing requirements

▶ Notices of general meetings do not have to be filed. A copy should be retained in the company's internal records.

Notes

▶ The members of a company have an absolute statutory right to appoint a proxy of their choice to attend, speak and vote at a general meeting. This cannot be overridden (any contrary clause in the company's articles is ineffective).

▶ Proxy rights in charities that are in other legal forms (including CIOs) will depend on the terms of the particular charity's constitution.

▶ Electronic communication can usually be used to despatch notices and for the return of completed proxy forms. The Companies Act sets out detailed provisions in relation to both matters for companies. For charities in other legal forms, these matters largely depend on the specific constitution of the particular charity.

Objects – alteration England and Wales

Introduction

▶ The law permits the alteration of charitable purposes within certain parameters (broadly the alterations must remain within the spirit of the original purposes) and provided that:

▷ the prior written consent of the Charity Commission is obtained; and

▷ the relevant procedures are followed (see further below).

▶ Any purported alteration of objects without the required consent of the Charity Commission is ineffective.

Checklist

▶ Alterations to the objects of a CIO do not take effect until the Charity Commission has recorded the changes in the CIO's public entry on the register of charities.

▶ Alterations to the objects of a charitable company do not take effect until the Registrar of Companies registers the required documents on the company's public record.

▶ In most other circumstances, an alteration of objects takes immediate effect (there are exceptions).

Procedure

▶ The procedure required varies depending on the legal form of the charity and, to some extent, the provisions of its constitution.

▶ Prior Charity Commission consent is required for any alteration of the objects of a registered charity in England and Wales.

Charitable company

▶ An alteration to the objects of a charitable company requires a special resolution of its members, passed at a general meeting. A 75%

majority vote in favour is necessary to carry the resolution (calculated on the votes cast).

▷ Alternatively, the resolution can be passed in accordance with the Companies Act 2006 procedures for statutory written resolutions of a company's members.

Charitable incorporated organisation

▷ A members' resolution is required. A 75 % majority vote in favour is necessary to carry that resolution (calculated on the votes cast at the relevant members' meeting).

Unincorporated members' association

▷ Follow the procedures set out in the power of amendment set out in the constitution. This will include a requirement for a members' resolution in favour of the proposed alteration.

▷ If there is no power of amendment, see further below.

Unincorporated trust

▷ Follow the procedures set out in the power of amendment in the trust deed. This will include a requirement for a trustees' resolution in favour of the proposed alteration. It may also require the execution of a deed of amendment (especially in older trusts).

▷ If there is no power of amendment, see further below.

Small unincorporated charities without power to amend objects

▷ If the charity has no constitutional power to alter its objects, does not hold land for its charitable purposes (or any part of those purposes) and has annual income under £10,000, the trustees may resolve to alter its charitable purposes provided they are satisfied that:

1. it is expedient in the interests of the charity for its current purposes to be replaced; and
2. so far as reasonably practicable, the proposed new purposes are similar to those they will replace.

▷ If the charity is a membership charity, the trustees must satisfy themselves on the above points and then obtain approval of the members to the proposed changes. A two-thirds majority in favour is required.

▷ Copies of the relevant resolution(s), with the trustees' reasons for making the changes, must be filed with the Charity Commission. The Commission can require the proposed changes to be advertised. If it does not think the changes are appropriate, the Commission can prevent them becoming effective. Otherwise, the changes take effect 60 days after the documents are provided to the Commission.

Charities that have land and are without power to alter their objects

▶ Legal advice should be taken. It may be necessary to obtain a Charity Commission scheme to make an alteration.

Larger charities without power to alter their objects

▶ Legal advice should be taken. It may be necessary to obtain a Charity Commission scheme to make an alteration.

Filing requirements

▶ A charitable company must file a copy of its articles including the altered objects, a copy of the relevant special resolution, a copy of the relevant Charity Commission consent and form CC04 (Statement of company's objects) at Companies House. Note that the change does *not* take effect until the Registrar of Companies places the resolution, articles and form live on the company's public record.

▶ Details of the altered objects and a certified copy of the relevant members' resolution (membership charities) or trustees' resolution (unincorporated trusts where the trustees exercised a power of amendment to make the change) must be filed with the Charity Commission.

▶ Note the additional filing requirements for small charities without constitutional power to alter their objects (summarised above).

Notes

▶ A 'cross-border' charity that is also registered in one or more of the other UK jurisdictions will also have to obtain prior consent to the proposed alteration from the other relevant charity regulator(s) (the OSCR and/or the Charity Commission for Northern Ireland).

Objects (charitable purposes) – Northern Ireland

Introduction

To be a charity in Northern Ireland:

1. an organisation must have objects (purposes) that are within the 'descriptions' of charitable purposes set out in the Charities Act (Northern Ireland) 2008; and
2. those objects must be 'for the public benefit' (in a charitable way).

Checklist

▶ The objects (i.e. the charitable purposes of the particular charity) are usually set out in the charity's governing document.

▶ The objects of the charity must fall within the descriptions of charitable purposes set out in the Charities Act (Northern Ireland) 2008.

▶ The objects must be for the public benefit (in a charitable way).

▶ Note that the Charities Act (Northern Ireland) 2008 uses the phrase 'charitable purposes' in relation to the objects of a charity. It sets out a list of 'descriptions' of purposes that are potentially charitable in Northern Ireland (see further below).

▶ Charities that are more recently established, or older charities that have altered their objects or fully updated their constitutions, often adopt the modern terminology 'charitable purposes' to describe what were previously termed their 'objects'.

▶ A charity must act within its objects at all times.

▶ A charity must ensure its funds and assets are applied in pursuit of its charitable objects.

List of potentially charitable purposes (Charities Act (Northern Ireland) 2008

▶ Note that not every purpose of an organisation that is within the *ordinary language* meaning of any of the entries on this list will be charitable. The particular circumstances will determine whether or not the specific purpose, in that particular organisation, does fall within the legal boundaries of any of these 'descriptions of charitable purposes'.

1. The prevention or relief of poverty.
2. The advancement of education.
3. The advancement of religion. 'Religion' includes:
    > a religion which involves belief in one god or more than one god; and
    > any analogous philosophical belief (whether or not involving belief in a god).
4. The advancement of health or the saving of lives. The advancement of health includes the prevention or relief of sickness, disease or human suffering.
5. The advancement of citizenship or community development. This includes rural or urban regeneration, and the promotion of civic responsibility, volunteering, the voluntary section or the effectiveness or efficiency of charities.
6. The advancement of the arts, culture, heritage or science.
7. The advancement of amateur sport, i.e. sports or games that promote health by involving physical or mental skill or exertion.
8. The advancement of human rights, conflict resolution or reconciliation or the promotion of religious or racial harmony or equality and diversity (this includes the advancement of peace and good community relations).
9. The advancement of environmental protection or improvement.
10. The relief of those in need by reason of youth, age, ill-health, disability, financial hardship or other disadvantage (this includes relief given by the provision of accommodation or care to the persons mentioned).
11. The advancement of animal welfare.
12. Any other existing purposes and analogous purposes.

Procedure

▷ The prior consent of the Charity Commission for Northern Ireland is required before a charity may change its objects.

▷ Any purported change made without the required consent is ineffective.

Filing requirements

▷ The objects of a charity registered in Northern Ireland will appear on its public entry on the Charity Commission for Northern Ireland's website: www.charitycommissionni.org.uk.

Notes

▷ Although in general company law allows companies to do anything lawful and it is no longer necessary for companies to have specific objects, this is not possible for charitable companies. This is because charity law requires a charity to have specific and purely charitable objects.

Objects – alteration Scotland

Introduction

The law permits the alteration of charitable purposes within certain parameters (broadly the alterations must remain within the spirit of the original purposes) and provided that:

▷ the prior written consent of the OSCR is obtained; and

▷ the relevant procedures are followed (see further below).

Any purported alteration of objects without the required consent of the OSCR is ineffective.

Checklist

▶ Alterations to the objects of a SCIO take immediate effect (unlike the position with regard to a CIO in England and Wales).

▶ Alterations to the objects of a charitable company do not take effect until the Registrar of Companies registers the required documents on the company's public record.

▶ In most other circumstances an alteration of a charity's objects takes immediate effect.

Procedure

▶ The procedure required varies depending on the legal form of the charity and, to some extent, the provisions of its constitution.

▶ Prior consent from the OSCR is required for any alteration of the objects of a charity on the Scottish Charity Register (including a cross-border charity that is constituted under the law of another territory, for example, England and Wales).

▶ The proposed altered purposes must be entirely charitable within the law of Scotland (this can cause difficulties for cross-border charities).

▶ By law, the charity must apply to the OSCR for consent at least 42 days before the date on which it proposes to make the change. In practice, the OSCR advises applying at least two months in advance.

▷ The relevant application form can be downloaded from the OSCR's website: www.oscr.org.uk.

▷ The application must be accompanied by relevant supporting documents, including a full copy of the charity's current constitution and a copy of the constitution including the proposed revised objects.

▷ As part of its assessment of the application, the OSCR will check whether the current constitution provides a power to alter the objects and check the precise procedures required to exercise that power. (Except in the case of charities where there is a statutory power to alter the objects, for example, charitable companies and SCIOs.)

▷ Provided the OSCR gives its consent, the relevant procedures for altering the objects must then be followed (see below).

Charitable company

▷ An alteration to the objects of a charitable company requires a special resolution of its members, passed at a general meeting. A 75% majority vote in favour is necessary to carry the resolution (calculated on the votes cast).

▷ Alternatively, the resolution can be passed in accordance with the Companies Act 2006 procedures for statutory written resolutions of a company's members.

Scottish charitable incorporated organisation

▷ A members' resolution is required. A 75% majority vote in favour is necessary to carry that resolution (calculated on the votes cast at the relevant members' meeting).

Unincorporated members' association

▷ Follow the procedures set out in the power of amendment set out in the constitution. This will include a requirement for a members' resolution in favour of the proposed alteration.

▷ If there is no power of amendment, see further below.

Unincorporated trust

▷ Follow the procedures set out in the power of amendment in the trust deed. This will include a requirement for a trustees' resolution in favour of the proposed alteration.

▷ If there is no power of amendment, see further below.

Unincorporated charities without a power of amendment

▷ Legal advice should be taken.

Filing requirements

▷ A charitable company must also file a copy of its articles including the altered objects, a copy of the relevant special resolution, a copy of the relevant consent from the OSCR and form CC04 (Statement of company's objects) at Companies House. Note that the change does *not* take effect until the Registrar of Companies places the resolution, articles and form live on the company's public record.

▷ Once the alteration has been made, the charity is obliged to notify the OSCR formally in writing (within three months of the change). A form is available on the OSCR's website for this purpose.

▷ A copy of the revised constitution, including the altered objects, should be enclosed with that notification.

▷ A charitable company should confirm to the OSCR the date the change took effect (i.e. the date on which the Registrar of Companies placed the required documents on the company's public record at Companies House.)

Notes

▷ A 'cross-border' charity that is also registered in one or more of the other UK jurisdictions will also have to obtain prior consent to the proposed alteration from the other relevant charity regulator(s) (the Charity Commission or the Charity Commission for Northern Ireland).

People with significant control (PSCs) – companies

Introduction

Company law rules and requirements relating to people with significant control (PSCs) apply to all companies, including charitable companies and trading subsidiaries of charities.

In essence a PSC is a person who has the specified level of control over a company.

Underlying the legal rules is the public policy aim that there should be transparency over who owns and/or controls UK companies (and certain other legal entities to which these requirements apply, such as limited liability partnerships – 'LLPs').

The relevant legal criteria that makes a person a PSC are specified by the Companies Act 2006 and related regulations.

In addition, Companies House issues statutory guidance on the PSC requirements. It is a legal obligation to 'have regard' to that guidance in interpreting 'significant influence or control' in the context of the PSC rules and requirements under the Companies Act (as amended by the Small Business, Enterprise and Employment Act 2015).

For charities and subsidiaries of charities, the practical application of these complex legal requirements and how the affected company must comply may be clear. However, in some situations matters will be complex and careful judgements will be needed. In such cases it will be appropriate to obtain specialist legal advice.

Checklist

▶ Establish whether the company has any PSCs – the company has a responsibility to make enquiries to establish whether or not it has any PSCs.

▶ If not, notify Companies House there are none.

▶ If one or more PSCs are identified, follow appropriate procedures to comply with the relevant legal requirements.

▷ Where PSC changes occur comply with relevant requirements to record and notify those changes.

Procedure

▷ Set up and maintain a register of PSCs (there must be a register, even if there are currently no PSCs to be recorded in it).

▷ If any one or more PSCs are identified, obtain the required information about each PSC and comply with the relevant legal requirements, in particular:

▷ make the required entries in the company's register of PSCs; and

▷ notify Companies House.

▷ When any subsequent changes occur to relevant information about PSCs (or new/different PSCs are identified) obtain required data and ensure the register of PSCs is updated and the necessary notifications are made to Companies House.

▷ Consider what procedures should be put in place in case of a public access request for access to the register of PSCs held by the company.

Filing requirements

▷ PSCs must be notified to Companies House.

▷ Changes amongst PSCs (e.g. if a new PSC is identified) or changes to the data for existing PSCs must also be notified to Companies House.

▷ If a company considers that it does not have any PSCs, Companies House must be notified.

Notes

▷ An individual will be a PSC if they meet one or more of the criteria specified in the Companies Act.

1. Holds more than 25% of the shares in a company limited by shares.
2. Holds more than 25% of the voting rights in a company.
3. Holds the right to appoint or remove the majority of the board of directors.
4. Has the right to exercise, or actually exercises, 'significant influence or control' over the company.*

▷ Where a trust or firm satisfies any of the above four conditions, an individual who holds the right to exercise, or actually exercises, significant influence or control over the activities of the trust or firm will themselves be a PSC of the company.*

▷ Modified, broadly comparable, criteria apply for determining whether an organisation is a PSC (for example, another company).

▶ Statutory time limits apply to meeting each legal obligation – the obligations to record details of a PSC or changes to the details in the register of PSCs, to notify Companies House of PSCs identified or changes amongst the PSCs or changes to PSC details, public inspection requests for access to a company's register of PSCs.

* The statutory guidance relating to 'significant control or influence' must be considered in relation to both of these.

More information

▶ See checklist 'Records' for more information on the PSC register which a company must keep, notifications to Companies House, public access inspection rights and applicable statutory time limits.

▶ Various guidance is available on Companies House website, including the statutory guidance:

'Statutory Guidance on the Meaning of "Significant Influence or Control" Over Companies in the Context of the Register of People With Significant Control'.

Proxies

Introduction

A proxy is a person who is appointed by a member of a charity to attend a members' meeting and exercise the member's rights on their behalf.

Whether or not a member of a charity can appoint a proxy will depend on the legal form of the charity or, for some legal forms, the terms of the individual charity's constitution.

Checklist

Charitable company

▶ Members of companies have a statutory right to appoint a proxy.

▶ This is an absolute right; any attempt to restrict it, in the company's articles or any other document, is ineffective.

▶ The member may choose whoever they wish as their proxy (they cannot be required to choose only from amongst their fellow members).

▶ The notice of a general meeting must specify that the members have the right to appoint proxies and that a proxy can be anyone the member wishes to appoint as their proxy.

▶ A proxy may speak and vote at the meeting, as if the proxy was the member who appointed that proxy.

▶ The proxy form (proxy document) that notifies the company of the appointment of the proxy should be in the form specified in the company's articles (if any style is specified). Otherwise in a common style of proxy.

▶ The articles will specify the deadline for submitting proxy forms prior to the meeting (this cannot be longer than 48 hours ahead of the meeting).

CIOs, SCIOs and unincorporated members' associations

▶ There is no statutory right for the members of a CIO, a SCIO or an unincorporated members' association to appoint a proxy.

▶ They may be given the right to do so by the particular charity's constitution.

▶ The constitution may impose some restrictions such as limiting the choice of who a member can appoint as their proxy.

Open or closed proxies

▶ Open proxies allow the proxy to decide how to vote on each resolution.

▶ Closed proxies instruct the proxy how to vote on each resolution.

Procedure

▶ For companies, most procedures relating to members' proxy rights, the appointment of proxies and the delivery of proxy documents etc. are governed by relevant Companies Act 2006 procedures.

▶ For a charity in some other legal form, procedures will depend on the terms of the individual charity's constitution.

▶ Proxy forms should be checked and validated in advance of the meeting.

▶ Care must be taken to ensure any votes validly given by proxy are properly counted when a vote is taken on any formal resolution at a members' meeting.

Filing requirements

▶ Proxy forms do not have to be filed at Companies House or with the charity regulators. They should instead be kept in the charity's own internal records of the relevant meeting.

Public benefit

Introduction

Charities must provide charitable public benefit. This is part of the most fundamental legal obligations that charities must fulfil.

There are also some specific legal obligations regarding public benefit (including reporting obligations) that charity trustees must meet.

This is an area in which the detailed legal rules do differ between the various UK jurisdictions (England and Wales; Scotland and Northern Ireland).

Checklist

England and Wales – public benefit

▶ A charity's purposes must be within the list of 'descriptions' of charitable purposes in the Charities Act 2011 and that purpose must be *for the public benefit* (in a charitable way).

▶ The charity must pursue its own stated purposes, for the public benefit and:

▷ its activities must be appropriate for those purposes;

▷ its funds and assets must be applied towards them; and

▷ the beneficiaries must be appropriate.

▶ Any private benefit that arises must be necessarily incidental to the charitable activities and the delivery of the public benefit through those activities.

England and Wales – trustees' duties

▶ Trustees must have regard to the statutory guidance that the Charity Commission has issued on public benefit:

▷ PB1 The Public Benefit Requirement (the legal requirement that a charity's purposes [as set out in its constitution] must be for the 'public benefit').

▷ PB2 Public Benefit – Running A Charity (public benefit in the context of running a charity).

▷ PB3 Public Benefit – Reporting (charity trustees' duty to report on how they have carried out their charity's purposes for the public benefit).

▶ Trustees must report in their trustees' annual report on the activities the charity has undertaken in the relevant year to further its purposes for the public benefit.

Scotland

▶ In Scotland, public benefit requirements form part of the 'charity test'.

▶ Trustees of charities on the Scottish Charity Register should consider the OSCR's guidance on that test, which includes guidance on the public benefit part of the test.

▶ In order to register on the Scottish Charity Register, held by the OSCR, and be a charity under the law of Scotland, an organisation must:

▷ have charitable purposes (under the law of Scotland); and

▷ provide public benefit in Scotland or elsewhere.

▶ This is an activities-based obligation (rather than a purposes-based test as is the case under English law).

▶ New organisations seeking initial registration must provide evidence to the OSCR that they will provide public benefit.

▶ In determining whether an organisation provides public benefit, the Charities and Trustee Investment (Scotland) Act 2005 requires a comparison to be made between the benefit to the public and:

▷ benefits to the organisation's members or third parties (other than as members of the public) (i.e. private benefits); and

▷ any 'disbenefit' incurred, or likely to be incurred, by the public.

▶ Where benefit is only provided to a section of the public and there are any conditions on obtaining the benefit (including any charge or fee), the Act requires consideration of whether those conditions are unduly restrictive.

▶ The OSCR addresses these issues when assessing a charity registration application from a new applicant organisation and when reviewing existing charities.

Northern Ireland

▶ The Charities Act (Northern Ireland) 2008 requires any organisation seeking to be a charity in Northern Ireland to meet these conditions:

▷ it must have purposes that fall within the 'descriptions' of purposes set out in the Act; and

▷ those purposes must be for the public benefit.

▶ Charity trustees must 'have regard' to the statutory public benefit guidance published by the Charity Commission for Northern Ireland.

Procedure

▶ Trustees generally have discretion as to the charity's current activities and how those deliver public benefit (subject to their obligation to have regard to the statutory guidance issued by the charity regulators).

▶ They also generally have discretion about changes they might make to improve the public benefit being provided.

▶ However, these discretions are subject to any legal restraints or constitutional limitations or obligations applicable to the particular charity and its situation, such as:

▷ restricted funds – can only be applied within the terms of the relevant restrictions;

▷ endowment must be applied within the terms of the special trust that apply to that endowment;

▷ some charity constitutions are quite prescriptive and/or narrow regarding the charity's powers or the activities it can, or must, undertake; and

▷ some charity constitutions are quite narrow with regard to the beneficiary group (e.g. age limits or geographical limits).

Filing requirements

▶ Note the reporting obligations (see above).

Notes

▶ Charities are subject to the public benefit requirements on a continuing basis (it is not merely a requirement for charity registration).

More information

▶ Charity trustees and charity advisers should familiarise themselves with the relevant public benefit guidance and other related guidance issued by the charity regulators:

▷ www.gov.uk/government/organisations/charity-commission.

▷ www.oscr.org.uk.

▷ www.charitycommissionni.org.uk.

▶ For additional information on reporting standards see SORP.

Quorum – general meetings

Introduction

The quorum for a general meeting is the minimum number of members that must be present and entitled to vote in order to constitute a valid meeting.

An inquorate meeting should not attempt to deal with substantive business or pass any formal members' resolutions.

The relevant quorum provisions in the charity's constitution will apply to all general meetings, including an annual general meeting.

Checklist

Companies

▶ The articles of the particular company normally specify the quorum.

▶ If the articles are silent, the Companies Act default rule is that, for a company with two or more members, the quorum is two 'qualifying persons'. Note that if the articles make provision for the quorum, that provision overrides this default position.

▶ For this purpose, a 'qualifying person' is:

  ▷ an individual who is a member of the company;

  ▷ an authorised representative of a corporation which is a member of the company; or

  ▷ a person who has been appointed as a proxy for a member.

▶ For a single member company the quorum is one, regardless of the provisions of the articles. It is rare for a charitable company to be a single member company.

▶ Proxies *must* be counted in calculating the quorum.

Other charities

▶ The quorum rule should be set out in the individual charity's constitution.

▶ Note that if the constitution does permit the use of proxies, it *may* provide they are to be counted in calculating the quorum.

Procedure

▶ Check the provisions of the charity's constitution with regard to the quorum.

▶ Consider whether proxies count towards the required quorum or not (in a company they *must* be counted).

▶ Ensure there is a quorum present before the general meeting proceeds to business.

▶ Note in the meeting minutes that a quorum was present.

Notes

▶ Some constitutions provide that a quorum must be present at the start of the meeting, while others state it must be present throughout the meeting.

▶ Usually a charity's constitution contains provisions as to how much time can elapse before a meeting at which insufficient members are present is to be declared inquorate and adjourned.

▶ Note that those not attending in a non-voting capacity must not be counted in calculating whether the required quorum is present (for example, non-member trustees, professional advisers or guests).

Quorum – trustees' meetings

Introduction

The quorum for a trustees' meeting (i.e. a board meeting) is the minimum number of trustees that must be present and entitled to vote in order to constitute a valid meeting.

An inquorate meeting should not attempt to deal with substantive business or pass any formal trustees' resolutions.

The relevant quorum provisions in the charity's constitution will apply to all board meetings.

Checklist

Companies

▶ The articles of the particular company normally specify the quorum.

Other charities

▶ The quorum rule should be set out in the individual charity's constitution.

Procedure

▶ Check the provisions of the charity's constitution with regard to the quorum.

▶ Ensure a quorum is present before the board meeting proceeds to business.

▶ Record in the meeting minutes that a quorum was present.

Notes

▶ Some constitutions provide that a quorum must be present at the start of the meeting, while others state it must be present throughout the meeting.

▶ Note that many constitutions include a provision that a trustee who has a personal interest may *not* be counted in the quorum.

Records

Introduction

Charities need to keep a range of records for both practical and legal reasons.

Which records are *legal requirements* for a particular charity depends on:

▷ the legal form of the charity; and

▷ the nature of its activities and its particular circumstances (e.g. whether it employs staff or is VAT registered).

Checklist

Records of meetings

▶ Charities should always keep records of formal meetings, both trustees' meetings and meetings of their members, such as the annual general meeting. These are usually kept as minutes (see checklist: 'Minutes').

Records of decisions taken other than at a meeting

▶ Charities should also keep records of formal decisions taken by their members or trustees other than at a meeting – for example, a formal decision taken by written resolution.

▶ The Companies Act requires a record to be kept of any written resolutions of the members of a company, made pursuant to the statutory procedures in the Act for the passing of written members' resolutions. This includes details of the text of the resolution, the type of resolution, the date it took effect and the names of the eligible members who signed the resolution.

Financial records

▶ All charities are obliged to keep financial records (i.e. internal accounting records).

Companies – statutory registers (general)

▶ A private company must keep statutory registers that comply with company law requirements. These legal requirements apply equally to charitable companies and the trading subsidiaries of charities.

▶ Registers can be kept in paper form in bound books or loose-leaf formats. Computer systems may also be used provided they can be reproduced in legible form. Whatever methods are chosen, the company must take adequate security steps to prevent and detect falsification or accidental loss or damage.

Companies – register of members

▶ For each member the details required are:

▷ name;

▷ address;

▷ class of membership (if there are different classes of members); and

▷ dates of admission and cessation of membership.

▶ With the exception of the first members (i.e. the initial subscribers on incorporation), the only persons who are legal members of a company are those who have agreed to be members and whose names have been entered in the register of members. Accordingly this register can be crucial if doubts arise over who the members are. It is therefore essential that the register of members is accurate and up-to-date.

▶ This register will need to be consulted for the proper corporate administration of the charity – for example, in verifying who is entitled to attend and vote at any annual or other general meeting.

▶ A company must be careful to record in its register of members all those who are its members for the purposes of company law.

▶ Other persons associated with the company but who are not members in law (e.g. 'supporters' or 'associates' or directors/trustees who are not also members) should not be recorded in this register. Separate records should be kept for such groups of people.

Companies – register of directors and secretary

▶ For directors (i.e. the charity trustees) this register must record:

▷ name;

▷ address;

▷ date of birth;

▷ business occupation (if any);

▷ usual country or state of residence (in the case of UK resident directors, this can be recorded as the relevant part of the UK, e.g. England or Scotland); and

> ▷ dates of appointment to and cessation of office.

▶ The address can be either the director's residential address or a 'service address'. The service address can be simply stated as 'the registered office'.

▶ Details of 'other directorships' are not required, but the director does have to give any name(s) by which they are, or were, known for business purposes. There is no longer an exception for a married woman's former name.

▶ If the company has (or has had) a secretary, this register must record:

> ▷ name;

> ▷ address; and

> ▷ dates of appointment and cessation of office.

▶ Again, the address can be either the residential address or a 'service address'.

Companies – register of directors' residential addresses ('RODRA')

▶ To support the rights of privacy for individual directors' residential addresses, companies must keep records of individual directors' residential addresses in the RODRA.

▶ This register is *not* open to general public access (though various investigatory and regulatory bodies have access rights).

▶ If the director has already entered their residential address as their service address in the register of directors, the RODRA need only state that fact. The exception is if the director's residential address is the registered office address, and the address given as the service address in the register of directors is 'the company's registered office'. In that case, the residential address must be given in full in the RODRA.

Companies – register of charges

▶ This must contain details of all charges that are subject to registration requirements.

Companies – register of people with significant control

▶ If a company has people of significant control ('PSCs'), as defined in the Companies Act, it must keep this register.

▶ All UK companies are obliged to ascertain whether they have PSCs and, if they identify any PSCs they are further obliged to enter their details in the company's register of PSCs and also notify their details to Companies House.

▶ In a wholly owned trading subsidiary of a charity, if the charity itself is the holder of all the issued shares, that charity will be a PSC for the purposes of these legal requirements.

▶ Where a charity is itself a company, it may have PSCs and so be obliged to record them in its register of PSCs and notify them to Companies House.

▶ A PSC's details must be recorded in the register within 14 days of the company becoming aware of the required information. The notification to Companies House must be made within a further 14 days, beginning on the day after the register entry was made.

▶ The same time limits apply to updating the register and notifying Companies House when PSC details change.

▶ When no changes have occurred during a 12-month period, the company must confirm this to Companies House.

▶ The register is open to public inspection, without charge. Where an inspection request is made, within five working days the company must either comply or apply to court for an order that it does not need to comply on grounds that the request is not made for a proper purpose.

▶ If the PSC is an individual, the following information is required:

   ▷ name;

   ▷ date of birth;

   ▷ nationality;

   ▷ country/state or part of the UK where the individual usually lives;

   ▷ correspondence address (also called a service address);

   ▷ usual residential address;*

   ▷ the date the individual became a PSC;** and

   ▷ which condition(s) for being a PSC are met by the individual.

   * This must be obtained and recorded, but if a public inspection request is made by any third party, the residential address must not be disclosed to them.

   ** If this was prior to 6 April 2016 (when these legal requirements initially came into force), that date should be used.

▶ Where the PSC is a corporate body, comparable details must be obtained and recorded.

▶ For further information, including the conditions for being a PSC, see checklist: 'People with significant control (PSCs) – companies'.

CIOs and SCIOs – statutory registers

▶ CIOs and SCIOs must keep a register of trustees and a register of members.

▶ Relevant regulations require particular information to be recorded in these registers; however, there is no set format, so a CIO or SCIO may keep the required details in whatever format it finds convenient.

▶ There is general public access to the register of trustees. Restrictions apply to the register of members which can only be accessed by the members themselves, the trustees and various public, regulatory and investigatory bodies.

Other statutory records (all charities)

▶ Other statutory records may need to be kept by charities because of general legal provisions, such as tax and VAT requirements or health and safety and employment legislation.

Unincorporated members' associations – membership records

▶ While unincorporated members' associations will normally keep some form of membership records (and are strongly advised to do so, for obvious reasons), there are no statutory requirements about the form and content of those records.

▶ The individual organisation's constitution may include some specific requirements, including access rights. If it does those requirements should be followed. Otherwise usual good practice standards should be observed.

Charity Commission records

▶ The Charity Commission's records of charities are public records that must be managed to comply with the Commission's statutory duties and responsibilities under the Charities Act 2011. It must also be managed in accordance with the Public Records Acts 1958 and 1967, particularly with regard to historical and archival material.

▶ Material relating to a particular *registered* charity is displayed on that charity's entry on the register of charities. This is open to public access via the Charity Commission website.

▶ Where a charity has been dissolved or otherwise removed from the register, some basic information about that charity, including the date of removal from the register, is available from the Commission's website.

▶ If the charity ceased to exist because of a merger, it is likely there will also be an entry on the register of mergers. This is also available for public access on the Commission's website.

▶ Historical and archival material relating to charities that is selected for preservation is normally transferred to the National Archives (no later than 30 years from the date of its creation).

Procedure

Location of statutory registers – companies

▶ The default position is that a company must keep its registers available for inspection at its registered office. However, regulations made under the Companies Act allow a company to specify a single alternative inspection location (SAIL), as an alternative to the registered office, where it may keep all or any of its public records available for inspection.

▶ The conditions that must be met in order to use a SAIL are:

1. the SAIL is situated in the part of the United Kingdom in which the company is registered;
2. the company notifies Companies House of that SAIL (form AD02); and
3. the company notifies Companies House which records are kept at the SAIL (form AD03).

▶ All records of a given type must be kept together either at a SAIL or the registered office; they cannot be split between two locations.

▶ A company must, within five working days, disclose the address of its registered office, and any address where it keeps company records available for public inspection (and the type of company records kept there), to any person it deals with in the course of its business who makes a written request to the company for that information. It must also state the SAIL address (if any), and which records are kept at the SAIL as at the return date.

Inspection of statutory registers – companies

▶ The relevant statutory regulations require a person wishing to inspect the company's records to give the company advance notice. The notice period is generally 10 days, but is two days in certain specified circumstances. The records must be available for inspection on any working day for at least two hours between 9am and 3pm.

▶ The current rules on access to and inspection of the register of members retain the general principle of public access to the register of members but also provide safeguards against potential abuses of the access right.

▶ The following rules apply to any request for access:

▷ The request must provide the name and address of the person making it.

▷ The request must say what the information will be used for, whether it will be shared with anyone else and, if so, who and for what purpose.

▶ The company has five days to comply with the request (or seek a court order that the request is not made for a proper purpose).

▶ Where any application to refuse an access request is made and the applicant disputes the company's decision that the access request was not made for a 'proper purpose', the matter might be taken before a court for an ultimate decision (this is clearly undesirable).

Filing requirements

▶ There are various statutory obligations to notify the Registrar of Companies and/or Charity Commission and/or other charity regulators of required information about members and trustees and of any changes to that information.

▶ These obligations are dealt with by electronic filing, usually by online notifications directly through the relevant regulators' websites, and sometimes by accessing those websites via approved third party company secretarial software.

Notes

Appropriate arrangements should be made to safeguard registers and records against loss, accidental damage, falsification and theft.

Directors' residential addresses – disclosure to Companies House and third party access

▶ Note that a director's residential address (and any change to that address) has to be provided to the Registrar of Companies. It is kept securely, with access only available to relevant authorities and credit reference agencies.

▶ The Registrar of Companies is, however, only required to protect residential addresses given officially and correctly. The Registrar is under no obligation to check that a residential address has not been given inadvertently, e.g. in the presenter's details on a statutory form (or equivalent electronic filing).

▶ A third party may want to know a director's residential address (either that a separate residential address has been given, or that the service address given is also the director's residential address). The circumstances in which this protected information may be disclosed (or used) by Companies House are as follows:

1. Companies House may use a residential address to communicate with the director.
2. The protected information may be disclosed to a public authority specified in regulations.
3. To a credit reference agency (as defined in the Consumer Credit Act 1974).
4. If a director consents to disclosure.

▶ The Secretary of State has made regulations setting out conditions that must be satisfied before such a disclosure may be made (the Companies (Disclosure of Address) Regulations 2009). These include reassurances about the security measures the agency has in place to protect the data and declarations about the purposes for which it is being sought.

▶ The regulations also set out the circumstances in which application can be made to prevent disclosure to a credit reference agency. Essentially there has to be risk of serious violence against the director or someone in their household in order to gain this added protection.

Register of charities

Introduction

In England and Wales some (but not all) charities are required to register on the public register of charities held by the Charity Commission.

In Scotland there is a comprehensive charity register. All charities constituted in Scotland or operating in Scotland must be registered on the Scottish Charity Register held by the OSCR.

When the new regulatory regime in Northern Ireland has been implemented there will be a comprehensive charity register for Northern Ireland, held by the Charity Commission for Northern Ireland.

Checklist

Register of charities England and Wales

▷ The register of charities for England and Wales is kept by the Charity Commission.

▷ Charity registration was first introduced by charity law reforms in the 1960s although a comprehensive register of charities has still not been established, as many charities are not legally obliged to register.

▷ Details of 'excepted' or 'exempt' charities are not included in the register of charities. Also, it does not provide details of small charities that are beneath the income level for compulsory registration (£5,000 annual income).

▷ Only charities governed by the law of England and Wales can be registered, so organisations established under the law of another territory (including charities constituted under the law of Scotland) cannot register.

▷ The information on the register of charities comes from the organisation's original charity registration application, its constitution and the annual reporting the charity must undertake to the Charity Commission.

▶ For smaller registered charities, that have exemptions from annual reporting, there is more limited information on the register. For the very smallest registered charities (income below £25,000) there is no financial information on the register because these charities are exempt from the obligation to file annual accounts with the Charity Commission.

▶ Although the Commission encourages charities to notify it of key changes during the year, and provides a simple online 'Update my charity' facility on its website, few changes *have* to be notified to the Commission as they occur. Instead, the annual reporting documents are the main route by which changes come to the Commission's attention and are recorded on the register.

▶ The entry for each charity is publicly accessible, via the Charity Commission's website. It provides details including:

▷ the name of the charity;

▷ the charity's contact details and the names of its trustees;

▷ the charitable purposes of the charity;

▷ a summary of the charity's activities and where they are mainly carried out;

▷ the registered charity number;

▷ a summary of the charity's financial history (unless it is exempt from filing accounts because it is very small);

▷ a summary filing record, including the applicable filing deadlines and, if those were not met, details of how late the charity was in providing the required items (or a statement that they remain overdue and how late they now are);

▷ copies of annual accounts and trustees' reports (unless the charity is exempt from filing these because it is very small); and

▷ various other details, such as the constitutional form of the charity (i.e. its legal form – unincorporated members' association, trust, CLG, CIO etc.).

Scottish Charity Register

▶ The Scottish Charity Register is kept by the OSCR. It is a comprehensive register of every charity constituted under the law of Scotland or operating in Scotland (including charities constituted under some other legal system, including the law of England and Wales).

▶ The entry for each charity is publicly accessible, via the OSCR's website, and provides details including:

▷ the name of the charity;

▷ the charity's principal office address;

▷ the charitable purposes of the charity;

> ▷ a summary of the charity's activities and where they are mainly carried out;

> ▷ the Scottish charity number; and

> ▷ various other details, such as the constitutional form of the charity (i.e. its legal form).

▶ Where it is necessary in order to protect an individual or the charity's premises, the address given may be the address of one of the trustees (this is rare).

▶ The charity trustees are not listed on a charity's entry on the Scottish Charity Register. The OSCR is not obliged to keep a register of trustees and states that it does not have the resources to keep a list on a voluntary basis. Interested parties are advised by the OSCR to seek a copy of the annual accounts, by contacting the charity directly, to ascertain who the trustees are.

▶ The OSCR does not make full copies of the charity's constitution available on the register, nor does it provide copies of the annual accounts and trustees' report (this may change in the future).

▶ The OSCR is obliged to ensure every organisation on the register meets the charity test. It must remove any organisation that does not do so and fails to address the areas of concern, after having been given an opportunity to do so.

▶ Other reasons for removal from the register include:

> ▷ voluntary removal at the request of the charity (steps would be required to protect any remaining charitable funds and assets before such a request could be granted);

> ▷ removal after amalgamation or winding up (a formal legal process would be necessary to carry out either); and

> ▷ compulsory removal by the OSCR at the end of a statutory inquiry or because the organisation had failed to comply with the OSCR's monitoring requirements.

Register of charities – Northern Ireland

▶ A comprehensive register of charities is being created by the Charity Commission for Northern Ireland under the Charities Act (Northern Ireland) 2008.

Procedure

▶ Public access to the UK's charity registers is principally web-based via the charity regulators' websites:

> ▷ www.gov.uk/government/organisations/charity-commission.

> ▷ www.oscr.org.uk.

> ▷ www.charitycommissionni.org.uk.

Filing requirements

▷ Increasingly filing requirements are met by charities using the online
   filing systems provided by the charity regulators on their websites. In
   some cases, paper filing is no longer available as an option (e.g. for
   the charity annual return to the Charity Commission).

Notes

▷ If a charity is in default in relation to its annual filing obligations,
   this will be clearly flagged by the charity regulators on that charity's
   register entry.

Resolutions of members – records and filing

Introduction

A members' resolution is a formal decision of the charity's members.

Such resolutions are usually passed at a meeting of the members (often called a 'general meeting'). However, they are sometimes passed as a written resolution.

Checklist

▶ Consider what, if any, statutory requirements apply because of the legal form of the particular charity.

▶ Note that CLGs, CIOs and SCIOs are subject to particular statutory requirements.

▶ Consider any relevant provisions of the charity's constitution regarding records of members' decisions and records of general meetings, or other formal decisions, of the members.

Procedure

Records of resolutions passed at meetings

▶ Charities should always keep records of formal meetings of their members, including any annual general meeting and any other general meetings.

▶ These records should include details of members' resolutions passed at those meetings.

▶ The records are usually kept as minutes (see checklist: 'Minutes').

Companies – records of resolutions passed at meetings

▶ The Companies Act requires companies to keep records of meetings of their members and the decisions taken at those meetings.

Companies – records of written resolutions

▶ The Companies Act requires a record to be kept of any written resolutions of the members of a company, made pursuant to the statutory procedures in the Act for the passing of written members' resolutions. This includes details of the text of the resolution, the type of resolution, the date it took effect and the names of the eligible members who signed the resolution.

CIOs – records of resolutions passed at meetings

▶ CIOs are required to keep records of proceedings at all meetings of their members. Those records must be kept for a minimum period of six years from the date of the meeting.

CIOs – records of other decisions of the members

▶ Decisions of the members of a CIO taken other than at meeting should also be recorded (e.g. written resolutions).

▶ The CIO regulations specifically require records to be kept of all appointments of the trustees (in many CIOs it is the members who appoint the trustees). Those records must be kept for a minimum period of six years from the date of the appointment.

Filing requirements

Charity Commission

▶ There is no general obligation to file copies of members' resolutions with the Charity Commission. However, some members' resolutions will relate to a matter that triggers a requirement for the charity to notify the Charity Commission – for example, the appointment of a new trustee.

The OSCR

▶ There is no general obligation to file copies of members' resolutions with the OSCR. However, some members' resolutions will relate to a matter that triggers a requirement for the charity to notify the OSCR because there is a change in the charity's registered details on the Scottish Charity Register (e.g. the appointment of a new trustee).

▶ Other resolutions will need to be notified because they relate to a notifiable change under section 17 of the Charities and Trustee Investment (Scotland) Act 2005 (e.g. a change to the charity's constitution).

Companies House

▶ The Companies Act specifies which members' resolutions a company must file at Companies House.

▶ All special resolutions must be filed.

▶ Certain ordinary resolutions must also be filed (e.g. an ordinary resolution to remove a director/trustee or to remove an auditor – note that these are exceptionally rare).

▶ Where a filing requirement applies to a particular resolution, it is usually necessary to include one or more statutory forms (or electronic equivalent).

▶ If there have been changes to the articles, a copy of the altered articles must also be filed.

Notes

▶ In CLGs, CIOs and SCIOs certain decisions must be taken by their members, not by their trustees. These include alterations to the articles (CLG) or constitution (CIO or SCIO).

▶ The constitution of an unincorporated members' association is likely to state that certain decisions must be taken by the charity's members, not by its trustees.

▶ Most members' decisions have immediate effect. However, a notable exception is an alteration of objects (i.e. charitable purposes). Such an alteration has *no* effect if the prior consent of the Charity Commission (and/or any other relevant charity regulator(s)) has not been obtained.

▶ In addition, in a CLG the change does not take effect until it has been registered on the company's public record by Companies House. In a CIO the change does not take effect until the Charity Commission has registered it on the CIO's entry on the register of charities.

Resolutions of members – types and majorities

Introduction

▶ A members' resolution is a formal decision of the charity's members.

▶ Such resolutions are usually passed at a meeting of the members (often called a 'general meeting'). However, they are sometimes passed as a written resolution.

Checklist

Companies – types of resolution and majorities

▶ The Companies Act provides for two types of members' resolution:

▷ ordinary resolution; and

▷ special resolution.

▶ An ordinary resolution is passed by a simple majority.

▶ A special resolution is passed by a majority of not less than 75%.

▶ The notice period for either type of resolution is normally 14 days; however, if the company's articles require a longer period that longer period of notice must be given. It is quite common for the articles of older companies (especially those incorporated prior to 1 October 2009) to require 21 days' notice period for a special resolution.

Companies – calculation of majorities (meetings)

▶ The *calculation* of the majorities required for resolutions is subject to different rules, depending on whether they are to be passed at a general meeting on a show of hands, or at a general meeting on a poll, or by written resolution.

▷ At a *meeting*, if the vote is taken on a show of hands the simple majority is calculated based on votes cast (i.e. the 'one person one vote' principle).

▷ At a *meeting*, if the vote is taken on a poll the majority is calculated by reference to the total voting rights of the members who actually vote on that resolution.

▷ Note that proxies and authorised representatives of corporate members may vote whichever method is used to take the vote.

▷ Those who abstain and those who fail to attend the meeting are not counted, in either case.

Companies – calculation of majorities (written resolutions)

▷ The calculation of majorities for written resolutions is based on majorities of votes from 'eligible members'. That is, the members who qualify to vote on the relevant resolution at its circulation date (i.e. the date on which copies of the draft resolution are sent or submitted to the members in accordance with the Companies Act rules).

▷ Note that there is a time limit for obtaining the required majority, otherwise the proposed resolution lapses. If the articles are silent, the time limit is 28 days beginning on the circulation date. However, if the articles specify an alternative time limit that will apply.

▷ The required voting percentages are:

▷ ordinary resolution – a simple majority of the *total voting rights* of the eligible members; and

▷ special resolution – not less than 75% of the *total voting rights* of the eligible members.

CIOs and SCIOs

▷ An alteration to the constitution of a CIO or SCIO requires a resolution of the members passed:

a) by a 75% majority of those voting at a general meeting; or
b) unanimously by the members, if it is passed otherwise than at a general meeting.

▷ If the constitution permits the use of proxies or postal voting, votes given by that method are counted in relation to (a).

▷ Other resolutions – the requirements will normally depend on the constitution of the particular CIO or SCIO.

Procedure

▷ The procedure required to pass a particular type of members' resolution depends on the legal form of the charity, whether the resolution is to be passed at a general meeting of the members or by written resolution.

▷ In some unusual situations, the particular circumstances will also affect procedural requirements (e.g. a proposed forcible removal of a trustee/ director or an auditor of a CLG – both of which are extremely rare).

Companies

▶ The relevant Companies Act procedural requirements must be followed. In addition the provisions of the articles must be considered.

CIOs and SCIOs

▶ For CIOs and SCIOs, most of the procedural requirements depend on the terms of the individual charity's constitution.

Other charities

▶ Most of the procedural requirements depend on the terms of the individual charity's constitution.

Filing requirements

▶ See checklist: 'Resolutions of members – records and filing'.

Restricted funds

Introduction

All funds held by a charity (whether as liquid funds or represented by assets) must be used to further that charity's purposes. Charitable funds must not be used outside that charity's charitable purposes or outside the scope of that charity's powers.

In addition, some funds have further legal restrictions on them that make those funds 'restricted'.

Checklist

▶ Restricted funds are held by a charity for a specific, restricted, purpose.

▶ This will be a purpose within the charity's overall charitable purposes but in some way narrower than those overall purposes.

▶ The restrictions may arise because:

▷ the donor imposed conditions on the original gift;

▷ the funds were provided as a grant for a particular limited purpose; or

▷ the funds were given in response to an appeal by the charity for funds for a specific purpose (e.g. a particular project or activity).

▶ Restricted funds are subject to specific trusts with regard to how those funds can be used (i.e. the restriction arises from what are sometimes called 'special trusts' that apply to those funds).

▶ Restricted funds may be income funds, where the entire sum can be spent within the terms of the restriction.

▶ Alternatively they may be capital funds, where the capital sum cannot be spent, only the income generated by that capital sum can be spent (on the relevant restricted purposes).

▶ Income generated from restricted funds (e.g. interest on a restricted sum that has been invested) is normally subject to the same restriction.

▶ Any asset purchased with restricted funds must be used in accordance with the relevant restriction.

Procedure

▷ The trustees must ensure the terms of the restriction are followed and that the funds are correctly applied.

▷ Restricted funds must be separately accounted for and reported separately in the charity's annual accounts. Information should be set out in the accounts about the nature of the restriction.

Notes

▷ A restricted fund should not be in deficit.

▷ A restricted fund should not be applied towards the charity's general running costs.

▷ Removal of restrictions from a restricted fund is quite a complex matter (and not always possible). Legal advice should be taken before attempting to remove or alter restrictions. Charity Commission prior consent may also be required.

▷ Depending on the relevant circumstances and the nature of the legal restrictions on the funds, it may be possible to alter or remove those restrictions with the original donor's consent. In other circumstances, including situations where donor consent is not possible (e.g. because the original donor is dead or untraceable) there may be other legal routes that can be purposed to alter or remove the restrictions.

Scottish Charitable Incorporated Organisations (SCIOs)

Introduction

A SCIO is a corporate body registered only with the OSCR (not Companies House) under the Charities and Trustee Investment (Scotland) Act 2005 and the SCIO specific regulations.

The SCIO legal form can only be used by a charity established under the law of Scotland (there are equivalent legal forms that may be established under the law of England and Wales and of Northern Ireland).

The SCIO legal form is specific to registered charities in Scotland, so it *cannot* be used by:

 ▷ a charity constituted under the law of any other territory (including the other territories within the United Kingdom); or

 ▷ a non-charity.

Checklist

Distinctive features of SCIOs

▶ Key distinctive features of SCIOs include:

 ▷ the members have a statutory duty (see below);

 ▷ conflicts of interest *must* be addressed in a SCIO's constitution; and

 ▷ the members are *not* liable to contribute to the assets of the SCIO if it is wound up.

Registration and regulation

▶ A SCIO is created by registration with the OSCR. It comes into being as that registration occurs (the equivalent of the date of incorporation of a company).

▶ There are SCIO specific regulatory requirements.

Statutory power

▶ A SCIO has statutory power to do anything that is calculated to further its charitable purposes or is conducive or incidental to doing so.

Principal office

▶ A SCIO must have a principal office in Scotland (this is the equivalent of a company's registered office).

Assets

▶ There is a statutory obligation for the SCIO to use and apply its property in furtherance of its charitable purposes and in accordance with its constitution.

Members

▶ A SCIO must have at least two members. (The English equivalent, the charitable incorporated organisation [CIO], is permitted to have a sole member).

Trustees

▶ A SCIO must have at least three trustees.

▶ They are responsible for the strategic management and the general control of the SCIO's administration.

▶ They have the general duties of charity trustees (under the law of Scotland) and also SCIO specific duties.

Constitution

▶ A SCIO's constitution must include:

▷ the SCIO's name and its charitable purposes;

▷ provisions about who is eligible for membership and how members are admitted to membership;

▷ provisions for the appointment of at least three trustees; and

▷ such other provisions as are required under the general SCIO regulations.

▶ The general SCIO regulations also require these further matters to be dealt with in the constitution:

▷ The SCIO's organisational structure.

▷ Procedural rules, including the convening of meetings, records of meetings, the quorum for meetings, voting rights of members, voting rights of trustees and how resolutions may be passed.

▷ The processes for withdrawal of members and removal of members and of trustees.

> Any additional restrictions on the circumstances in which trustees may be remunerated, which go beyond the permissive provisions of section 67 of the Charities and Trustee Investment (Scotland) Act 2005.

> Procedures for dealing with any conflict of interest.

> Dissolution provisions regarding the purposes to which the final funds can be transferred on winding up or dissolution of the SCIO (which must be purposes that are the same as, or closely resemble, the SCIO's own purposes).

▶ Any restrictions on the SCIO's powers must also be included in the constitution.

Constitution – alterations

▶ A SCIO may alter its constitution by resolution of its members.

▶ The requirements of the SCIO's constitution with regard to the convening and conduct of general meetings of the members must be observed (including notice period, contents of the notice, delivery methods, the use of proxies, quorum rules, chairing of the meeting and voting rights and practical arrangements).

▶ Prior consent of the OSCR is required for certain alterations, including any alteration to the charitable purposes.

▶ The resolution must be passed:

> by a 75% majority of votes cast, if the relevant resolution is proposed at a general meeting of the SCIO's members; or

> unanimously, if the resolution is to be passed otherwise than at a general meeting (e.g. in writing).

Members' statutory duties

▶ The members of a SCIO have some of the legal duties of charity trustees, specifically:

> to act in the best interests of the SCIO; and

> to seek, in good faith, to ensure the SCIO itself acts in a manner which is consistent with its charitable purposes.

Statutory members' meeting

▶ A SCIO *must* hold a members' meeting not more than 15 months after the previous members' meeting. No 'opt out' is available.

Public accountability

▶ The SCIO's entry on the Scottish Charity Register is accessible to the public via the OSCR's website: www.oscr.org.uk.

▶ A SCIO's annual accounts and trustees' annual report must be filed with the OSCR. There are no filing exemptions for smaller SCIOs.

▶ In addition to annual reporting obligations, SCIOs are subject to a range of public accountability obligations and requirements:

▷ Obligations to disclose the SCIO's name in documents signed or issued by or on behalf of the SCIO.

▷ An obligation to include a statement that the organisation is a SCIO in all documents signed or issued by or on behalf of the SCIO.

▷ Obligations to disclose various other details and information on certain documents and in communications:
   a) business letters;
   b) emails;
   c) the home page of a website operated by or on behalf of a SCIO;
   d) advertisements, notices and official publications;
   e) any document which solicits money or other property for the benefit of the SCIO;
   f) promissory notes, endorsements and orders for money or goods;
   g) bills rendered;
   h) invoices, receipts and letters of credit;
   i) statements of account prepared to comply with the relevant accounting regulations applicable to the SCIO;
   j) educational or campaign documentation;
   k) conveyances which provide for the creation, transfer, variation or extinction of an interest in land; and
   l) contractual documentation.

▷ Bills of exchange that are not cheques within the meaning of section 73 of the Bills of Exchange Act 1882.

▷ The requirement to include 'Scottish Charitable Incorporated Organisation' or 'SCIO' at the end of the organisation's name.

▶ Note that there are criminal sanctions against any charity trustee or other person who issues, or authorises the issue of, signs or authorises the signature of, an item that does not comply with these requirements.

Amalgamations

▶ There are specific statutory provisions and related procedures for the amalgamation of two or more SCIOs.

Transfer of undertaking

▶ There are specific statutory provisions and related procedures for the transfer of a SCIO's undertaking to another SCIO.

Conversions

▶ There are specific statutory provisions and related procedures for the conversion of certain other legal types of charity into SCIOs (charitable companies and charitable industrial and provident societies).

Procedure

▶ Some procedures are subject to statutory provisions, which are in many circumstances mandatory (e.g. the procedure to alter a SCIO's constitution).

▶ Other procedures will be subject to the provisions of the particular SCIO's constitution.

Regulatory consents

▶ A SCIO must obtain prior consent from the OSCR before it can take certain actions or make certain changes (e.g. a proposed alteration to its charitable purposes).

Statutory members' meeting

▶ The legislation does not specify the business to be dealt with at this meeting.

▶ Check the constitution, as it may make provision for what business is to be dealt with at this statutory meeting. Otherwise, the business will be a matter for the trustees to decide.

▶ The requirements of the SCIO's constitution with regard to the convening and conduct of general meetings of the members must be observed (including notice period, contents of the notice, delivery methods, the use of proxies, quorum rules, chairing of the meeting and voting rights and practical arrangements).

Filing requirements

▶ SCIOs have a range of filing obligations in these areas:

▷ annual accounting and reporting; and

▷ event/transaction notifications to the OSCR (some of these obligations are SCIO specific rather than simply general charity obligations).

More information

▶ See:

▷ Chapter 7 of the Charities and Trustee Investment (Scotland) Act 2005.

▷ The Scottish Charitable Incorporated Organisations Regulations 2011.

▷ SSI 44 of 2011.

▷ The Scottish Charitable Incorporated Organisations (Removal from the Register and Dissolution) Regulations 2011, SSI 362 of 2012.

▷ The Scottish Charitable Incorporated Organisations (Removal from the Register and Dissolution) Amendment Regulations 2013 SSI 362 of 2013.

Seal

Introduction

A seal is an official seal used by companies and certain other incorporated bodies, to authorise and authenticate important documents.

Seals were once commonplace and were once compulsory for companies (under previous company law) but are now less so.

Checklist

Companies

- The Companies Act 2006 provides for the company seal to be optional, so a company may choose to have a seal or not.

- If it has a seal, it may execute documents under its seal or choose to use any of the alternative execution methods now available to companies under the Companies Act 2006.

CIOs

- A CIO may choose to have a seal.

- If it has a seal, it may execute documents under that seal, in accordance with the CIO general regulations, or use the alternative execution method for CIOs specified in the regulations.

Other charities

- Charities in other incorporated legal forms may choose to have a seal (e.g. charitable industrial and provident societies or charities incorporated by Royal Charter).

- An unincorporated charity will not have a seal, because the charity itself does not have independent identity and legal competence to enter into agreements, contracts etc. in its own right.

International/cross-border matters

- An incorporated organisation that undertakes international activities and/or cross-border or overseas transactions may encounter practical difficulties and legal queries if it does not use a seal on major documents. This can be the reason for some organisations opting to retain a seal and use it on certain documents.

Procedure

Initial adoption of a seal

▶ Initial adoption of a seal should be by formal resolution of the trustees.

▶ The decision should be recorded in the minutes of the meeting.

▶ It is good practice to make an impression of the new seal in the margin of those minutes.

Authorising use of the seal

▶ Ensure any use of the seal is properly authorised and recorded.

▶ In the case of a company, its articles will normally specify who can authorise use of the seal (probably the board of trustees) and who can be authorised to countersign the seal on a document.

▶ The articles may permit non-trustees to be authorised as countersignatories to a document that is being sealed, or they may only permit authorisation of trustees (and perhaps any company secretary) for this purpose.

▶ At least two countersignatories are usually required. They should be present when the seal is placed on the relevant document, as their signatures witness the sealing.

Recording use of the seal

▶ As it is usually the board of trustees who must authorise use of the seal on a particular document, the decision should be recorded in the relevant board meeting minutes.

▶ The minutes should also record authorisation of the relevant countersignatories.

▶ It is good practice to keep a copy of the sealed document with the relevant minutes.

▶ Some charities will choose to keep a register of sealings to record all documents sealed by the charity. In the case of a charitable company, this is a non-statutory register (i.e. an optional register).

Filing requirements

▶ The use of a seal does not have to be notified to charity regulators or Companies House.

Tax and VAT

Introduction

Charities do not have blanket exemption for direct taxation or from VAT. They do, however, have access to a wide range of charity tax exemptions and reliefs provided:

▷ the organisation satisfies the conditions to be a charity for tax purposes; and

▷ the necessary conditions for the particular relief or exemption are satisfied.

Checklist

▶ Access to charity tax exemptions and reliefs is not automatic.

▶ Recognitions as a charity *for tax purposes* must be formally obtained by application to HMRC.

▶ The conditions for charity tax status are set out in the relevant legislation (Finance Act 2010).

▶ A charity's donated and investment income is not normally subject to tax, provided it is properly applied to the charity's charitable purposes. Gifts of securities (including shares) and real property (i.e. land and buildings) to a charity are usually tax free as are gifts made to a charity under a will.

▶ Income generated from the charity's primary purpose trading (that is trading in *direct* pursuit of the charity's charitable purposes) is generally exempt from tax provided it is applied exclusively to the charity's charitable purposes.

▶ Fundraising trading income is *not* subject to a blanket tax exemption, although there is a small scale trading exemption (see below).

Conditions for charity tax status

▶ These conditions must be satisfied in order for an organisation to be regarded as a charity for tax purposes:

▷ the organisation is established solely for charitable purposes;

▷ it meets the jurisdiction condition;

▷ it meets the registration condition; and

▷ it meets the management condition.

▶ The jurisdiction condition – this means that the organisation is subject to the control of a court in the exercise of the court's jurisdiction with respect to charities.

▶ The registration condition – this means the organisation must be registered with the relevant charity regulator as required under the law of the territory in which it is established (e.g. the Charity Commission of the OSCR).

▶ The management condition relates to the probity of the members of the governing body and the organisation's managers – the 'fit and proper persons test'.

Fit and proper persons test

▶ The Finance Act 2010 sets out a definition for tax purposes of charities (and certain other organisations) that may be entitled to UK charity tax reliefs. The definition includes a requirement that, to be a charity, an organisation must satisfy the 'management condition'.

▶ For a charity to satisfy this condition, its trustees and other senior managers must be fit and proper persons. There is no definition in the legislation of a 'fit and proper person'. However, HMRC publishes guidance on its website setting out how HMRC applies this test to those who have the general control and management of the administration of the charity.

▶ HMRC states that it assumes that all people appointed by charities are fit and proper persons unless they have information to show otherwise. Provided charities take appropriate steps on appointing personnel then they may assume that they meet the management condition at all times unless, exceptionally, a challenge is made by HMRC.

▶ Positive action to check candidates, prior to appointment, is expected and is clearly both appropriate and advisable.

▶ HMRC does not offer a clearance service itself for charities to confirm that particular managers are fit and proper persons. It is a matter for the boards of individual charities to ensure they decide what checks are appropriate and ensure those are properly carried out for each proposed appointment to the board (and to senior management posts) in that charity.

▶ Where HMRC finds a manager of a charity is not a fit and proper person, a charity will not necessarily lose entitlement to the charity tax reliefs. As explained below, HMRC is able to treat a charity as having met the management condition where either the manager has no ability to influence the charitable purposes of the charity or the application of its funds, or the circumstances are such that it is just and reasonable to treat the charity as having met the management conditions throughout the period the manager has been in office.

▶ Factors that HMRC states may lead it to decide that a manager is not a fit and proper person include, but are not limited to, individuals:

  ▷ with a history of tax fraud;

  ▷ with a history of other fraudulent behaviour, including misrepresentation and/or identity theft;

  ▷ for whom HMRC has knowledge of involvement in attacks against or abuse of tax repayment systems; or

  ▷ who are barred from acting as a charity trustee by a charity regulator or court, or being disqualified from acting as a company director.

▶ HMRC states that a charity's tax reliefs and exemptions will not be withdrawn during an enquiry into whether it meets the management condition. HMRC may however decide not to make repayments of tax during an enquiry, depending on the circumstances. Where the management condition is ultimately found to be satisfied, or HMRC treats the management condition as being met, then the charity will qualify for tax reliefs and exemptions throughout the period of the enquiry. HMRC states that it will then make any outstanding repayments at the conclusion of its enquiry.

▶ Where HMRC has found someone is not a fit and proper person, it will normally advise the person of its decision and that person may ask for the relevant review process to be followed on the decision. If at the end of that process HMRC still considers the person is not fit and proper, HMRC will ask them whether they intend remaining as a manager of the charity. If the person stands down as a manager HMRC will not inform the charity. However, if they remain as a manager HMRC will notify the charity that it considers that the manager is not a fit and proper person if the charity is not already aware. HMRC is not able to disclose specific concerns about the person to the charity without the person's permission but will explain that, because the manager is not a fit and proper person, the management condition is not met so tax relief may be in jeopardy. HMRC will also, where appropriate, advise the charity what it must do, and by when, if HMRC is to apply its discretion to treat the charity as having met the management condition throughout the period of the person's term in office.

Small scale trading exemption

▶ There is a tax exemption for income raised by small scale trading by a charity. The exemption is available provided the funds raised do not exceed 25% of the charity's total incoming resources (up to a maximum income threshold of £50,000 a year).

▷ Modest levels of direct fundraising trading can therefore usually be carried out directly by the charity without incurring a tax charge.

▷ Note that this exemption does not apply to trading subsidiaries of charities.

Business rates exemption

▷ Where a charity occupies and uses premises for its charitable purposes it is entitled to 80% mandatory rates relief from non-domestic rates (i.e. business rates).

▷ Various conditions apply, including a requirement that the premises must be used wholly or mainly for the charity's charitable purposes.

▷ The relevant local authority may grant the additional 20% relief on a discretionary basis.

▷ Note that this exemption does not apply to trading subsidiaries of charities.

VAT

▷ There is no blanket exemption from VAT for charities.

▷ There are some limited VAT reliefs available to charities. These do not apply to the trading subsidiaries of charities.

Tax agents

▷ HMRC defines a tax agent as someone who is appointed to discuss, correspond or transact with HMRC about tax matters on behalf of another person.

▷ A charity may choose to use a professional adviser to assist it with its tax and VAT affairs and that person may therefore need to be formally appointed as a tax agent and notified to HMRC.

▷ The charity must give its adviser proper authority to act on its behalf and this must be verified to HMRC as otherwise HMRC cannot:

  ▷ discuss the charity's financial and tax affairs or any other relevant information about the charity with that adviser;

  ▷ exchange information with them; or

  ▷ send them certain forms, letters and returns relating to the charity's tax affairs.

▷ The process for authorising and notifying an agent to HMRC can be done on paper or online via HMRC Online Services: www.hmrc.gov.uk/online.

▷ The authorisation lasts until the organisation withdraws it.

Procedure

Fit and proper persons checks

▶ Checks should be carried out before appointments are made or, at the very least, before appointees take up their responsibilities.

▶ As a bare minimum, charities should use a self-certification declaration based on the model available on the HMRC website, along with basic identity and residential address verifications.

▶ It is preferable to go beyond that – for example, by also carrying out a disqualified director search on the Companies House website (this can be done online free of charge). Note that disqualified directors are also barred from holding charity trusteeships.

▶ Also consider carrying out a County Court judgement and bankruptcy search (or Scottish equivalent). Such searches are available at a modest cost from a variety of search agents.

Filing requirements

▶ There are a variety of filing and notification/returns requirements in relation to tax and VAT. Almost all of them can be done online via the HMRC website or by other electronic means. Some can only be dealt with electronically (there are no longer paper alternative options).

Notes

▶ Tax and VAT issues can be complex and potentially risky. Appropriate specialist professional advice about the particular charity and its own situation should always be taken.

More information

▶ HMRC provides a wide range of charity specific guidance and some helpful tax related toolkits on its website: www.hmrc.gov.uk.

Trading

Introduction

Charities may undertake trading activities, within a range of legal and regulatory parameters and restrictions.

However, this is a complex and potentially high risk area for charities. Specialist professional advice should be obtained on all relevant issues, including legal, regulatory, constitutional, tax and VAT issues.

Checklist

▶ Careful judgements must be made as to what trading is lawful and possible, as well as what trading is appropriate.

▶ Considerable care must be taken as to how any trading activities are structured and carried out (including whether the trading in question can be carried out directly by the charity or whether it should, or must, be placed through a trading subsidiary).

▶ Charitable funds and assets should not be put at undue risk in trading activities.

▶ The charity's reputation and good standing must be considered and safeguarded.

▶ It is important to ensure that trading is carried out properly as there are personal liability risks to the trustees, as well as risks to the charity, if the charity trades ultra vires (beyond its powers) or otherwise unlawfully.

Trustees

▶ The board of trustees has ultimate responsibility for all trading activities carried out by or on behalf of the charity.

▶ The trustees should ensure that they discharge their duties and responsibilities diligently in relation to all trading activities and trading relationships.

▷ Trustees should consider how any proposed or current trading activities fit into the charity's overall strategy and that they are consistent with the charity's ethos.

▷ Trustees must ensure the charity trades within the terms of the charity's own constitution and within all applicable legal restrictions and requirements.

▷ Trustees should read and consider all relevant guidance from HMRC and the charity regulators. They should also obtain and consider appropriate professional advice.

Risk management

▷ Risk management must be adequately addressed (for all major risks, including reputational risks, not simply the financial risks).

Management, monitoring and review

▷ Trading should be actively managed, with clear objectives and regular monitoring of performance against those objectives.

▷ A broader annual review by the board of the charity's overall trading activities is good practice.

Investments

▷ Some trading arrangements will be subject to the charity law rules and restrictions regarding charity investments (including investment in trading via a trading subsidiary).

Primary purpose trading

▷ Primary purpose trading is trading by the charity in direct pursuit of its charitable purposes.

▷ Examples of primary purpose trading might include charging an entrance fee to an exhibition in a charitable art gallery or selling tickets to performances at a charitable theatre (provided that the exhibition or performance directly furthers the charitable purposes of the particular charity, for the public benefit).

Non-primary purpose trading

▷ All other trading is non-primary purpose trading; this includes trading to raise funds that are subsequently applied to the charity's charitable purposes.

▷ Trading to raise funds is not, of itself, a charitable purpose. So a charity cannot simply have 'fundraising' stated in its constitution as its charitable purpose.

Public benefit

▶ Considerable care must be taken that trading activities do not give rise
to private benefit that could prejudice the charity's charitable status
(including benefit to individuals or commercial organisations). Only
minor private benefit is permissible from a charity's activities (i.e. that
which is necessary and incidental to the carrying out of the charitable
purposes of that charity, for the public benefit).

Conflicts of interest

▶ Considerable care must also be taken to identify, and correctly
manage, any potential conflicts of interest in relation to trading
activities and trading relationships.

Notes

Charity shops

▶ Traditional charity shops, selling second-hand goods donated to the
charity by the public, are not regarded as commercial trading. The sale
of a donated item in this way amounts to the cash conversion of a free
gift from the person who donated the goods in question. HMRC will
not seek to tax the funds this conversion of donated goods provides
for the charity.

▶ However, the sale of purely donated goods must be distinguished
from:

  ▷ the sale of goods as agent for the supporter who provides those
goods to the charity, where that supporter agrees to donate back
to the charity the proceeds of the sale (usually with Gift Aid,
provided the donor meets the Gift Aid conditions); or

  ▷ the sale of new goods, bought in by the charity for direct sale to
the public.

▶ Both of these involve very different legal arrangements and
transactions and can have very different legal, regulatory and tax
consequences. Appropriate professional advice should be taken
before embarking upon such arrangements.

More information

▶ Trustees, charity senior managers and professional advisers assisting
charities should consider the Charity Commission guidance 'Trustees,
Trading and Tax: How Charities May Lawfully Trade' (CC35) which is
available on the Commission's website.

Trustees – duties and responsibilities

Introduction

Charity trustees hold a position of utmost trust and are subject to a range of legal duties and responsibilities. They must discharge these duties and responsibilities diligently and honestly.

Checklist

▶ Under English law, trustees' duties are a mix of common law duties and specific duties under the Charities Act 2011 and associated legislation.

▶ The overriding duty of a charity trustee is to act at all times in what the trustee honestly believes to be the best interests of the charity's charitable purposes.

▶ Most of the specific statutory duties of a charity trustee relate to public accountability and reporting, the protection and correct application of charitable funds and assets or particular transactions (e.g. land transactions).

▶ Some specific statutory duties only apply to the trustees of particular legal forms of charity (e.g. the statutory investment duties under the Trustee Act 2000 are only compulsory for the charity trustees of unincorporated charities in England and Wales).

Companies – directors' general duties

▶ The trustees of charitable companies have the usual general duties of company directors, as well as their duties as charity trustees. Note that company law modifies some of those duties in their application to charitable companies (the summary below takes account of those modifications).

▶ The general duties are:

    ▷ to act within the charity's constitution and to exercise their powers as directors for the purposes for which those powers were conferred;

ss. 171–177
Companies Act 2006

▷ to promote the success of the company in achieving its charitable purposes;

▷ to exercise independent judgement;

▷ to exercise reasonable skill, care and diligence;

▷ to avoid conflicts of interest;

▷ not to accept benefits from third parties; and

▷ to declare direct and indirect personal interests in proposed transactions or arrangements.

▶ Much of this is both common sense and reflects the common law general duties of charity trustees.

Companies – directors' specific duties

▶ There are additional specific duties for directors under the Companies Act 2006.

▶ For directors of charitable companies, most of those relate to public accountability and reporting (including duties to ensure the company meets its filing obligations and provides required documents and information to Companies House, in accordance with the applicable time limits).

▶ Such reporting and filing obligations are not difficult to deal with in practice, as almost all the required items and information can now be filed quickly and easily online via the Companies House website: www.companieshouse.gov.uk.

CIOs – trustees' duties

▶ The trustees of a CIO have the usual charity trustee duties under the law of England and Wales.

▶ They also have CIO specific duties under the CIO specific provisions of the Charities Act 2011 the CIO regulations. See checklist: 'CIOs – trustees'.

SCIOs – trustees' duties

▶ The trustees of a SCIO have the usual charity trustee duties under the law of Scotland.

▶ They also have SCIO specific duties under the SCIO specific provisions of the Charities and Trustee Investment (Scotland) Act 2005 and the SCIO regulations. See checklist: 'Scottish Charitable Incorporated Organisations (SCIOs)'.

Liabilities for breach of duties

▶ The exact consequences of a breach of duty depend on the relevant duty and the particular circumstances. They may involve:

▷ personal liability for the trustees (regardless of whether the charity is incorporated or not);

▷ an obligation to compensate the charity for losses it has suffered as a result of the breach of duties;

▷ an obligation for the trustees to account to the charity for any improper payments they, or individuals or organisations connected with them, have received; and

▷ an obligation to restore property to the charity.

Improper contracts that benefit trustees or connected persons

▶ Where a contract has been entered into that benefits a trustee or connected person, in improper circumstances, that contract may be void and/or unenforceable by, or for the benefit of, the relevant trustee or connected person.

▶ The relevant trustee (and, depending on the exact circumstances, possibly also the other trustees) may be personally liable for breach of duties (see above).

▶ Note that the law protects a bona fide third party who has acted honestly.

Trustees' duties – Scotland

s. 66(1) Charities and Trustee Investment (Scotland) Act 2005

▶ Charity trustees have statutory general duties under the law of Scotland.

▶ A charity trustee is required to act in the interests of the charity and, in particular, to:

▷ seek, in good faith, to ensure the charity acts in a manner which is consistent with its charitable purposes; and

▷ act with the care and diligence that it is reasonable to expect of a person who is managing the affairs of another person.

▶ In addition, the trustees must:

1. ensure the charity complies with any direction, requirement, notice or duty imposed on it by the Charities and Trustee Investment (Scotland) Act 2005; and
2. if there has been any breach of the statutory duties of trustees, to take such steps as are reasonably practicable for the purposes of ensuring:
   a) that any breach of the two principal statutory duties (see above) is corrected by the trustee concerned and not repeated; and
   b) that any trustee who has been in serous and persistent breach of either or both of those duties is removed as a trustee.

▶ In relation to a *charity trustee who is appointed by any other person*, that trustee has particular statutory duties in relation to conflicts of interest. In circumstances capable of giving rise to a conflict between the interests of the charity and the interests of that other person (i.e. the appointor), the relevant trustee must:

▷ put the interests of the charity before the interests of the appointor; and

▷ where any other duty prevents the trustee from doing that, the trustee must disclose the conflicting interest to the charity and refrain from participating in any deliberation or decision of the trustees with respect to the matter in question.

Breach of statutory general duties of trustees (Scotland)

▶ Any breach of the general statutory duties of trustees under the 2005 Act is to be treated as misconduct in the administration of the charity.

Trustees – key responsibilities

▶ Charity trustees have ultimate responsibility for the charity and its affairs.

▶ Key areas trustees should focus on include strategic leadership, effective monitoring, financial management, the security of funds and assets, the correct application of funds and assets, pursuit of the charity's own charitable purposes and the delivery of public benefit.

▶ The key responsibilities of charity trustees are:

▷ pursuit of the charitable purposes and the delivery of the public benefit for which the charity is established;

▷ governance (acting together as the governing body of the charity);

▷ strategic direction of the charity;

▷ safeguarding and correct use of all charitable resources;

▷ financial management and solvency;

▷ compliance with the charity's constitution, charity law and regulatory obligations and the general law;

▷ public accountability of the charity and its compliance with public reporting obligations;

▷ identification and the correct management of conflicts of interest; and

▷ risk management.

Procedure

▶ The procedures trustees should or must follow are in part determined by applicable law and in part by the legal form of the charity and the terms of its own constitution.

Trustees – recruitment and appointment

Introduction

Every charity must have trustees. It is vital to ensure that the right people are appointed, to provide the leadership and oversight that the charity needs.

Checklist

▶ Consider eligibility – check the constitution for any specific eligibility criteria (e.g. that only members of the charity can be appointed to serve as trustees).

▶ Be aware of and observe the general legal rules on capacity, charity trustee disqualification etc.

▶ In some charities it will be appropriate (or may be a legal obligation) to carry out particular checks on potential candidates for reasons of safeguarding children and other vulnerable beneficiaries (e.g. criminal records and barring checks).

▶ Minimum age – if the charity is a company, the statutory minimum age for directors applies (16 or over).

▶ Ensure there is a vacancy to which the proposed trustee can be appointed (the constitution may specify a maximum number of trustees).

Procedure

Pre-recruitment

▶ If appropriate, carry out (or update) a skills audit of the current board members to identify key needs, skills gaps, etc.

▶ Consider whether a person specification should be drawn up or at least a summary of key skills, competencies, experience, etc. being sought by the board in recruiting new trustee(s).

▶ Check that the trustee role description is up-to-date.

▶ Review and update the documents and information in the trustee induction pack.

Recruitment

▶ A variety of methods can be used to identify potential trustees, including:

▷ word of mouth/personal recommendation;

▷ the charity's networks of contacts;

▷ the charity's members;

▷ the existing trustees' network of contacts;

▷ charity networks and support bodies (some offer free or chargeable advertising options for individuals seeking trusteeships and charities seeking potential trustees);

▷ advertising in the press and media (some organisations offer free or low cost advertising for charities seeking trustees);

▷ social media/the charity's own website;

▷ business electronic social media (e.g. LinkedIn) and business networking groups (e.g. local Chambers of Commerce); and

▷ recruitment agencies/headhunting services – there are a small number of agencies that include trustee search/board candidate headhunting services in their portfolio of recruitment services (however the cost is likely to be unaffordable to many charities).

Verifications and checks

▶ Note that the identity and bona fides of any potential new trustee should be verified.

▶ The charity should comply with the 'fit and proper persons' test.

▶ It should also undertake other appropriate security checks before proceeding with the appointment of a candidate identified as a potential new trustee, for example:

▷ disqualified director search (Companies House website, there is no fee);

▷ removed trustee search (Charity Commission website, there is no fee); or

▷ bankruptcy and County Courts judgement search, or local equivalent in Scotland or Northern Ireland (this can be done via a suitable search agent for a modest cost).

Appointment procedure

▶ The procedure for the appointment of a trustee largely depends on the provisions of the particular charity's constitution.

Induction

▶ Appropriate induction activities, as well as reference materials, should be arranged and provided for all new trustees. This is a matter of good governance, it also helps the new trustee feel welcomed and valued, as well as assisting them to begin contributing confidently to trustee board discussions and decisions.

▶ Appropriate reference documents/links to electronic versions and relevant reference material should be provided.

▶ As a bare minimum the new trustee needs access to:

▷ the trustee role description;

▷ the charity's constitution;

▷ the most recent annual accounts and trustees' report; and

▷ at least two immediately previous periods' management accounts.

▶ Consider how to familiarise the new trustee with the main activities undertaken by the charity.

▶ Arrange introductions to key staff and volunteers.

▶ Provide the annual calendar of board meetings and other key dates (for example, the date of the next AGM).

Records

▶ Details of any appointment made at a meeting of the trustees or the charity's members should be recorded in the minutes of that meeting.

▶ Charitable companies, CIOs and SCIOs must enter details of a new trustee in their register of directors/register of trustees.

▶ All trustees who served during any part of the year should be listed in the trustees' annual report for that year. The date of appointment should be stated alongside the name of any newly appointed trustee.

Filing requirements

▶ The appointment of a new director *must* be notified to Companies House. This can be done online via the Companies House website.

▶ CIOs *must* notify the Charity Commission of any changes amongst their trustees and SCIOs *must* notify the OSCR.

▶ Details of trustees held by the relevant charity regulator(s) should be kept up-to-date for all charities so, whatever legal form the charity takes, in practice do ensure that notification of the appointment of the new trustee is made to the Charity Commission and/or the OSCR and/or the Charity Commission for Northern Ireland.

▶ These notifications can be dealt with online via the relevant regulator's website.

Notes

▷ When addressing trustee recruitment, trustee boards should consider the range of skills, knowledge and experience the trustees currently serving on the board have, as well as identifying areas where there are gaps or the need to strengthen the board. They should also be aware of the need for periodic fresh blood to bring new perspectives and ideas.

▷ The charity's constitution may specify a period of service for trustees and it may allow trustees to be appointed for additional periods of service, perhaps with a final 'stop' point (or break period) after a certain length of service.

▷ Some constitutions place no limit at all on the length of time that a trustee may serve. This can make it difficult to ensure periodic turnover of trustees and to introduce fresh blood or required skills (especially if the constitution also specifies a maximum number of trustees).

▷ Where a constitution's provisions are hindering trustee recruitment, rather than assisting with it, the charity should consider altering its constitution to adopt more flexible, modern and suitable provisions.

List of removed charity trustees

▷ The Charity Commission holds a list of those who have been removed as a charity trustee by the courts or by the decision of the Charity Commission. There is a search facility available via the Commission's website.

▷ Note that this list does not include details of those who are disqualified from being a charity trustee by other means or for other reasons.

More information

▷ Search facilities relating to disqualified directors can be accessed on the government website – see: www.gov.uk/search-the-register-of-disqualified-company-directors.

▷ Safeguarding – Disclosure and Barring Service see: www.gov.uk/government/organisations/disclosure-and-barring-service/about.

Websites

Introduction

Websites are extremely useful to charities as part of their general communication processes and, increasingly, as one of a range of ways in which they seek public support and deliver services to their beneficiaries. There are a number of legal and administrative issues that need to be addressed in relation to websites that a charity operates itself or otherwise uses.

Checklist

▶ Ensure all relevant charity disclosure requirements are met (e.g. that the charity's name, charitable status and registered charity number(s) are set out on the website.

▶ Consider other applicable disclosure requirements (e.g. company law requirements, if the charity is a CLG).

▶ The general law applies to websites and statements and information made available on them (including the law of defamation, law relating to e-commerce and electronic communications and data protection law).

▶ If a website allows orders for goods or services to be placed and/or payments made for goods and services, consider the applicable legal requirements regarding e-commerce, consumer credit transactions and regulations relating to payments by credit or debit cards. Note that, in some circumstances, the law requires the purchaser to be allowed a 'cooling off' period.

▶ Other areas of particular importance to address include:

▷ data protection law and regulations;

▷ the regulations relating to cookies;

▷ fundraising law and regulations;

▷ fundraising standards and relevant codes of practice;

▷ cyber security, anti-fraud measures and protections against other potential criminal activities or other forms of abuse of the charity, its charitable assets or its reputation; and

▷ risks of any other abuse or misuse of web-based facilities (e.g. harassment and cyber bullying, infringement of copyrights or trademarks, libellous statements).

Cookies

▶ Cookies are widely used to help smart phones and other electronic devices such as laptop computers to interact with the websites; they also profile site users (e.g. for website development or marketing purposes).

▶ If an organisation uses cookies on its website, it must provide particular information to website visitors and seek their consent to cookies being placed on their device. In summary, the organisation must:

▷ tell people if cookies are being used on its website;

▷ explain what those cookies are doing; and

▷ obtain the site user's consent to any cookie that will be stored on that user's device.

▶ The Information Commissioner's Office receives significant numbers of public complaints about misuse of cookies and non-compliance with the regulatory requirements. It can and does take enforcement action against non-compliant organisations, so charities should take care that they are following the legal rules correctly (financial penalties for breaches can be significant and there are also potential criminal penalties).

Electronic Communications Act 2000

▶ There are general legal provisions relating to electronic communications and electronic signatures in the Electronic Communications Act 2000.

Companies Act 2006

▶ The Companies Act 2006 includes a range of provisions regarding electronic communications:

▷ to a company by an individual member (Schedule 4); or

▷ by a company (either by a company to its own members or by a corporate member to the company of which it is a member) (Schedule 5).

▶ These include provisions regulating the use of a website for notices of general meetings of the members and making documents relating to such meetings available to the members, as well as enabling members to access a copy of the company's annual accounts via the company's website.

▶ These requirements apply regardless of any other provisions in the company's articles.

▶ The provisions are detailed and complex. Care should be taken to interpret and apply them correctly in all formal company/member communications via a website.

Notes

▶ There are tricky legal and practical issues to address where a charity is represented on another party's website or uses a shared website.

More information

▶ Information Commissioner's Office: www.ico.gov.uk.

▶ Get Safe Online: www.getsafeonline.org.

▶ Code of Fundraising Practice (available on the Fundraising Regulator's website).

▶ Charity communications standards and effectiveness: www.charitycomms.org.uk.

Written resolutions – members

Introduction

A members' resolution is a formal decision of the charity's members.

While such resolutions are usually passed at a meeting of the members, sometimes they may be passed as written resolutions. Whether or not this is possible depends on:

▷ the legal form of the particular charity;

▷ the nature of the resolution to be passed (some resolutions must be dealt with at a meeting); and/or

▷ the provisions of the individual charity's constitution.

Checklist

Companies

▶ A private company, including a CLG, may pass a written resolution of its members in accordance with the procedure set out in the Companies Act 2006 (i.e. the statutory written resolution procedure).

▶ A written resolution may *not* be used to remove a director or remove an auditor.

▶ Otherwise, a written resolution may be used to pass either an ordinary or a special resolution.

▶ Only eligible members may vote. An 'eligible member' is a member who qualifies to vote on the relevant resolution at its circulation date (see further below).

CIOs

▶ A CIO's constitution may, or may not, include provisions for the passing of written resolutions of the members.

SCIOs

▷ A SCIO's constitution must contain provisions as to how members' resolutions are to be passed.

▷ A particular SCIO's constitution may, or may not, include provisions for the passing of written resolutions of the members.

▷ Note that the regular statutory meeting of a SCIO's members, required by the SCIO regulations, must be held as a meeting (see checklist: 'Scottish Charitable Incorporated Organisations (SCIOs)').

Other charities

▷ The charity's constitution may, or may not, include provision for passing written resolutions of its members.

Procedure

Companies

▷ The board approves the circulation of a draft written resolution to the members.

▷ The draft is circulated to the members.

▷ Provided that the required percentage of the company's eligible members signify their consent to the resolution, within the relevant time limit, the resolution is passed. Otherwise it lapses.

▷ The resolution may be sent or circulated in hard copy or by electronic means or via a website. The Companies Act specifies particular procedures that must be followed if electronic communication or a website is to be used.

▷ The date on which the draft resolution is sent or circulated to the members is the circulation date. This is important for calculating the time limit within which the resolution must be signed by the required majority (otherwise it will lapse).

▷ The calculation of majorities for written resolutions is based on majorities of consents from 'eligible members'. An eligible member is a member who is qualified to vote on the relevant resolution at its circulation date.

▷ The circulation date is the date on which copies of the draft resolution are sent or submitted to the members, in accordance with the Companies Act rules.

▷ The Companies Act specifies that consent to the resolution must be obtained from a relevant percentage of the eligible members. The required percentages are:

  ▷ ordinary resolution – a simple majority of the *total voting rights* of the eligible members; and

▷ special resolution – not less than 75% of the *total voting rights* of the eligible members.

▶ Note that there is a time limit for obtaining the required majority, otherwise the proposed resolution lapses. If the articles are silent, the time limit is 28 days beginning on the circulation date. However, if the articles specify an alternative time limit that will apply.

▶ Agreement to the resolution may be given by the member or by someone acting on the member's behalf. Usually, it is given by the member signing the resolution.

▶ The signatures may be placed on one single document or on more than one (provided the documents are all in the same form – i.e. the same text of resolution must be signed as being approved by the relevant members).

▶ The Companies Act provides for authentication via electronic communication, which may be used as an alternative to signature of a hard copy. Note that the Act specifies detailed procedures which must be carefully followed for this to be effective.

▶ The date of the resolution is the date of the last signature.

▶ A copy of the resolution and a record of the members who signed it must be retained by the company.

Other charities

▶ Follow the procedure set out in the charity's constitution.

Filing requirements

▶ If the resolution would have required filing if it had been passed at a meeting, then a copy of it must be filed at Companies House.

▶ This must be done within 15 days of the resolution becoming effective.

▶ See checklist: 'Resolutions of members – records and filing'.

Notes

▶ If a written resolution is to be used in relation to certain share transactions and authorisations, there are additional procedural requirements. This would not be relevant to a CLG (which does not have a share capital) but would apply to relevant situations in relation to a charity's trading subsidiary limited by shares.

Written resolutions – trustees

Introduction

A trustees' resolution is a formal decision of the charity's board of trustees.

Most trustees' decisions require due consideration of background information and active discussion of the issues, before the formal decision is taken. So most trustees' resolutions are passed at board meetings.

However, some trustees' resolutions may be passed as written resolutions. Whether or not this is possible depends on factors such as:

▷ the nature of the resolution to be passed; and

▷ the provisions of the individual charity's constitution.

Checklist

▶ Is the resolution suitable to be dealt with in writing?

▶ Consider whether prior consideration of appropriate background information and a board discussion are needed. If so, the resolution ought properly to be addressed at a board meeting.

▶ Does the charity's constitution permit the passing of written resolutions of the trustees?

▶ What is the specified procedure?

▶ Check the provisions in the constitution with regard to the percentage consent required to pass a written trustees' resolution. This is likely to be unanimity (rather than the majority vote usually required to pass a resolution at a trustees' meeting).

Procedure

▶ Follow the procedure specified in the charity's constitution.

▶ Ensure a record is made of the written resolution.

▶ The record should include the text of the resolution, its date and details of the names of the trustees who signed the resolution (note the constitution may require unanimous agreement, in which case all trustees will have signed the resolution).

Notes

Companies

▶ There is no specific statutory provision in the Companies Act empowering the board to pass written resolutions (unlike the position with regard to written resolutions of the members of a company). So a charitable company's trustees may only use written resolutions if the particular company's articles empower them to do so.

CIOs

▶ There is no specific statutory provision in the Charities Act 2011 or the CIO regulations empowering CIO trustees to pass written resolutions.

▶ The regulations do require a CIO's constitution to set out various matters in relation to trustee decision making and voting.

▶ The regulations also specify that, if the trustees are to have power to make decisions by resolutions in writing (or by electronic means outside board meetings) the individual CIO's constitution must include provisions to deal with this. Therefore, if the constitution is silent on the matter that the CIO's trustees will not have power to pass written resolutions.

SCIOs

▶ There is no specific statutory provision in the Charities and Trustee Investment (Scotland) Act 2005 or the SCIO regulations empowering SCIO trustees to pass written resolutions.

▶ The regulations do require a SCIO's constitution to set out various matters in relation to trustee decision making and voting.

▶ A particular SCIO may include provisions in its constitution dealing with written resolutions of trustees.

Other charities

▶ Check whether the particular charity's constitution enables the trustees to pass written resolutions.

Web directory

Useful contacts – regulators

Companies House
Website: www.gov.uk/government/
organisations/companies-house

Charity Commission
Website: www.gov.uk/government/
organisations/charity-commission

Charity Commission for Northern Ireland
Website: www.charitycommissionni.org.uk

Fundraising Regulator
Website: www.fundraisingregulator.org.uk

OSCR (The Office of the Scottish Charity Regulator)
Website: www.oscr.org.uk

Useful contacts – general

Action Fraud
The UK's fraud information, advice and reporting service, operated by the National Fraud Authority.
Tel: 0300 123 2040
Website: www.actionfraud.police.uk
Email: action.fraud@nfa.gsi.gov.uk
To report suspected fraud go to www.actionfraud.police.uk/report_fraud

Association of Charitable Foundations
Tel: 020 7255 4499
Website: www.acf.org.uk

Association of Chief Executives of Voluntary Organisations (ACEVO)
Tel: 020 7014 4600
Website: www.acevo.org.uk

Association of Chief Officers of Scottish Voluntary Organisations
Tel: 0131 243 2755
Website: www.acosvo.org.uk

Charities Aid Foundation
Tel: 03000 123 000
Website: www.cafonline.org.uk

Charity Comms
Tel: 020 7426 8877
Website: www.charitycomms.org.uk

Charity Finance Group
Tel: 0845 345 3192
Website: www.cfg.org.uk

Charity Law Association
Tel: 01634 373253
Website: charitylawassociation.org.uk/

Charity Retail Association
Tel: 020 7255 4470
Website: www.charityretail.org.uk

Charity Share

Tel: 020 7250 7070

Website: www.charityshare.org.uk

Charity Tax Group

Website: www.ctrg.org.uk

Charity Technology Trust

Tel: 020 7324 3380

Website: www.ctt.org

Charity Technology Exchange

Tel: 0845 456 1823

Website: www.ctxchange.org

Direct Marketing Association

Tel: 020 7291 3300

Website: www.dma.org.uk

Directory of Social Change

Tel: 020 7391 4800

Website: www.dsc.org.uk

Disclosure and Barring Service

Website: www.homeoffice.gov.uk/agencies-public-bodies/dbs

Equality and Human Rights Commission

Tel: 020 3117 0235

Helplines:
England: 0845 604 6610
Scotland: 0845 604 5510
Wales: 0845 604 8810

Website: www.equalityhumanrights.com

Fraud Advisory Panel

Tel: 020 7920 8721

Fax: 020 7920 8545

Website: www.fraudadvisorypanel.org
Email: info@fraudadvisorypanel.org

Gambling Commission

Tel: 0121 230 6666

Website: www.gamblingcommission.gov.uk

Get Safe Online

Get Safe Online is a public/private sector partnership supported by HM Government and leading organisations in banking, retail, internet security and other sectors. It provides information and signposts resources relating to online safety.

Website: www.getsafeonline.org

Health & Safety Executive

Redgrave Court,
Merton Road,
Bootle,
Merseyside L20 7HS

Tel: 0151 951 4000

Website: www.hse.gov.uk

HM Revenue & Customs (HMRC)

Various locations

Website: www.hmrc.gov.uk

HMRC Charities

HMRC Charities,
St John's House,
Merton Road,
Bootle,
Merseyside L69 9BB

Tel: 0845 302 0203 (8.30 am–5 pm, Monday–Friday) (also for VAT queries and in place of previous contact number for Gift Aid, Payroll Giving, Gifts of Shares and land and trading queries).

Website: www.hmrc.gov.uk/charities

Identity Theft

The UK's major investigatory and police authorities, including the Serious and Organised Crime Agency, the Metropolitan Police and the City of London Police, and other official agencies provide identity theft information and advice.

Website: www.identitytheft.org.uk

Information Commissioner

Wycliffe House,
Water Lane,
Wilmslow,
Cheshire SK9 5AF

Tel: 0303 123 1113

Website: www.ico.gov.uk

Institute of Fundraising

Park Place,
12 Lawn Lane,
London SW8 1UD

Tel: 020 7840 1000

Website: www.institute-of-fundraising.org.uk

ICSA: The Governance Institute

Saffron House,
6–10 Kirby Street,
London EC1N 8TS

Tel: 020 7580 4741

Website: www.icsa.org.uk

Institute of Legacy Management

Website: www.ilmnet.org

Intellectual Property Office

Concept House,
Cardiff Road,
Newport NP10 8QQ

Tel: 0300 300 2000

Website: www.ipo.gov.uk

iT4Communities

National IT volunteering.
c/o Information Technologists Company,
39a Bartholomew Close,
London EC1A 7JN

Tel: 020 7796 2144

Website: www.it4communities.org.uk

Lotteries Council

Website: www.lotteriescouncil.org.uk

Media Trust

4th Floor,
Block A,
Centre House,
Wood Lane,
London W12 7SB

Tel: 020 7871 5600

Website: www.mediatrust.org

National Association for Voluntary and Community Action

The Tower,
2 Furnival Square,
Sheffield S1 4QL

Tel: 0114 278 6636

Website: www.navca.org.uk

National Council for Voluntary Organisations

Society Building,
8 All Saints Street,
London N1 9RL

Tel: 020 7713 6161

Website: www.ncvo-vol.org.uk

New Philanthropy Capital

3rd Floor,
185 Park Street,
London SE1 9BL

Tel: 020 7620 4850

Website: www.philanthropycapital.org

Northern Ireland Council for Voluntary Action

61 Duncairn Gardens,
Belfast BT15 2GB.

Tel: 028 9087 7777

Website: www.nicva.org

Philanthropy Impact

www.philanthropy-impact.org

REACH

89 Albert Embankment,
London SE1 7TP

Tel: 020 7582 6543

Website: www.reachskills.org.uk

Remember a Charity

Encouraging legacy giving
Park Place,
12 Lawn Lane,
London SW8 1UD

Tel: 020 7840 1030

Website: www.rememberacharity.org.uk

**Scottish Charity Finance Directors'
Group**

Tel: 0141 560 4092

Website: www.scfdg.org.uk

**Scottish Council for
Voluntary Organisations**

Mansfield Traquair Centre,
15 Mansfield Place,
Edinburgh EH3 6BB

Tel: 0131 556 3882

Website: www.scvo.org.uk

**Small Charities Coalition/
Charity Trustee Network**

24 Stephenson Way,
London NW1 2DP

Tel: 0207 391 4812

Website: www.smallcharities.org.uk

Tenant Services Authority

Maple House,
149 Tottenham Court Road,
London W1T 7BN

Tel: 0845 230 7000

Website: www.tenantservicesauthority.org

Timebank UK

Royal London House,
22–25 Finsbury Square,
London EC2A 1DX

Tel: 0845 4561668

Website: www.timebank.org.uk

Volunteer Development Scotland

Jubilee House,
Forthside Way,
Stirling FK8 1QZ

Tel: 01786 479593

Website: www.vds.org.uk

Volunteer Now

129 Ormeau Road,
Belfast BT7 1SH

Tel: 028 9023 2020

Website: www.volunteernow.co.uk

Volunteering England

Regent's Wharf,
8 All Saints Street,
London N1 9RL

Tel: 020 7520 8900

Website: www.volunteering.org.uk

Volunteer Scotland

Website: www.volunteerscotland.org.uk

Volunteering Wales

Website: www.volunteering-wales.net

Wales Council for Voluntary Action

Baltic House,
Mount Stuart Square,
Cardiff Bay,
Cardiff CF10 5FH

Tel: 0800 288 329

Website: www.wcva.org.uk

Index

Lightning Source UK Ltd.
Milton Keynes UK
UKHW011908010219
336590UK00003B/500/P